YOGI ADITYANATH

Blend of Spiritualism and Political Realism

YOGI ADITYANATH

Blend of Spiritualism and Political Realism

Prof. Shekhar Adhikari

PENTAGON PRESS

YOGI ADITYANATH: Blend of Spiritualism and Political Realism
Prof. Shekhar Adhikari

First Published in 2018

ISBN 978-93-86618-45-0

Published by
PENTAGON PRESS
206, Peacock Lane, Shahpur Jat
New Delhi-110049
Phones: 011-64706243, 26491568
Telefax: 011-26490600
email: rajan@pentagonpress.in
website: www.pentagonpress.in

Printed at Avantika Printers Private Limited.

CONTENTS

FOREWORD

निन्दन्तु नीतिनिपुणा यदि वा स्तुवन्तु
लक्ष्मीः समाविषतु गच्छतु वा यथेश्टम्।
अद्यैव वा मरणमस्तु युगान्तरे वा
न्याय्यात्पथः प्रविचलन्ति पदं न धीराः।।
(नीतिषतकम्)

"Worldly wise may insult or praise, wealth may come or go by itself, they may die today or may live for hundreds of years but men of patience never divert from path of justice".
Nitishatkam

As a historian I always believe that reality is uncovered only after we breakdown the surface of appearances and Yogi Adityanath has fearlessly and truthfully burdened himself with this task. As a Mahant and Mathadari of Gorakhnath Math Yogi Adityanath has always been worried about peaceful and progressive India of which Uttar Pradesh is an integral part. He made varied efforts in various areas, be it diversification education, development of literacy programmes, spiritual teachings, organization of self help programmes, empowerment of women, facilitating girl child protection and promotion of multiculturalism Yogi Adityanath left no stone unturned. But ultimately he felt that weak desires bring weak results just as small amount of fire makes small amount of heat.

He realized that he was master of his fate and captain of his soul and therefore changing the atmosphere of India was possible by treating darkness as absence of light but not its contradiction. In order to remove the darkness of misrule, corruption, crime, non governance and other vices of caste system he assigned to himself the task on larger scale by participating in electoral politics and blending spiritualism of a Mahant with reformation of a statesman. It is in this process, that we come across a visionary such as Yogi Adityanath who is imbued with the idea of spiritualism and political realism. Yogi Adityanath seriously felt that if the fate of humanity has to be retrieved from getting into doldrums there has been a continuous thread from Vedas to Vyasa, Kapila to Sankhya, Buddha to Ramakrishna and Aurobindo to present day spiritual masters. In India it is often debated whether spiritualism and political realism can go side by side. Earlier also great visionary Mahants, Swami Sivananda, Mahant Digvijanath, Mahant Avaidyanath and other saw the world not only in the light of spiritualism but were also engaging with India's political, social and economic realities. In the same spirit, Yogi Adityanath's work is a rare combination of Indian spiritualism and political realism that adds a new meaning to suit to his well articulated thought on nation building. He has dealt with these issues from spiritual perspective. The core of Hinduism is spiritualism with a political and social base. He says that the base and soul of nation is culture and a particular religion or sect cannot replace it.

Yogi Adityanath believes that though India's boundaries have been changing but its culture has remained as bedrock. In time of crisis like war or natural calamities, the entire country unites and faces the problem together and this is our culture. India was created by saints, Sufis and leaders and the country was neither a piece of land nor a political unit but it was actually a cultural unit. The feeling of integrity and unity is part of Indian identity. Indian soldiers, on the one hand, protect our territorial integrity and, on the other hand, saints and social workers promote our culture and nationalism. Thus, war and peace or spiritualism and political realism also are important facets of nation-building.

While trying to integrate every aspect of human being and behavior Yogi Adityanath vividly describes how the Indian culture evolved nearly 5000 years ago and has come to us as a rich human legacy. To elaborate this, he quotes extensively from *Vedas, Upanishads, Vedanta, Yoga, Bhakti and Sufi* literature.

Being a spiritual leader, there is no doubt, that Adityanath was thoroughly engrossed in the development of India in general and the state of Uttar Pradesh in particular. He is very much engaged in promoting Hinduism by highlighting the cult of harmonious culture that could be a binding force. Hence, he talks of the ethos of a nation's culture which is imbued with the idea of political restructuring of states. He says that simply depending on power politics in India has been a factor that brought deterioration in the social and economic conditions of India in general and Uttar Pradesh in particular. He left no stone unturned in sarcastically critiquing the dual character of some other political parties because of their misdeeds and malfunctioning that landed our country into crisis at times.

Yogi Adityanath is also harsh in condemning the acts of terrorism and naxalism that India is facing at present times. The author has devoted full chapters on the issues of terrorism and naxalism. Both have become a disease that has to be cured. Hence, he focuses on the concept of security and development. He emphasises that India faces threat from external and internal forces. India is in search of identity for its security in an era of strategic uncertainty.

Indian history can also be described as a chronicle of military disasters. Paradoxically, during war, security issues are high on the Indian agenda. Yogi Adityanath says though India is a peace loving country and was earlier protected by our geography and culture. But this jinx was broken when China attacked India in 1962. From thence, onward, Yogi asserted that today India cannot compromise with its national security. But, at the same time, he questions securing our borders will not be enough.

More than this is proper development of our country in general and Uttar Pradesh in particular becomes more important than security because security is only one aspect of development. Yogi Adityanath believes that development means a progressive enhancement of nationalism. As such it can be said that a physical and material factors are important for the development of a nation. These factors have integral relationship. Even Yogi Adityanath cannot escape from this logic. To him, the state of Uttar Pradesh is in trouble because of lack of resources and this is a negative indicator of state's growth that is why he has recently invited investors from all over the world and India to successfully upgrade the economic structure of the state.

What is important for Yogi Adityanath is to eliminate and reduce the negative indicators like pollution, violence, corruption, illiteracy, poverty and ignorance. He believes that removing these evils from society will add strength to our culture and strengthen the national identity, unity and integrity of India. Thus, if Uttar Pradesh has to progress it has to deal with the present and future threats. Here, Yogi Adityanath does not mind in taking the stringent measures to set the system right. Here one can quote Kautilya & Machiavelli. Both believed in the dictum that where there are good laws there are good arms and there are good arms there are good laws. What does this mean? A state prosperity lies in the welfare and protection of the people even the rulers have/had to adopt harsh measures some times. Similarly, Yogi Adityanath wants to check organized crime in the state by introducing the bill on Uttar Pradesh Control of Organized Crime Act. This could be the right step in eradicating the evils of terrorism, naxalism and criminalization of politics from the soil of Uttar Pradesh.

Professor Shekhar Adhikari the author of this book and a senior academic has done a commendable job by exploring the vision of Yogi Adityanath and other aspects of his personality as a politician and spiritual master. It establishes the fact that simple accumulation of knowledge in any field is not end in itself but knowledge leads to virtue and it is virtue alone that distinguishes man from man. Yogi Adityanath has that virtue which distinguishes him from other saints and politicians.

This book is the product of serious fascinating efforts and provides a truly multifaceted account and way of understanding Yogi Adityanath and his political and spiritual mission from multiple perspectives.

Professor (Dr) Rattan Lal Hangloo
Vice-Chancellor
University of Allahabad
Uttar Pradesh, India

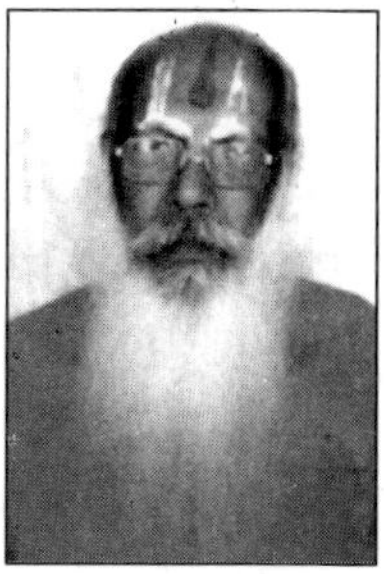

FOREWORD

The Book on Yogi Adityanath, written by Professor Shekhar Adhkari, is neither urged by an instinct nor is a result of a premeditated plan. It is a book to make aware the people of the past and present Indian culture. Destiny has afforded the author to deal with such vital issues that India is facing today. Yogi Adityanath's contribution in the sphere of spiritualism can not denied. Still, he is an able statesman who is truthfully engrosed in dealing with such vital issues that is necessary for country's growth. His narration of overall development of India in which Uttar Pradesh is an integral part of India, has led to critical analysis of India's strategic relations with western and eastern culture, the colonial legacy and contrasting value systems with the country's structural organization.

Yogi Adityanath, as I know, occupies a central position in spiritual and political fields in the 21st century. His life was full of dedication to work for a noble cause of promoting Indian culture and preserving the national unity and integrity. Following the footstep of his Guru Mahant Avaidyanath, he took active interest in India's politics, in general, and Uttar Pradesh, in particular. He wanted to give a new meaning to the state of Uttar Pradesh.

Indian subcontinent has been the home of the longest continuing civilization going back to the Vedic age and is still maintaining its essential features in the 21st century. Yogi Adityanath belonged to the class of Mahant who believed in Sanatan Dharma which has been well spelled out in ancient Sanskrit Literature, comprising the Vedas, Upnishadas, Puranas and the two great Epics- the Ramayan and Mahabharat. This has been well taken up in chapter "Spritualism vs. Political Realism." This reality was seen in early days of his life, because Uttar Pradesh, now Uttarkahand, became a fertile ground for like minded people like him to move ahead with his own spiritual and political agenda. This makes Yogi Adityanath an extraordinary person who tried to solve the existing problems through the prism of spiritualism and political realism.

Fascination and concern about the development of Uttar Pradesh made Yogi Adityanath a great critics of those vested groups who tried to promote there ownself interest and were not sincere in promoting India's age old traditions and culture. To Yogi Adityanath, "the soul of the nation is culture and religion or sect can not replace it." His contribution towards the development of Uttar Pradesh cannot be underestimated. Being called a 'Bimaru State' he has chanellised all his energies in making Uttar Pradesh a 'Shandar State.'

I am happy that the book on Yogi Adityanath has come out at such a crucial time when India in general, and Uttar Pradesh, in particular, is surrounded by negative trends that has hampered the growth of India as a nation. Professor Shekhar Adhikari has done a commedable work in laying out Yogi Adityanath's spiritual and political philosophy of national integration and unity that could well serve the interest of Indian people in future. Despite its vast canvas, the text is succinct to those who have great interest in India's spiritual and political development. I am happy to recommend the book to a wide readership.

Shri Mahant Sureshdas Ji Maharaj
Shri Mahant Akhil Bhartiya Shripanth Ramanandiya
Digambar Akhara, Ayodhya, Faizabad (U.P.)

ACKNOWLEDGEMENTS

I wish to extend my sincerest and heartfelt gratitude to hon'ble Vice-Chancellor, Professor Rattan Lal Hangloo, for his constant encouragement and support. I am also grateful to Mahant Shri Suresh Das Ji for his initial moral support and invaluable suggestions through the successive drafts.

My gratitude to Mr. Raj Bhushan Singh Rawat (OSD to Chief Minister of U.P.) and Mr. Rana Yaswant Pratap Singh, State Convenor, Bhartiya Janta Yuva Morcha, who introduced me to Mahant Yogi Adityanath. They were instrumental to write something on him. I am grateful to them for providing me necessary materials on the subject. Their suggestions on the contents and structure of the book have very helpful. I also wish to express my thanks to Mr. Umesh Rai, OSD, CM for his valuable suggestions. I personally thank Dr. Ragvendra Pratap Singh, Mr. Dilip Kumar Maurya, Mr. Uday Pratap Singh and host of other academicians for their expert inputs.

I shall fail in my duty if I do not acknowledge with thanks the assistance provided by Dr. Anand Kumar Srivastava, Dr. Urmila Srivastava, Mr. A.K. Singh, Mr. Akhilesh Kumar Srivastava and Sambhu Nath for going through the manuscript and making necessary corrections. I was fortunate to get good support from my computer operator Mr. Sudhanshu Sharma, who inspite of his busy schedule helped me in completing the book within a limited framework.

A special thanks to Mr. Rajan Arya, Pentagon Press for publishing the book. Last, but not the least, I am grateful to my wife and son, Mrs. Pratibha Adhikari and Janmajay Adhikari, for showing great patience while the book got completed.

Prof. Shekhar Adhikari

1

INTRODUCTION

Man, by his character and need, is a social and political living being. Since ancient times, his method of corporate life has been in accordance with some form of authority or control. Being a rational human being, he always thinks about how to improve his socio-economic condition so that it can lead to the growth of spiritual and political consciousness. Inherent in it is the unity and national integrity of the country that lies not only in moral and spiritual power but also in restructuring the political process. This is necessary as it would protect the people from overt and covert threats. The thrust on stable social orders with prosperity and diversity in unity attracted the attention of more and more men of intellectual bent.

Yogi Adityanath belongs to that class that has fearlessly and truthfully been burdened with the task of improving the condition of India. As a spiritual and political leader, he has always worried about peaceful and progressive India of which the state of Uttar Pradesh is an integral part. He realised that he was a master of his fate and captain of his soul and felt that the past political and social environment of India had severely affected its cultural growth. To improve the darkness of misrule, corruption, crime, non-governance and vices of the caste system, he assigned himself the task on a larger canvas by participating in electoral politics and blending the spiritualism of a mahant with the reformist tradition of a statesman.

It is in this process that we come across a visionary like Yogi Adityanath who is thoroughly engrossed with the idea of spiritualism and political realism. He planned the architecture of social and political reforms by dint of his courage and determination that could bind the nation into one single unit. How he has fared is the question that has been debated recently in great depth. It is found that spiritual and political ambitions were one way of gathering social, political and economic ideas related to the structure of the state government and the corporate model of security and development. As such, his contribution was not confined to the spiritual world but it was beyond this realm. It was the other-world power politics that formed an essential ingredient in understanding the State and society as such.

Early Life

Visionaries are not born in a day. When the fate of humanity is in the doldrums and the nation's hope for a bright future seems to be bleak, the country needs such spiritualists and political realists who can raise the hopes of people by their good deeds. In a country like India is it possible to develop these two different stream's for national integration? The answer is 'yes' and Yogi Adityanath is a glaring example of this unity of streams and who saw the world in the light of spiritualism and simultaneously realised the political and socio-economic realities of India.

Yogi Adityanath, in his early days, was known as Ajay Mohan Singh Bisht. He was born on 5 June 1972 in a village called Masalgaon in Uttarkashi district of Uttarakhand. He was a simple boy and knew that one day he would be a leading spiritual and political leader. Right from then, Ajay's fondness towards animals enabled one commentator to state that he was an environmentalist too. Today, laying emphasis on yoga, his love for animals, nature and environment and Indian Prime Minister Narendra Modi's Swachh Bharat Abhiyan and his strong stand against corruption, lawlessness and growing threat from various quarters, Yogi Adityanath, unlike others, showed his dedication to develop his personality to suit the changed environment that India, in general, and Uttar Pradesh, in particular, was passing through.

His early life shows that he got a good education from various institutions, whether it was in Thangar of Yamkeshwar block or Rishikesh where he was enrolled as a B.Sc. student with Physics, Chemistry and Mathematics along with English and Hindi. His primary education in Thangar is important to assess his capability as a youth. The Professor of History at the Mahayogi Guru Gorakhnath Yamkeshwar, Dr. Umesh Tyagi said that the Yamekeshwar area had a long history of association with its spiritual and nationalist leaders. The area was important because it became a breeding ground of young revolutionaries. That is why this area was called 'baaghi' area by the Britishers. It is not unlikely that the religious nature of his was profoundly influenced by the political happenings in the small town of Yamekeshwar.

In 1989, Yogi Adityanath joined the PG Government College in Kotadwar to pursue graduation with a science background. As a student he was quite reserved. The transformation of his personality was happening in the right direction. In his university days, he helped his classmate, Babita, when she fought for the post of joint secretary in the college. The incident is quite interesting. Once, after canvassing, he sensed uneasiness in Babita's mind about not reaching home within the prescribed time. Buses would not stop in the evenings and this was only means to return to Kotdwar. It was the humanness of Yogi Adityanath that forced him to stop the bus just a few inches away from him. His only worry was somehow to get the whole group safely to Kotdwar. This incident, later, influenced his normal behaviour. It shows that since childhood he had great respect for women. Today, the same is reflected in the Yogi administration when he took a drastic step for the safety and security of women in Uttar Pradesh by deploying Anti-Romeo squads.

Yogi Adityanath's awareness about politics rose early. His relatives earlier convinced him to join the Student Federation of India (SFI) but he was not convinced of its ideology. Thereafter, he joined the Akhil Bharatiya Vidyarthi Parishad (ABVP). The reason was that the country's political, economic and social condition was in the doldrums. He took up these problems and Kotdwar became the fertile ground to fulfil his revolutionary zeal to serve the small city and then thought of working on a larger canvas by leading various political and social movements. His first election in college did not yield any positive result.

After his election in Kotdwar, there has been no looking back and he has not lost any parliamentary elections till date. He won the Lok Sabha Parliamentary seat for five consecutive terms. During this span, he was very active and his long visionary zeal enabled him to ponder over the issues of national integrity, promotion of culture and security of Uttar Pradesh. Being radical in his approach, he draws not only the attention of the masses but became a well-known personality beyond India.

The year 2017 was the turning point of his career when the Bharatiya Janata Party (BJP) won the Uttar Pradesh assembly in a comfortable position. The question was who would head the state? The decision was taken by Narendra Modi. He had no better choice but to declare Yogi Adityanath the Chief Minister of Uttar Pradesh. Looking back into the early history of Uttarakhand when the State was well acquainted with the oppressive rule of the British Raj political leaders like Govind Ballabh Pant, Hemvati Nandan Bahuguna and Narayan Dutt Tiwari were towering figures who fought against the British system. Later, when Indian gained independence, they became chief ministers of Uttar Pradesh. Today, the nation sees Yogi Adityanath as the fourth chief minister of Uttar Pradesh hailing from Uttarakhand.

As an active parliamentarian, Yogi Adityanath raised issues important for the development of national integrity and culture. They included issues like a uniform civil code for the country, non-payment to sugarcane farmers, pitiable conditions of Eastern Uttar Pradesh, suitable measures for animal foods and the inclusion of Bhojpuri in the Eighth Schedule of the Constitution which drew the attention of not only the people but also of the media.

He also headed various committee constituted by the parliamentary board and was also a member of various parliamentary committees that visited different countries like Cambodia, Malaysia, Nepal, Singapore, Thailand, and the USA.

Nath Sampradhya

There is no denying that Yogi Adityanath had great respect for the Nath Sampradhaya because of his long association with it which goes back to his students days. The year 1992 is important as it was then that he first visited Gorakhpur and met Mahant Avaidyanath. The spiritualistic vision of Avaidyanath had left a deep impact on his personality. In November 1993, Yogi Adityanath left his abode in search of spiritualism and again came into contact with Mahant Avaidyanath. In February 1994, he was appointed a Nath Panti Yogi by his guru.

The Nath Sampradhyais well known for spreading spiritualistic ideas among the masses. At the same, it was also committed and involved in government work. This aspect must have taken people by surprise. Nath Yogis had considerable influence in South Asian politics for centuries. They have historically obtained power by emphasising their porous religious boundaries.

The term 'Nath' denotes 'Lord or protector '.[1] In Sanskrit, Adinatha means 'first' or 'original lord' and is synonymous with Lord Shiva. When Mahant Avaidyanath taught the 22-year-old Ajay Singh Bisht in 1994, he was called Yogi Adityanath who had appeared on the scene not only to promote religion but also to serve the people in a larger perspective.

Generally, it is said about the Nath Sampradhya that it combines the ideas of Shaivisism, Buddhism and Hath Yoga of India. Many consider Nath as a medieval cult[2] with Guru Matsyendranath as the founder of the Nath Sampradhya. He, along with his disciple, Guru Gorakh Nath, structured and collected all the teachings of the Nath tradition. According to Hazari Prasad Dwivedi, [3] the main sect of Nath Panth Yogis is the Gorakhnath Yogis. They are called Kanphata or *darasani* sadhus, and it is said that the name 'Kanphata' relates to yogis piercing their ears and wearing a special earring made of mud, ivory or gold. Gorakhpur sadhus are found in various parts of India.

It could well be argued that the Nath Yogis were well-established during the sultanate for other worldly activities. It was only during

Mughal rule that they began to gain political power and had good relations with other state rulers. Both Hindu and Mughal kings patronised the Sampradhya through land grants and other facilities in exchange for supernatural support, blessings and alchemical elixirs. Even the Mughal rulers held them in high esteem as alchemists. Similarly, Prithvinarayan Shah of Nepal and Man Singh of Jodhpur were also devotees of Nath yogis and their power.

The advent of the modern age has seen the decline of the Nath Yogis because of the popularity of *bhakti*, the rise of neo-Hindu groups and constant rivalries with the British raj. It is said that by the middle of the 19th century, these Yogis went into political and spiritual oblivion. A good example of this was that the Nath yogis of the 19th century in Jodhpur found no place during the British raj.

For the next 80 years, not much was known about the Nath sampradhya, including the yogis of Gorakhpur although some Nath yogis claimed yogic powers for centuries. The Sampradhya as a whole was lost somewhere. It was not until Mahant Digvijay began to consolidate the identity of the Sampradhya that political authority began to rise. This tradition was followed by Mahant Avaidyanath and Yogi Adityanath. Despite being spiritual leaders, they did not stay away from Indian politics. What was common in both was that by following the Nath traditions they propagated Hindutva philosophy to reawaken the masses that were lost in worldly gains.

Internal Power Politics

Adityanath's main concern was how India could be transformed into a progressive and peaceful country without diluting its ancient traditions and culture. In 2017, in one of his statements, Yogi Adityanath has categorically stated that the soul of a nation is its culture and religion or a sect cannot replace it. He elaborated this by saying that modern Europe was not the result of religion but the political unification that became the cornerstone policy of these small nations. They found the solution in binding the country into one single entity. This was done by compulsory military service. So, in modern European politics, the role of religion declined by the time the French revolution came. It was relegated to secondary position.

With the rise of modernism in the eighteenth century, one saw many intellectuals appearing on the international arena with Communist ideology. Most of the struggling states of Europe and Asia have survived on communist ideology. But in the Indian context, Yogi Adityanath has vehemently opposed such ideology which has divided the country and hampered the growth of Indian culture. He called this ideology as something imposed on the people by external powers. Though in the initial period there was some ray of hope that they could do something for the masses, the method adopted by them became a curse rather than a cure to wipe out the evils that were present in Indian society. Today, as we see it, in the name of communism, the people have rejected them as could be seen from various state elections. This issue has been dealt with in detail in one of the following chapters.

Yogi Adityanath was equally harsh on the working pattern of the Congress party. At one point, prior to the second World War, the party fought against imperialism, colonialism, caste politics and worked for the upliftment of the downtrodden masses. In between, the Congress lost its identity to solve the problems that India had to face. From time to time, it had to modify the Constitution with the inclusion of such words like socialism and secularism. Even our Constitution was a copy of the constitutions of 26 or 27 countries and, in my opinion, the country succumbed to political pressure from the then ruling party and we saw colonialism in new a form known as 'constitutional colonialism'. India still does not have an independent Constitution. This shows the rivalry and selfish interests of the Congress party because it promoted its own interest at the cost of nationalism. Moreover, the party which was meant for the masses had been converted into dynasty rule under Nehru. The political leadership has become a family matter. The hegemonistic design of the Congress party has kept them away from the masses because it failed to deliver a clear mass ideological, political and economic base against the rising tide and the people were adversely affected. Hence, the Congress had to pay a heavy price because it failed to negotiate with other national parties in search of a real identity of India. As a consequence, it lost the opportunity to evolve a viable and effective long-term strategy in combating the evils that have crept into Indian society. Yogi Adityanath says that the fault lies within the party structure and the duality of its approach in tackling political and economic problems which has led it to go in for appeasement politics. This aspect has been well discussed in Chapter III.

Yogi Adityanath feels that in spite of 70 years of India's independence, the then ruling parties failed miserably to bring a fresh lease of life in the minds and hearts of the Indian masses. Whatever progress we saw has become a serious issue. During these years, the national character was degraded. The Hindu's feeling of spiritualism and dedication were on the wane. On the contrary, corruption, illiteracy, caste politics and the deteriorating law and order situation hindered the growth of Indian culture. Yogi Adityanath is correct in his analysis when he says that 70 years is not a small period for a nation to progress. With India's independence, many nations became independent. Where are we today? India is still groping in the dark to find the reality of Indian politics. The time has come for us to free ourselves from the shadow of the Cold War and internal politics. The BJP in the Centre and Uttar Pradesh are working in a positive direction but the opposition never wants a party with Hindutva ideology to rule. These rival parties should know that for the past 70 years of 'imported ideology' India got nothing and as a result the masses rejected them.

Major Challenges

The biggest challenge Yogi Adityanath had to face come from Islamic terrorism and naxalism. Today the entire world is engulfed in such problems. The crisis erupted because of a corrupt and incapable political leadership. He calls it incapable because the political leadership could not fulfil the wishes of the common man and failed to protect the religious culture and historical sites that have been made the target by rival political parties. With the rise of global terrorism, a new chapter was added to our culture, i.e., breaking up India into a thousand pieces. Today Kashmir is bleeding and burning. Terrorism has been defined by Adityanath in these words: "A terrorist is a person who has been bred specifically to carry out violent activities in the name of a cause that will result in maximisation of deaths and injuries to the target groups. So while you may argue that there are street thugs, rapists, mafia goons and the like who terrorise people, they all do so as a means to achieve a deterrent end." He says that terrorism has no boundaries and any part of the world can be its target. In one of his articles, 'Idiot Mujahedeen' such terrorist outfits like HUJI, Indian Mujahadeen, Laskhar-e-Toiba, Jaish-e Mohammad and Deendar Anjuman are there to perpetrate more violent activities in Kashmir and the rest of India so that they can obtain their real objectives.

Thus, Islamic terrorism has become a serious concern for Indian security planners. He raises a bundle of questions before us. Why are Indians targeted in Afghanistan and Pakistan? Why has terrorism in Bangladesh reached the ultimate stage? Why do Muslims in Russia and China demand autonomy? Why did Yugoslavia disintegrate? Why are Chechnya, Kosovo and the Valley of Kashmir in the grip of terrorism outfits? Yogi Adityanath believes that all these outfits have a deep connection with *madrassas*. The issue of terrorism has been discussed in detail in Chapter Five.

One important fact to mention here is that Yogi Adityanath is fighting for a noble cause against terrorism. His stand on terrorism got ample support from US President Donald Trump. Like Yogi Adityanath, Donald Trump maintains that every nation has an absolute duty to ensure that terrorists find no quarter on their soil. Terrorists do not worship God but worship death. They, therefore, should not find a place in this world.

Security and Development

Elimination of terrorism and naxalism from Indian soil leads to another important issue, i.e., security vs development. Yogi Adityanath lays much emphasis on these terms because both are important ladders in the promotion and protection of our culture. India, like any modern state, is cautious of its security. Today, the kinds of threats that have emerged today have enabled India to search for its security in an era of strategic uncertainty. It is well said that Indian history is a history of chronicles of military disasters.

Let us not forget our past in which we were slaves to foreign powers. Even today, from time to time, we see many military conflicts. It is interesting to note that when both the first and second World War ended the world saw peace but a peace dominated by power politics. The strange understanding among the superpowers prevented further wars, though they had different ideologies. But in the Indian case, a peaceful formula was propagated by the Indian and Chinese prime ministers in 1954 to bring peace. However, where did peaceful formula take India? It brought a humiliating defeat for us. From thence onward, the issue of security and development was debated. Today, however one looks at these terms, one finds that they are associated with the well-being of individuals. Individuals are well connected with the social and cultural environment to which they belong. To Yogi Adityanath development is a progressive enhancement of society. In structuring a full-fledged society, physical and economical factors are important for national security. To him, today, the State of Uttar Pradesh is in doldrums because lack of resources and technology, deteriorating law and order, corruption, caste politics, etc. These factors have hampered the State's growth and hence, overall, Indian society has suffered a lot. Yogi Adityanath says unless these negative factors are not solved, Uttar Pradesh cannot be a secure State. Thus, if Uttar Pradesh has to progress, it has to deal with present and future threats. Here, Yogi Adityanath does not mind in taking the strongest measures to make the system right. In this context, the preaching of Kautilya and Machiavelli become important when they say where there are good arms there are good laws and where there are good laws there are good arms. In the worst scenario, they believed a State or society can flourish only when they adopt cruel measures. Then, the people will be contented and lead a harmonious life that will be good for a country's culture and national integrity. In a similar vein, Yogi Adityanath has proposed a bill to contain criminalisation of politics. The Uttar Pradesh Control of Organised Crime Act is a timely planned step by him to eradicate the evils of terrorism, naxalism and communalism from Uttar Pradesh. Here, he endorses the Narendra Modi slogan of '*Sabka Saath Sabka Vikas.*' But one can hope that with timely action by Yogi Adityanath as Chief Minister, lots of issues can be resolved through various methods. The author has devoted an entire chapter to Uttar Pradesh.

Yogi Adityanath's elevation as the Chief Minister of Uttar Pradesh has made the Hindu Yuva Vahini the core of the State. At one time, the organisation was discredited as a fringe and because the tag of Hindutva was placed it. Today, it has assumed greater importance in taking the lead by raising the social and economic issues of the people that are vital for their survival. To the organisation, various functions like formation of cow vigilante groups, anti-Romeo Squads, protests against religious conversion which was once thought to be radical, illegal and even categorised as moral policy, now appear to be 'attuned to the socio-economic philosophy of Yogi Adityanath. Though there are certain sections of the Muslim community that are radical and hence have no respect for others their plea is that the organisation is anti-national and justifies criminal activities by citing religious scriptures. These kinds of charges against the Hindu Yuva Vahini are not correct because Yogi Adityanath has always emphasised the victory of good over evil. In fact, those propagating these ideas are responsible for damaging the image in general and Uttar Pradesh in particular about the present state of affairs. If this is not checked, it will spread like a disease and then India will have no answer but will succumb to such pressures that are bent on dividing society. In this situation, where the political and social systems are in turmoil and economic crisis is on the rise then it becomes a daunting problem for the State to progress. But Yogi Adityanath has an answer that has been dealt with extensively in one of the chapters.

International Power Politics

Yogi Adityanath is correct in his assessment when he says that national incidents affect international politics. In the case of India, the planners earlier had to search for an independent identity when the world was on the verge of another major war. Indian foreign policy then had to be protected through its national interest. National interest at that time was not to align itself with any major power. Hence, the policy of non-alignment became the cornerstone of India's foreign policy. Even the policy of alignment was met with criticism from all over the world. Though international politics has undergone major changes Yogi Adityanath stood by the political philosophy of Kautilya and Pt. Deen Dayal Upadhyay. Kautilya has described foreign policy not in terms of a great empire like the Mauryan but in how small warring states indulged in incessant conflicts. Today, the conflict has to be overcome by a cooperative approach adopted by the State. If conflict dominates the other aspects of the State's development, it will suffer and lose its credibility.

Today, the nature of the Indian polity has become more of conflict rather than cooperation. Yogi Adityanath more or less lays stress on India as one unit. The same content was earlier described by ancient political thinkers. In ancient times, the king was a force to be reckoned with and he had great power to bring about social stability. Similarly, in spite of having diversity in various forms, the Indian Constitution is federal but with a strong central government. Furthermore, decentralisation of power between the Centre and the States has helped the State in times of natural calamities and war. Yogi Adityanath was quite aware of the conflicting nature of both national and international power politics. He has also accepted the relationship between morality and political action but this has to be viewed on a rational basis.

The question of spiritualism and political realism raises doubts about the credibility of Yogi Adityanath as a pragmatic thinker. The pertinent issue is in which category should he be placed. Is he an idealist or a realist? I believe he belongs to the school of political realism. One should be clear here that international or national politics do not signify the Plato philosophy of abstract reasoning. Yogi Adityanath dealt with national and international issues by resorting to rational and logical reasoning. To him, national integration, unity and promotion of culture have to be assessed in a realistic manner rather than drawing an idealistic picture. The reasons cited by him were that the deteriorating condition of India has forced the Government to take harsh measures so that its real identity can be retained at any cost. Hence, Yogi Adityanath's spiritualism and political realism have their proper place. Against this background, the author has examined the contribution made by Yogi Adityanath in painting a real picture of India and then solving its problems with his own rational reasoning.

NOTES

1. Wolf-Dieteer Strol: *Shiva: The World God of Power and Ecstasy* Inner Tradition, 2004, pp 5, 258.
2. http://www.britannica.com/topic/Nath
3. See H. P. Dwivedi, *Nath Sampradhya*, Hindustan Academy, UP, Allahabad, 1950.

2

SPIRITUALISM VS. POLITICAL REALISM

When the fate of humanity is in the doldrums, it becomes rather difficult to justify the hopes and aspirations of a nation especially in the present circumstance. This become equally important when one comes across a visionary who could justify the validity of spiritualism and political realism. In a country, is it possible to develop these two different streams for national integration? Can spiritualism and political realism go side by side? Like western thinkers, India too has had great visionaries like Swami Vivekananda, Aurobindo, Swami Sivananda, Mahant Digvijaynath, Mahant Avaidyanath and others who saw the world in the light of spiritualism and realised the political and socio-economic realities of India.

In the same spirit, the writings of Yogi Adityanath on nation building cannot be ignored. As a key spokesman of spiritualism, he is well aware of India's political reality arising from the worldwide environment in general and the situation in India in particular. The significance of Yogi Adityanath's contribution is a collective breakthrough beyond the nation's cultural and revolutionary horizons. To him the concept of spiritualism and political realism further added a new meaning to suit his well-articulated thought.

To Yogi Adityanath, spiritualism could lead to the development of the Indian mind which would have a great impact in attaining the goal of national integration. Aurobindo once said that the "work of the renaissance in India must be to make this spirit, the higher view of life and a sense of deeper potentiality for more creative movement."[1] Taken in this sense, spiritualism encompasses all human objects—the arts, politics, economics, society—which are key factors in the development of national integration. In other words, it could also be said that these factors are important in realising the objectives of power, peace, unity and harmony of the divine nature of humanity. Such indulgence by a nation could lead to the development of culture. Here, it is necessary to point out that culture does not mean civilisation. Taken together, civilisation and culture are the redeeming features of national integrity and unity. Civilisation denotes the ethics of the State or society which includes the mental life including the arts and learning. Aurobindo in "The Foundation of Indian Culture" has rightly commented that "civilisation is harmony of spirit and body." Will Durrant, in his work "The Story of Civilisation," has understood civilisation in terms of social organisation, moral order and cultural activity. Such a civilisation could be interpreted as in an advanced stage of social development which embraces economic provisions, political organisation, moral tradition and pursuit of knowledge and art. Culture, on the other hand, is the way that leads to an individual's moral and intellectual development. Culture comprises various activities of the cultivated aesthetic being. Yogi Adityanath regards culture as the sum total of the people's institutions, customs and the arts. Civilisation is the outer way of a country's conduct and culture is its internal beauty.

As far as Indian culture is concerned, it includes the idea of life, religion, a secret sense and human existence. To Yogi Adityanath, the core of Hinduism is spiritualism with a political and social base. On the 48th death anniversary of Mahant Digvijaynath and the third death anniversary of Mahant Avaidyanath, Yogi Adityanath said that the "base and soul of a nation is culture and a religion or sect cannot replace it. In 1947, Pakistan came into existence but the country was again divided in 1971. It proves that religion is not the sole base of a nation."[2] Adityanath further elaborated by citing the case of small European nations that were built on the concept of religion. In the Western world, the modern age began when one saw the disintegration of the medieval structure based on religion.

He says that "though India's boundaries have been changing, its culture has remained the same. In difficult times like war on natural calamities, the entire country unites and faces the problem together which is in our culture."[3] India was created by saints and leaders and the country was neither a piece of land nor a political unit but was actually a cultural unit. The development of the nation is the result of thousands of years of traditions, cultural norms and values. The Western notion of a nation is very different from that of India.[4] Thus, the feeling of integrity and unity is the identity of India. Indian soldiers, on the one hand, protect our territorial integrity and on the other hand, saints and social workers promote our culture and nationalism. Thus, war and peace or spiritualism and political realism are important facets of nation-building.

Modern Hindu spirituality highlights some of the basic issues that have led to the development of the positive orientation of the tradition towards the world and also the universal relevance of the Hindu philosophy of spirituality. In this light, Yogi Adityanath explains the spiritualistic dimension of present Hinduism. Any further analysis requires a comparative study of the Western and Indian notions of spiritualism and then to remove certain anomalies that exist in both the worlds.

Western Notion of Spiritualism

There are two ways to think about human development. First, how is spiritualism seen by the people? Second, taken as a whole, the focus on spirituality is how people develop a sense of national integration between bio-psychological-social and spiritual aspects and its relation with other beings and the Universe. In the West, spiritualism is an aspect of religious tradition and also of existential value systems. Elkins states "spirituality which comes from the Latin word *spiritus*, meaning breath of life, is a way of being and experiencing that comes about through an awareness of a transcendent dimension and that is characterised by certain identifiable values in regard to self, others, nature, life and whatever one considers the 'Ultimate'." Decker defines "spirituality as the search for purpose and it involves both transcendence (the experience of existence beyond the physical and psychological) and immanence (the discovery of the transcendent in the physical and psychological), regardless of religious affiliation."[5] To Carson, spiritualism has a deep connection with the soul. It is the way we create meaning in our lives. It is the recognition of the presence of the spirit within us and cultivation of a style of life consistent with that presence. Spirituality provides a perspective to foster purpose, meaning and direction to time. It may find expression through religions."[6]

Often in the Western world, people are rather confused on the concept of spiritualism as religion and faith are usually regarded as interchangeable terms. There is no proper way to define faith because it conveys different meaning to different persons. For some, it is a general religious attitude and for others it is a personal acceptance of a specific set of beliefs. It is worthwhile to note that faith is defined as a general religious attitude of an accepted set of personal beliefs which was not present in the Greek and Roman cultures. Hellwig opines that faith has directly originated from the Hebrew scriptures. Faith has been a part of religion.[7] On the other hand, J. W. Fowler describes faith as "the most generic and most profound process of being human, the process of meaning."[8] Faith to him is, therefore, often but not necessarily religious. Further elaborating, Fowler states "faith is so fundamental that none of us can live for very long without it, so universal that when we move beneath the symbols, rituals and ethical patterns that express it, faith is recognisably the same phenomenon in Christians, Marxists and Hindus, yet it is so infinitely varied that each person's faith is unique."[9]

Furthermore, Fowler also discusses the relationship between faith and imagination. He specifically calls it the "ultimate environment".[10] The ultimate environment is the means by which we find order and shape our actions based on what we see what is going on around us. In imagination, faith forms a comprehensive unit of what we see in the world and deposits value and power in it with regard to self, others and the world. Generally, the ultimate environment influences a person's response to life. Taken in this sense, faith, then, becomes a complex phenomenon because it involves both the objectives and subjective interpretations. As such, faith is related to making, maintenance and transformation of human beings. It could be summed up as a developmental process of knowing, finding and making sense as a human activity.

As stated above, it seem in the Western world, to some, spiritualism, religion and faith are used as synonymous terms. But it reflects one school of thought. There are others who use these terms in different ways. Love and Talbot[11] provide a discussion of spirituality and the development of spiritualism but do not provide a valid distinction between the two terms. The important question is how spiritualism and religion are equated with fate. Related to each other, they are developed on the foundation of faith. To define religion is quite a difficult task. But one can say that religious practices are related to a super human being.[12] For sociologists, religion is viewed as a "stable cluster of values, norms, status, role, groups developed around a basic social need."[13] In other words, religion can be seen as a set of beliefs and practices that revere a god or a centre of power and value. As such, a person indulges in the act of worshipping or praying or showing reverence to 'God.' It is a state of doing. Similarly, the Webster Dictionary defines spiritual as the spirit or the soul as distinguished from the body on material matters. Spirituality is imbued with spiritual character, quality or nature. Hence, to be spiritual or have spirituality, people attempt to live a life guided by the spirit of their faith. Persons may mediate, pray or make conscious decisions regarding their actions based on how they sense the spirit that influences them. In short, this activity could be described as a state of being.

In the modern period, in the Western world we come across certain terms that deserve our attention. Spiritualism could be visualised as secular and techno-spirituality.

Secular spiritualism: Secular spiritualism is adherence to a spiritual philosophy without religion. It emphasises the personal development of the individual rather that a relationship with the divine. According to Robert Solomon, "spirituality is co-existence with religion and it is not incompatible with or opposed to science or the scientific temper. It is one of the goals, perhaps the ultimate goal of philosophy."[14] Instances of secular spirituality are mediated differently. For example, we can be encouraged through a diversity of unique environments and situations. In the 21st century, individuals increasingly connect with secular spirituality through technology.[15] Secular advocates of spirituality emphasises the importance of traditional religious practices such as yoga and meditation. Meditation and yoga can be practised and cherished to promote empathy and manage selfish drivers of behaviour with solicitude and forgiveness. Spirituality, in a sense, may be referred to nurture thoughts, emotions, words and actions that are in harmony with a belief that everything in the universe is mutually dependent. However, some philosophers suggest that everything in secular spirituality does not refer to theisms, supernatural or any other worldly construct and therefore it cannot be truly considered spirituality.[16]

Du Toit defines secular spirituality as a contemporary phenomenon experienced in spheres separated from structured institutionalised religion.[17] He argues that as a contemporary phenomenon secular spirituality is different from earlier spiritualities. There are various reasons for change in the concept. The concept of spirituality means something different in the current techno-scientific world than it was in a world of phantoms, magic, gods and demons in which humans believed themselves to be at the mercy of forces they could not control.[18] Further, Du Toit argues that industrialisation has led to an increase in materialism in the West. Materialism has contributed to a more individualistic Western culture which underpins secularism. Thus, secular spiritualism assumes a spiritual quality that is not limited to any one religion or transcendent realm. In this way he tries to establish a relationship between secularism and individualism.

Peter Van der Veer suggests secular spiritualism began with the emphasis on forming group identities, both national and political, and the need for these communities was to share a spiritual identity. To him, secular spirituality arose in communities through the simultaneous rise of secularism and spirituality as well as their interaction in the context of 19th-century globalisation.[19] He identifies spirituality, secularism and religion as three interacting but independent concepts that create a framework for different systems of belief. Secular spirituality reflects individualism and self reflexivity through forming group identities outside of a modern geopolitical context. Secular spirituality, in reality, does not reject modern ideas of liberalism, socialism and science but instead exists as a parallel reading of the discourse with contemporary society. He identifies the use of these contemporary ideas in order to establish communities of individuals who share secular interests in a system of awesome belief as instances of secular spirituality.[20]

Techno-Spiritualism: In modern times, this term has assumed much importance. What does it mean? In the present time, science and technology have made spiritual practices more and more mediated through technology.[21] For many religious people, technology can be seen as an alienating force, the encapsulation of human rationality that competes with religion and spirituality.[22] Technology leads to such ideas like freedom, knowledge, happiness and peace. But sociologists have not taken this idea seriously. Since the period of Enlightenment, religion in the West argues that secular spiritualism as a phenomenon recognises the relations between technology and spirituality.

Spiritualism in Indian Perspective

Before examining Indian spiritualism, one can readily agree that Western knowledge is the science of facts and spirituality is the science of the soul. But in India, spiritualism has focussed both on action as well as value or cognitive thought that shaped the culture of a country. That is why Yogi Adityanath often speaks of culture as the soul of the nation. He tries to integrate every aspect of human beings and their behaviour.

Spirituality, as Yogi Adityanath sees it, is as old as mankind. It is not a new phenomenon. People are surprised that innovations in the sphere of spirituality originated in India. Hence, it is comparable with Indian cultural values. Old traditions are still carried on in the present time. It would also be interesting to dwell on the issue of cultural values as understood by UNESCO. The UNESCO book on

"Traditional Culture of South East Asia" has regarded culture as the total accumulation of material objects, ideas, symbols, benefits, sentiments, value and social forms which are passed from one generation to another in any given society." In other words, "culture is the refinement of minds and manners and also cultivation of aesthetic faculties in a particular society.

The question then arises: what is the spiritual aspect of Indian culture? The spirit is the non-material, animating and immortal part of mankind. Yogi Adityanath was influenced by Indian philosophers. As Aurobindo says "spirit is the self existence being with infinite power of consciousness and unconditional delight."[23] He has defined spirituality as "the attempt to know and live in the highest self of the divine, the all-embracing unity and to raise life in all parts to the divinist, possible value." Spirit without mind, spirit without body is not the type of man, therefore a human spirituality must not be little of the mind, life or body or hold them in small amounts: it will hold them in high account, of immense importance, precisely because they are the conditions and instruments of the life of the spirit in man".[24]

Indian culture is a growing process and is not like the Babylonian, Egyptian, Greek and Roman cultures. These cultures, though important to them, have declined sharply in terms of historical values. The root of Indian culture is still alive. Swami Ranganathananda has vividly described "how the Indian culture arose nearly 5000 years ago, how it was developed and has come to us as a rich human legacy," and this is a rather interesting and thoughtful study.

Vedic Period

In ancient India, during the Vedic age, the Aryans were a spontaneous race of people. They worked at both levels—material and mental. At the material level, Aryans showered love of life and were involved in composing poems with fighting as a passion. On the other hand, at the mental level, they were involved in the spiritual and philosophical life of society. The Vedas were written at that time. There were Rigveda, Yajurveda, Samaveda and Atharvaveda. The

Rigveda is the first ever written record of humans and lays heavy emphasis on spiritualism. The Vedic rishis excelled in devising mystic and metaphysical sciences for realising the immortal and divine self of which life and death are but shadows.[25] Aurobindo held "the Veda was to these early rishis the world discovering the truth and clothing in image and symbol the mystic significance of life. It was a divine discovery unveiling of the potencies of the world, of its mysterious revealing and creative capacity, not the world of the logical and reasoning or the aesthetic intelligence, but the intuitive and inspired rhythmic utterance, the mantra.[26]

Quoting much from Vedas, Yogi Adityanath was thoroughly engrossed in spiritualism and saw the positive side of the Vedic Indians who were eager to "know the soul." Later, it found supreme expression in various forms of Vedic lore, i.e., Upanishads, Brahman treatises, Aranyakas, Karakas, Dharsans, Sutras and Smitris. Yogi Adityanath believed that the world is dynamic and in a state of evolutionary process. In spite of this speculation, the world is full of mystery and the mystery deepened with the advance of knowledge. The world becomes a family and devoted to the welfare of all human beings. In the modern age, we come across the ideal of a global village, though the application of the term may be different.

Upanishads

Yogi Adityanath was also inspired by the Upanishads. They emphasise the scientific pursuit of the truth of life and the reality of the 'Ultimate'. In a similar tone, Aurobindo has stated that they are a record of the deepest spiritual experiences—documents of revelatory and intuitive philosophy of an inexhaustible light, power and largeness. The further development of Indian culture was influenced by Upanishadic philosophy. For instance, Buddhism and Sufism with all their developments were only restatements though they tried to give a new meaning and reasoning to truth and the reality of the ultimate.

While mentioning the Upanishads one cannot ignore the Bhagavad Gita which deals with a complete philosophy of life as far as human culture is concerned. Being also inspired by the

Bhagavad Gita, Yogi Adityanath attaches much importance to the yoga of knowledge which has been taken in an unique way. In it, action and devotion—Jnana, Karma and Bhakti—hold supreme expression in his thought. The absolute means of meditation and yoga systems have been secured by moral purity and intense aspiration for change of consciousness. It has provided a spiritual base for the future of Indian culture.

The Mundaka Upanishad (II(ii)-8) describes the world as blissful and immortal. The Isha Upanishad describes God as a divine poet-seer. These statements strengthen the argument that the Vedas and the Upanishads were not the only guiding principle of Indian spirituality but encompass all Indian art, poetry and literature. Taken as a whole, Yogi Adityanath finds the Vedas are spiritual and the psychological seed of Indian culture and that the Upanishads were regarded as the truth of the highest spiritual order.

Vedanta

The revelatory gnosis of the Vedas culminates in Vedanta. In the literal sense, it means the essence of all knowledge. Vedanta is based on immutable spiritual laws in the form of a common religion and worldwide spiritual traditions. The traditional Vedic Karmakand was practised to guide society to self-knowledge and more *jnana*. In Hinduism, meditation is seen as a means to gain self-knowledge. In the achievement of the ultimate goal of salvation, self-knowledge separates *maya* from reality. Yogi Adityanath also agrees that meditation, self-discipline and spiritual connectivity are well related to the Vedic religion.

Today, India is dominated by Hindu pluralism. It is very closely related to spiritualism because of the religious plurality of India. In the 19th century, Hinduism churned various regional traditions such as vaishnavism in the west, shaivism in the south and the shakti cult in the east. The credit to construct a doctrine of pluralism goes to Vivekananda. From time to time, he emphasised that Vedanta was the universal religion for those who believed in spiritualism. Vedanta then was the highest truth of all religions. He firmly believed that it was a transcendental religion. Later, Gandhi also recognised

Hinduism as the most tolerant of all religions because it enables a man to admire and assimilate the good in other faiths.

Ethics has Vedanta as its basis. For a Hindu, feeding a single sage or a mahatma means feeding the entire world. This Hindu ethics is based on the sublime philosophy of Vedanta. It highlights the philosophy of oneness and unity of consciousness. Ethics and doing good to others are the manifestation of this oneness. *Atman* is present in all forms. Universal love leads to the belief that the world is 'Vasudhaiva Kutumbakam'. Hindu ethics leads eventually to self-realisation. In this sense, ethics becomes a means to attain Yoga.

Post-Vedic Period

In the post-Vedic period, spiritualism, instead of speculation, became more experimental. As such, spiritualism was more associated with ritualistic priest craft but still continued to dominate the Indian way of thinking and belief. The great epics—the Ramayana and the Mahabharata—were written during this period.

Another system that was acknowledged during this period was tantra yoga. In the words of Aurobindo, tantra yoga raised "nature in man into manifest power of spirit." The cult of shakti worship also developed in the people. Shakti had a deep connection with the energies of nature—physical, biological, mental and spiritual. Even today, shakti is worshiped in various forms, viz., in the form of Kali, Chandi, Durga and the Devil.

About the fifth century BC, the spiritual content of Indian culture got a setback. But in the changed environment, Mahavira and Buddha's appearance gave a new meaning to spiritualism. Buddhism sets new values that are most suitable to the common man. Hence, it proved to be a great creator in the sphere of arts, i.e., a phase of re-interpretation of life, society and politics. The teachings of Jainism were similar to Buddhism. In spite of these developments, the Vedic tradition was well preserved. In such an environment, Shankaracharya, Ramanuja and others favoured the Vedanta philosophy. Shankaracharya had depicted the universe as "waves of beauty." His poetic collection is on intellectual echo of the "voice of the Upanishads and manner of the Gita." He was deeply engrossed in explaining Advaita, Vishisht Advaita and Dvaita.

It was in the medieval period that spiritualism received a setback because Sanskrit became the language of the pundits. Still, numerous works of literature like the Ramayana of Kritibas, Bengal; Bhavartha, Ramayana in Marathi, Ranganatha Ramayana in Telegu, Adityatma Ramayanam in Malayalam and Ramcharita Puranam in Kannada laid emphasis on the need of a disciplined life in a cultured society. Along with this, we saw the emergence of the Bhakti movement that inspired the life of the rich and the poor. Ramdas, Tukaram and Tiruvalluvar stressed the need for the moral upliftment of the masses in their respective regions. In the east, Chaitanya, Bidyapati and Chandidas brought a new awareness among the masses. In north India, one cannot forget the names and works of Tulsidas, Surdas, Kabir, Mirabai, Nanak and others for highlighting the religious aspects of Indian culture. Here, Sufism with its method of salvation also inspired the people. During the Mughal rule, it was seen that both the cults flourished and there was no clash between these two distinct schools.

Modern Period

In modern times, spiritualism received a setback because of the rising tide of the physical sciences. In the case of India, the materialistic Western civilisation hampered the growth of Indian culture because Indian society was in a chaotic stage. History proves that all great reformist movements of modern times amply studies European spiritualism and then tries to co-relate it with Indian conditions. For instance, the Brahmo Samaj favoured the idea of large cosmopolitanism. The Arya Samaj in Punjab and other regions tried to re-interpret the truth of the Vedas and an attempt was made to apply the Vedic principles of life to contemporary conditions. It was seen that from time to time, Vedic enlightenment was in the doldrums but it reappeared with much vigour and force with the writings of Ramakrishna, Ramana Maharishi, Swami Dayanand and Aurobindo. Today, the national pride and sentiment connected with Indian spiritualism and nationalism are well carried by Yogi Adityanath.

Yoga

Yoga has been discovered at various levels. Yogi Adityanath is well aware of the importance of yoga in developing the human personality. The primary question is: what is yoga? The word 'yoga' comes from the root 'Yuj' which means 'to join'. Yoga is the restraint of the activities of the mind and unites the individual soul with the Supreme Soul. Generally, Yoga is a philosophy that connects the body, mind, spirit and soul within ourselves and with one another. The Gita also defines Yoga as evenness temper."[27] It is a union of the *jivatma* (soul) and *parmatma* (god). Philosophers have established the relationship between ethics, spirituality and religion. There is no denying the fact that without ethics one cannot attain the spiritual path. Thus, ethics is the real base of yoga and a gateway to God-realisation.

Commenting on ethics as the gateway to religion, Yogi Adityanath believes in the principle that one who leads a moral life will attain freedom, perfection or *moksha*. Good conduct is the root of material and spiritual prosperity. Conduct gives fame. Since ancient times in India, good conduct has prolonged life and destroyed all calamities and evils and brought eternal happiness. As such, good conduct becomes the highest *dharma*. Good conduct also paves the way to the attainment of righteousness, truth and good works, power and prosperity. History has proved it that the rise and decline of a state depended on the good conduct of the kings and governments. Yogi Adityanath feels that Hindu morality is great and Hinduism has given great importance to ethical discipline. Yama (self-restraint) and Niyama (canon) are the foundation of Yoga. Rules of conduct have also been laid down by Manu and Yajnạvalkya the sage.

The ethics of the Hindus is subtle, sublime and profound. The basis of Hindu ethics is "there is one all prevailing Atman. It is the innermost soul of all beings. It is a pure consciousness. Rightfully, it has been perceived that if you injure any other creature you really injure yourself because the whole world is nothing but your own self." This is Hindu ethics. The Upanishads or Srutis lay great stress on the primary truth of religion and ethics as its base.

It is pertinent to dwell on the question whether the term 'yoga' has been mentioned in the Vedas. Yoga is not directly mentioned. Instead 'dhira' has been mentioned in all Vedas. Dhira means self-realisation. Asana, pranayam, mudras, meditation techniques, yam and niyama, dharanas are explained in the Vedas. The Vedic yoga was the result of several Vedic seers of the aniras and bhrigu families and the seven most important great seers were Vahistha, Vamadeva, Bharadwaj, Gritsamada, Vishvamitra, Kanwa and Atri. All believed in the spiritual path of humanity. There is no denying that while studying spiritualism, Yogi Adityanath has given enough space for such discussion. The Nath Sampradaya lays emphasis on Hatha Yoga and Kundalini Kriya Yoga.

Hatha Yoga has a deep connection with the practice of asanas (posture). The syllable 'ha' denotes the pranic (vital) force that rules the physical body and denotes the mental force. These make hath yoga a catalyst for the awakening of the two energies that rule our lives. Its application harmonizes and purifies the body systems and the mind becomes more alert and prepares for more advanced Chakras and Kundalini Kriya Yoga.

In the Kundalini Yoga system, the psychic centres of chakras is important because it exists in every human being. There are six main chakras in a human being. The human mind consists of several layers. Each layer has a deep connection with higher levels of consciousness. In such yoga, higher level chakras along with high psychic centres are awakened. In order to arouse awakening, methods such as asanas, pranayama, mudra and bandh are used to obtain perfection. Perfection is also, as Yogi Adityanath states, important in hatha yoga which will lead to higher states of awareness and meditation.

Yoga Order in Natha Sampradaya

The Natha Sampradaya's tradition and lineage are heterodox siddha tradition. It contains many sub-lineages: Matsyendranath was its founder. A story of the origin of the Natha Sampradaya says that Matsyendranath was swallowed by a fish. Inside the fish, he overheard the teachings given by Shiva to his wife, Parvati.

According to legend, the reason behind Shiva imparting teaching at the bottom of the ocean was in order to avoid being overheard by others. In the form of a fish, Matsyendranath exerted his hearing in such a manner to absorb the teachings of Shiva. After being rescued from the fish by another fisherman, Matsyendranath took initiation as a sannyasin from Siddha Carpati. Gorakshanath Babaji added further to his knowledge. Gorakshanath is even today considered by many to have been the most influential of the ancient Nathas. It was Gorakshanath who developed Hatha yoga which are commonly known as kaya-sadhana, pinda-sadhana, etc. The practices of the Nathas include internal alchemy leading to immortality. For many centuries, the Nath cult transferred knowledge through lineage from guru to disciple. Therefore, Yogi Adityanath has kept the tradition alive even today. During this period, various spiritual systems of India borrowed methods of Hatha yoga from the Nathas. These two seers are also revered in Tibetan Buddhism as Mahasiddhas having great powers and who devoted themselves to spiritual attainment. Among the numerous ascetic traditions existing in India, the lineage of Nathas is the most ancient with remarkable traditions. Nathas are also called Yogis because the foundation of their order is based on yoga. The primary goal of the earlier Nath Siddhas was to achieve liberation during their current lifespan. Yogi Adityanath, as a follower of the Natha Sampradaya, places great importance on the practice of yoga, mysticism and spirituality.

Yogi Adityanath acknowledge the importance of Patanjali in formulating Yoga Sutras. The texts written by him are often quoted and his translated versions are studied even today in yoga centres all over the world. The text contains spiritual guidance for using the physical body to yoke consciousness to the Divine source.[28]

The Four Paths of Hindu Yoga

Yogi Adityanath was not far behind in accepting the four paths of yoga. These were Karma Yoga, Bhakti Yoga, Raja Yoga and Jnana Yoga. Before him, there were philosophers like Vivekananda, Aurobindo, Swami Sivananda, Digvijaynath, Avaidyanath and today Yogi Adityanath who have made notable contributions in obtaining the goal by following these four paths. Their acceptability of these paths prompts them to comment that each method leads independently to the realisation of non-duality. Yogi Adityanath does not see the different methods as being in conflict with one another. Each one is adapted to a different nature and temperament. Vivekananda, moreover, generalises the various human beings into four types. The first, is the active, energetic temperament, the worker, for whom karmyoga is meant. The second is that there is an emotional aspect of man who discovers an appropriate method in the form of bhakti yoga. Jnanayoga is meant for the assimilation of the philosophical and national mind. Lastly, Raja yoga serves the purpose of mystically-oriented persons.[29] It would be rather interesting to dwell on these different paths of Hindu Yoga.

Karma Yoga: It is the path of action which leads to the attainment of God through selfless work. It is the yoga of renunciation of the fruits of action.[30] It teaches us how to work for work's sake and how to channelise the greater part of our energies for best use. Work is worship. The Karma Yogins are not bound by Karmas. "Yoga Karmaasu Kausalam" which means that yoga is still in action. A rigid moral discipline and control of senses are indispensable for the practice of Karma yoga. To realise the goal, every man should perform his duties in accordance with his own varna, ashrama, caste and stages of life.[31] Similarly, Vivekananda has mentioned Karma yoga as an independent path of liberation and described it as free from all doctrines and dogmas. He says "the Karma yoga need not to believe in any doctrine whatever. He may not believe even in god, may not ask what his soul is, nor think of any metaphysical speculation. He has got his own special aim of realising selflessness and he has to work it for himself. Every moment of life must be realisation because he has to solve by mere work without the help of theory"[32] Karma yoga, if it is of the lowest order, will lead to personal desire and attachment.

Vivekananda's philosophy assumes importance only when one follows the doctrine of Advaita. The problem here arises when he tries to establish the relationship between karma yoga and moksha. As such, thinking has becomes imprecise and then visualises the need to reformulate the nature of the problem and the goal that has to be attained. Thus, it may be well said that the Advaita perception of humility has been well associated with service of others and, thus, is an important instrument to take advantage of non-dual knowledge. On the issue of the elimination of ignorance that Advaita often understands, Vivekananda's stand is not clear, i.e., how far reaching deductions can be made or how far they are self-evident.

Bhakti-Yoga: To Yogi Adityanath, bhakti is well connected to intense love for the 'Supreme' or 'Ultimate'. It is the path of systematic devotion for the achievement of union with the Últimate'.

Like Vivekananda, Yogi Adityanath also believes that bhakti is mental work and begins with ordinary worship and ends in a supreme intensity of love for the 'Ultimate'. There is a marked difference between Karma yoga and Bhakti yoga. Karma yoga is more an activity-oriented work and Bhakti yoga is devoted purely to emotional temperament and does not indulge in abstract or philosophical definition or speculation of God. In achieving the bhakti goal, worldly desire and craving are obstacles in the way of devotion.

Ramanuja's contribution to bhakti yoga cannot also be ignored. He says there are two stages for bhakti yoga. The first one is *gauni* or the preparatory stage where there is a need for myths, symbols, forms, rituals and repetition of names. The second stage is *para bhakti* or supreme devotion. This is the stage where the devotees do not even hope for salvation but persist that God is loved because He is loveable. Once this is established, man is free from fear. The end result will be 'anand'. In the fulfilment of the divine will *Aatma* will make a man to distinguish between right and wrong. Qualities like equanimity, equality and universality will dominate a man's life. The power of truth, then, becomes more important which Aurobindo called 'Mind of Light.'

In Bhakti yoga, there is no place for caste, creed, family, colour or race among the devotees. God is above all these things. Bhakti believes in purifying the heart of devotees. No one can resist a man from becoming a devotee of the Lord. History is full of examples.

Nanda, an untouchable; Rai Das a cobbler; Kannapan, a hunter; Kabir, a weaver; Sabari, a bhil woman, were all devotees of God.

Jnana Yoga: Jnana yoga is the path of knowledge. Moksha is attained through knowledge of the highest order in Indian society. The importance lies in the realisation of the identity of the individual through the supreme soul or Brahman. Generally, it has been perceived that jnana yoga is a suitable path of the highest order and for most exceptional minds. Jnana path is the most difficult but the solution is quick. Even Vivekananda believed that there was no difference in the realisation of the objective of jnana, bhakti and rajya yoga but the means are different. Jnana yoga is source of strength for those who are neither mystical nor devotional but they are more rational. If janas shakti is influenced by Maya, ignorance will dominate man's behaviour. Out of this, fear and ego will become disturbing elements in the realisation of real knowledge. Contrary to this, emphasis on divinity will make a man contented and fearless.

Thus, logic and rationality become the most distinctive quality of Jnana yoga. It is different from selfless activity or worship. It is above these and Indian philosophers have called it pure *vidya*. Intellectual knowledge helps in the realisation of knowledge of the Absolute. To achieve this, different means are discrimination, dispassion, the six-fold virtues, tranquillity, restraint, renunciation, endurance, faith and concentration. Besides this, to achieve jnana yoga there are seven stages. These are aspiration for the right, philosophical enquiry, subtlety of mind, attainment of light, inner detachment, spiritual vision and supreme freedom.

Raja Yoga: Raja yoga is the way to connect with God through self-restraint and control of the mind. It deals with the control of the senses and mental thought that comes from the mind. Yogi Adityanath believes that Hatha yoga is physical discipline and Raja yoga is the discipline of the mind. Patanjali discuses Raja Yoga in detail while stressing the importance of yoga sustras. He believed that Raja Yoga consists of the eight-fold sustras. These are yama, niyama, asana, pranayama, pratyahara, dharama, dhyana and samadhi. Yana and niyam are the ethical disciplines that purify the heart. In Yana, ahimsa, satya, brahmacharya, asteya and aparigraha are the constituent elements. Niyama reflects observance. Yama and niyama are good to practise yoga. Asana, pranayama and pratyahara are preliminary elements to yoga. Asana is a steady pose. Pranayama is regulation of the breath. Yogi Adityanath has said that "all asanas (postures) in Surya Namaskar and Pranayama activities are similar with the way Namaz is done by our Muslim brothers. But nobody ever tried to bring them together because a few people were interested only in 'bhoga' and not in Yoga."[33] Pratyahara is withdrawal of the senses from their objects. Dharana is concentration of the mind on any object. Dhyana is meditation related to one particular object. In samadhi, mediator and the meditated become one. All these lead to non-functioning of mind and samskaras, impressions and vasanas are not a hindrance in any way in the realisation of the goal. Ultimately, the Yogi is freed from birth and death and attains final freedom.

Yoga of Synthesis

In the study of Indian spiritualism, we often across the term of synthesis of yoga. In this context also, Yogi Adityanath's contribution cannot be ignored. There are some who advocate that Karma yoga can be attained through salvation. Some advocate the idea of devotion to connect with God. There are others who feel in the attainment of wisdom of the final goal wisdom which is the only means. Still then, there are some who believe that all the three paths are equally efficacious to bring about perfection and freedom.

Yogi Adityanath was clear in this perception that the mental state of mind comprises will, feeling and thought and all of them are at loggerheads. From this, it becomes clear that to eliminate will, emotion and thought is not an easy task. Similarly, devotion and knowledge go side by side. Thus, it cannot be said that the most important form of sadhana is the synthesis of Yoga. The mind is marked by three defects, viz., mala or impurity, vikshipa or tossing and avarana or veil. To remove these defects there are methods. By practising Karma yoga, mala or impurity can be removed. Worship would lead to the removal of vikshipa or tossing. By Jnana yoga one could put an end of avarana or veil. Then what is left? Yogi Adityanath says that self-realisation, then, becomes important. The Yoga of synthesis is the only method to bring integral development that will ultimately lead to perfection. If all these are harmoniously balanced it will lead to an ideal religion. These three different paths, in fact, become one constituent element and then Yoga becomes the easy path by which self can be seen, loved and regulated. Yogi Adityanath has pledged, after taking charge as Chief Minister, that there will not be any discrimination on the basis of religion. Showering praise on the Prime Minister for making yoga a global phenomenon, Yogi Adityanath said, "Modi deserved all the credit for the global recognition which yoga has got" and referred to the UN declaring International Yoga Day on June 21." The number of countries that participated in the International Yoga Day celebrations in 2015 was 175, which went up to 192 in the subsequent year.[34]

Hindu Temples and Festivals

At the dawn of India's spiritual history, the belief was that God held the supreme position in the minds of the Hindus. Hence, people could offer prayer anywhere and worship any visible part of nature as god. Yogi Adityanath believes that following the Indian glory of religion and cultural tradition, people keep fasts and celebrate festivals with great enthusiasm. Whether it is Raksha Bandana or Vijyadasmi or Holi or Deepawali all indicate the faith, belief and happiness of the people that they have carried from ancient times to the modern age. It is well documented in the Yajur Veda.[35]

> *He through whom the heaven is strong and the earth firm,*
> *who has steadied the light and the sky's vault and*
> *measured out the sphere of cloud in the mind air*
> *Who is the Deity we shall worship with our offerings?*

The relevant question is who is the deity we shall worship with our offerings. It is an instinctive worship of all nature. For example, the Rig Veda mentions the manifestation of devas in terms of ra and satya. It is known as vibhuti yoga of the Vedas. Usas, Asvins, Marut, Sarasvati, Indra and Vayu were part of people's devotion to god. In the past, the Yajna vedi was the sacrificial spot. The people kindled a fire and worshiped God by placing their offerings in the flames. One can says that the idea of a temple came for the first time which was well conceived by our ancestors.

K. Bharadvaja tried to vaguely trace the worship of icons in our Vedas. In the Atharva Veda, it is mentioned that Athara, a saga, pays obeisance to a "prasthara" (stone) which belongs to sages and is sanctified by some Divinity. "Prasthara" is precursor of the colloquial "patthar" and it is thus clear that some sacred stone is referred to in the Vedic verses.[36] Furthermore, in the Puranas, the term 'devasthan' appears. It means a temple. It could be believed that the erection of a shed around the object of worship had started. Archaeologists have unearthed temples of the Puranic cult. This apathy shows that even the Puranic people made good use of these principal images of Vedic times for the sustenance of the temple. It is doubtful whether the Vedas mention temple ritualism but one thing was noticed that the people felt that they needed space apart from the dwelling place to offer prayers where the world did not intrude.

Yogi Adityanath has given importance to Hindu spirituality in his personal efforts to recognise and early realise the need of raising a temple for its unique qualities of its culture that has led to an awareness of the national spirit within individuals. This was possible only through worship of icons and got ample spiritual impulsions of the environment and had been greatly supported by Indian art and literature. In the words of Aurobindo, "An Indian temple, to whatever godhead it may be built, is most reality an altar raised to the divine self, a house of the Cosmic Spirit, an appeal and aspiration to the infinite."[37]

Temple worship, as Yogi Adityanath says, took firm root during the Ramayana and Mahabharata periods. History proves that Hindus, Jains and Buddhists built bigger and more artistic places of worship. He felt that the temple's activities were conducted in the form of festivals. Amongst the Indians' enduring and diversified fasts and festivals, Makar Sankranti is of supreme importance to Yogi Adityanath. While pointing out the great truth of the physical world, Rig Vedic saints spoke of the sun as the soul of the visible and living world. According to astrology, the skyway of the sun is known as Kantikrit which is divided into twelve different rashis. The Sun, the soul of the Universe, revolves around twelve rashis throughout year and when the sun crosses from one to another, it is called Sankranti. Similarly, when the sun enters makar rashi from danu then the festival of Makar Sanskranti occurs. This festival is basically a grand festival of sun worship. Every year, the sun moves according to the rashis and enters the phases of uttarayan and dakshinayan. The Sun is in the position of uttarayan from makar to mithun rashis. This period is good for six different types of religious traditions. When the sun is in uttarayan, the days, as compared to nights, are of shorter duration.

When the sun enters makar rashi in the month of magh, bathing and donations have special importance in Indian culture. In different parts of India, it is celebrated in different forms with great enthusiasm and vigour. In the Hindi-speaking belt, it is generally called khichidi or donation of a mixture of rice and pulses. In Maharashtra, on this occasion, til (fry) and jaggery (gur) are used. In Bengal, it is called Tilwa Sankranti and in the south it is known as the festival of Pongal.

All over India, Makar Sankranti is celebrated with great vigour because people's faith and belief are associated with it. This holy festival has a deep connection with Mahayogi Gorakhnath and Gorakhpur has its own importance. It is recorded, as Yogi Adityanath says, that in the treta yuga, once Mahayogi Guru Gorakhnath, while travelling, reached Jwala Devi in Kangra district. Seeing the Mahayogi, the goddess appeared before him, welcomed him and invited him for bhiksha. There Gorakhnath refused to have a tamsi meal. Instead, he pleaded that he will only eat khichidi. The goddess asked him to bring rice and pulses. It is said that from there, in search of khichidi, Gorakhnath entered Ayodhya which today is called Gorakhpur in the name of Gorakhnathji. Seeing the peaceful and isolated place, Mahayogi was deeply involved in meditation in the foothills of the Himalayas. Then, he returned back to Kangra where, under the influence of Jwala Devi, the water was boiling. Because of the growing popularity of the uttarvarti nath, gradually and in large numbers the people started entering Srinath temple during

Sankranti. This tradition is still alive and every year the number of devotees increases day-by-day.

To Yogi Adityanath, the temple is the centre of learning because of the great teachers associated with it. Of all the temples in North India, Gorakhnath temple in Gorakhpur holds supreme importance for him. There are many idols of different gods which highlight the high tradition and culture of India. Besides this, the city has Yoga training and health centres which are equipped with modern infrastructure. Dharmasalas are constructed for the devotees. In the surroundings of the temple, there are hospitals and the Sanskrit Mahavidyalya. As stated above, the temple is the source of great learning. Hence one finds a large library associated with the Hindu religion, philosophy and yoga. Today, the temple is working towards the attainment of much required goals that could bend the people towards the national stream.

Yogi Adityanath, with great respect, describes in detail the work and personality of Mahayogi Gorakhnath which he considers as epoch making. On the one hand, Yogi Adityanath highlights the spiritual aspect of Mahayogi Gorakhnath in the form of simplicity, control and morality in yoga sadhana and on the other hand he has opened the door of yoga sadhana for all castes and creeds. His great works and impact in different phases of his life have been well documented in Indian historical writings. Shah Rajvansh of the Hindu rastra of Nepal came into existence because of the blessings of Gorakhnathji. Its founder Prithvinarayan Shah was able to unite the country because of Gorakhnathji's blessings. In the eighth century, in Mewar, the creator of the great royal dynasty, Vir Bappa Rawal, owes his victory to Mahayogi Guru Gorakhnath. The elder brother of Vir Vikramaditya, Britharai was blessed by him and was instrumental in making Brithari mahayogi. The credit is again given to Mahayogi Gorakhnathji for giving yoga diksha to Queen Mainavatti of Bengal and King Gopichand.

The influence of Mahayogi Gorakhnath, in the words of Adityanath Yogi, was not limited to India only but its charm spread to Burma (now Myanmar), Tibet, China and Mongolia. The influence of Mahayogi Gorakhnath was an important factor in glorifying the

Gorakhnath temple. Such was the personality that people started pouring into the city. Soon it became the hub of learning and training and today it is known as Gorakhpur city and the district is named after it.

Thus, Yogi Adityanath says that temples are the source of inspiration for integrating the country. The year 2019 will be the best opportunity for demonstrating India's spiritual strength. It would be, then, necessary to present to the world the spiritual and scientific temper of India which the country has been witnessing for ages. In this way, he emphasised the spiritual aspects of Indian culture that revolved around "the truth of life." Unless, people are aware of this, the growth of Indian culture leading to national integration and unity will face more and more problems as we see today. Summing up Western and Indian spirituality, today, one has to analyze in terms of secular spiritualism and secularism. In the Western world, secularism was an important factor in the activities conducted by the Church and State. Hence, it gave birth to debate on religion and politics and thence it became a turning point of Western political and social thought. Though secularisation was deeply connected with modernism and the advancement of science and technology, secularism was understood as an alternative to religion. In India, one can say that secularism was related to tolerance and spiritualism. But Yogi Adityanath notes that secularism is a big lie. This statement of Yogi Adityanath has been debated extensively elsewhere. Therefore, spiritualism becomes a method to achieve the goal of Hindutva, based on nationalism. Behind, the idea of spirituality lies the theory of political realism.

Political Realism

Being a spiritual leader, there is no doubt, that Adityanath was thoroughly engrossed in the development of India and particularly of the state of Uttar Pradesh. As such, it would be interesting to debate on the issue of political realism and then find out whether he was a political realist. It said that in his writings, both spiritual and political realism assume much importance because he thought in terms of development of India culture that would be the binding force besides his emphasis on national integration and unity.

Yogi Adityanath has said that the soul of a nation is its culture and religion or sect cannot replace it. In 1947, Pakistan became a free nation but the country was divided in 1971. It proves that religion is not the base of a nation. He gives the classic example of small European nations where religion was not the base of a nation. But what was important there was political unification and the binding force was war and not religion. In the case of India, its boundaries have been changing but its culture has remained the same. In difficult times like war or natural calamities the entire country unites and faces the problem together that hinders Indian culture.[38] To him, India was created by saints and leaders and the country was neither a piece of land nor a political unit but actually a cultural unit. The development of India is unlike the Western notion of a nation and it cannot be explained by the philosophy of Aristotle. He says we need to concentrate more on the political thought of Kautilya and Deen Dayal Upadhyaya.[39] What is important is the feeling of integrity and unity in actual terms that determine the identity of India. Indian soldiers protect our borders whereas saints and social workers work for Indian culture and nationalism.[40]

Adityanath's observation needs more elaboration. This could be divided into three heads. An attempt will be made to debate on the political though of Aristotle, Kautilya and Deen Dayal Upadhyaya; second is security and development and third is the 1971 war. Then, probably we can draw some conclusion on Yogi Adityanath's political contribution towards the growth of nationalism.

Aristotle, Kautilya and Deen Dayal Upadhyaya: These political philosophers were concerned with the protection of society and state from any kind of threat. To protect society is the real art of the state. The primary concern was related to practical administration. Kautilya's reference to people suffering from anarchy, as illustrated by "a large fish swallowing a small one" first elected Manu to be the king and allotted one-sixth of the grains grown and one-tenth of the merchandise as sovereign dues. Fed up by this payment system, kings took upon themselves the responsibility of maintaining the safety and security of their subjects when the principle of levying just punishments and taxes had been violated. Hence saints also provided the king with one-sixth of the grains gleaned by them thinking that it is payable to "him who protects us."[41]

To Kautilya, the state is composed of human elements, i.e., people. Without an articulate population, the state is "as useless as a barren cow." The state is meant for the protection of life and prosperity of the people so that society can progress. It is quite clear from the "Arthasastra" that though Kautilya mentions the material welfare of the people and the state, the moral and ethical philosophy have been taken seriously by him. Kautilya, in this context, differs from Aristotle, the Greek philosopher. To Aristotle, the state was a foreign ideal which assisted not only in the solution of man's ethical problems but also to achieve his highest goal. Further, he emphasised that the individual and the state stood in the closest relationship to each other and the family and the social and religious life of the Greek people and his self-realisation were determined by the state. He was more concerned with the city-state whose territory and population were limited but not thought of as an empire. Kautilya, on the other hand, was an unequivocal champion of a large kingdom that could grow into a mighty empire. Depicting the political situation of the state during Kautilya's time, one finds drastic changes in the system. The Mauryan king maintained an army that could overthrow not only the mighty Nandas but also compelled the most powerful western contemporary rulers who had acquired Punjab from Alexander and made Chandragupta Maurya the undisputed king of an area stretching right from the boundaries of Gandhara to those of Bihar. It shows that constant combat amongst the Indian kingdoms brought to Kautilya's mind the necessity of a strong and unified state and centrality of force in politics.

Kautilya's thinking might have influenced Yogi Adityanath in the sense that the real function of the state is the protection and welfare of society. The protection of the people could lead to an idea of a welfare state. Like Kautilya, Yogi Adityanath must have discarded the theory of the theology of a state but rather propagated the idea of a welfare state. Aristotle was more concerned that the king must have force in order to maintain law. On this, he seems close to Kautilya's view on *danda* which was meant to maintain the state by protecting its subjects. A Hindu's thought of the past, present and future and the scope of the state's action were not limited. It extended from the solidarity of the narrow social unit of the city-state to humanity.[42] Hence, L. N. Rangarajan regarded Kautilya as a great preceptor of statecraft whose teachings had universal validity.[43]

Furthermore, Kautilya's writings were based on rationalism and realism. As such, he ascribed the supremacy of ideas and helped him renounce the theological background of the origin of kingship. The state, then, is amenable to human control. It also shows that he was not a believer in fate but believed in pragmatic politics. In other words, he emphasised the positive side of politics and gave importance to reason and experience.

Yogi Adityanath was also influenced by the political philosophy of Pandit Deen Dayal Upadhyaya. Pandit Upadhyaya has envisioned "Integral Humanism" as the essence of India. Internal humanism advocates an integrated approach towards life and politics. It endeavours to synthesise organically the material and the spiritual, the individual and the collective and hence aspired to introduce a decentralised system of governance with partnership between the citizen and government. It aspires to make the economy self-reliant through an indigenous model in order to create a compassionate and egalitarian society.

Furthermore, Pandit Upadhyaya believed that the over-emphasis of the Western concepts of individualism, consumerism, materialism or capitalism will not do justice to the basic character of India. He believed that 'integral humanism' can propagate and realise the true essence of Bharatiya culture. He maintained that true swaraj could be possible within the framework of internal humanism where the human being is basically seen as a spiritual being. His perspective can be understood as a middle path between capitalism and socialism where science can be given its due but with a synthesis of heritage and science.

Pandit Upadhyaya has given more importance to spiritual well-being as compared to material well-being because we are not merely a material body but primarily we are souls. In this, we have to awaken our national soul and 'ethos' to create a new India. He believed that political life shall be in sync with spiritualism and through political restructuring the values of the Hindu way of life and the cultural ethos of India will be promoted. In this way, Yogi Adityanath also talks of the ethos of a nation's culture which is imbued with the idea of political restructuring of states. While explaining this aspect, religion should not act as an obstacle in promoting the national interest of India.

Security and Development: The above analysis leads to an important issue, i.e., India's security and development. Yogi Adityanath lays much emphasis on these terms as both are important for the development of Indian culture and prosperity and thereby promoted national unity and integrity in spite of diversity preserved in the Indian system. One is aware of the fact that concern for the security of the nation is as old as the nation-state itself. In a way, it can be traced back to the evolution of civil society when man transformed himself from the state of nature to civil society. India, like any other modern state, is conscious of its security. Today, India faces threats from external and internal sources. Yogi Adityanath has very vividly pointed out that, today, externally not only India but the entire world is engulfed with Islamic terrorism and internally by naxalism supported by Maoist forces that has affected the country's security. Moreover, today, India is in search of its security in an era of strategic uncertainty. Both terrorism and naxalism have been examined in detail elsewhere.

India's history can be well described as a chronicle of military disasters.[44] Paradoxically, during active conflict or war, security issues are high on the Indian agenda. The justification for this is that India is a peace-loving country and does not threaten any other country. Moreover, it could be explained by such factors like geography, history, culture and the colonial legacy. For instance, Indians have long regarded the mountains and seas as protective barriers against outside interference and invasion.[45] Geography has made India essentially an inward-looking state. But this jinx was broken when China attacked India in 1962. From thence onward, the issue of security vs development became an important agenda for discussion.

Today, how do we look at these terms? Both the terms have acquired much relevance not only in sociological, political, economic and environmental spheres but are also focussed on the associated studies undertaken by various social sciences. Both the terms indicate a state associated with the well-being of an individual. The performance of an individual's well-being is related to such a social environment and cultural structure to which he belongs. In the West, it is said that "security is development and development is security." It is true in the Indian context also. But, what is development? As Yogi Adityanath believes it means a progressive enhancement of society. As such, it can be said that physical and monetary factors are important for national security. The physical factor includes the physical features and material resources. The monetary progressive enhancement is related to economic development. In other words, both are inter-related with each other. Even Yogi Adityanath cannot escape from this logic. To him, the state of Uttar Pradesh is in the doldrums because of a lack of resources and this hampers its growth. That is why recently he invited investors from all over the world and other parts of India to upgrade the economic development of the state. What is important is the elimination and reduction of negative indicators like disease, pollution, violence, corruption and ignorance. These need greater attention not only in our state but throughout the country. He believes that removing these evils from society will add strength to our culture and strengthen the national identity, unity and integrity of India. Thus, India's perspectives on security and development are based on its power potential indicating the present and future threat perceptions.

Division of Pakistan: Yogi Adityanath says though Pakistan became an independent country in 1971 but the domestic compulsions divided it into two halves in 1971. The legacies of events played a crucial role in domestic politics and cast a shadow over international relations among them. Critics often focus on the historical development crisis behaviour of the political actors and groups and misperception of leaders. These have largely influenced the ongoing public discourse, political relations and religious identity of Pakistan. Thus, Yogi Adityanath's perception of the division of Pakistan could be viewed from the neo–realist view where the separation of Pakistan into two halves was highly predisposed not only because of violence perpetrated by Western Pakistan political leaders but also by domestic compulsions and challenges imposed on East Pakistan.

One is aware of the fact that Pakistan was created out of Muslim-majority regions in the North-east and North-west of the Indian subcontinent. Both the areas were separated by one thousand miles of Indian territory. But within the span of 24 years of Pakistani independence, it fought three wars with India. The 1971 war was important because Pakistan as a nation further crumbled and that led to the division of the nation. From the neo-realist perspective, Pakistan failed to address the imbalance created by internal and external sources and failed to unite the nation into one political unit.

Yogi Adityanath feels when Pakistan was carved out as a state for Muslim in 1947 and that the leadership in West Pakistan used the communal basis for identity as a means to unify a geographically and ethically diverse country. In the words of Stephen Cohen, Pakistan began the process of official myth-creation in earnest. A large central-bureaucracy was created to manufacture an ideology for Pakistan, one that glorified the army as the state's key institution."[46] This makes Yogi Adityanath comment that Islamic ideology and identity were extensively propagated and used for greater military cohesion and effectiveness of the army.

More important was that Islamic identity was seen as a key element of the ideological make-up of the Pakistani ruling elite and supremacy towards Hindus in India and Bengalis in East Pakistan. Since its inception, West Pakistan was almost exclusively Muslim (97 %) while a very sizeable minority remained in East Pakistan (22 %). Pakistani elites also viewed the Hindus in East Pakistan as generally overrepresented in all strata of education, deliberated the idea of weaning away Bengali Muslims from Islam to secularism and syncretism. As Yogi Adityanath perceived the situation, the people in East Pakistan demanded legitimate and fundamental political rights which was seen in West Pakistan as a direct threat to the core Islamic ideology of Pakistan. Thus, this kind of ideology, besides other factors imposed on the people of East Pakistan, became important in the bifurcation of Pakistan and the creation of an independent nation known as Bangladesh.

Global Pressure after Second World War

Any analysis of national and international politics after 1945 has to be examined in terms of state identity and solidarity of its political and social institutions. Political realism, then, was more governed by the nation's quest for power and the inevitability of conflict among states. In such an environment, India had to keep pace with the developments in international politics. Important to note was that these developments affected India in terms of national identity, national interest and the means to achieve national interest. Though international politics has undergone major changes, still Yogi Adityanath sticks to the political philosophy as propounded by Kautilya, Kamandaka, Bhanbhatt, Somadeva Suri, Sukracharya and others.

Like Kautilya, it seems that as a political realist Yogi Adityanath thinks that a nation-state works to produce maximum power and national interest. Thus, moral principles in the political activities of the nation are missing in his writings. He further observed that a nation looked to the security of its interests in the event of natural calamities or at the time of war. War or peace are dependent upon a country's national interest. According to Burton Stein, Kautilya describes foreign policy not in terms of a great empire like Mauryan, but as small warring states that indulged in incessant conflicts such as India had experienced before the Mauryan empire.[47] Similarly, later on, Kamandaka says that the king's assertion and the formation of policy will serve the interest of the state. If he is affiliated with calamities, he causes its ruin. In one of the extracts (VI-23) he, after dividing the state into two units, the king and the territory forming its inner and outer parts respectively, stresses that these two should be regarded as one because of their interdependence. Like Kautilya, Kamandaka too views the state as a means for preserving order and prosperity. How is the state to be preserved? It is because of some political control, i.e., the king could protect the state in times of internal and external crises.

Describing India as one national unit, Yogi Adityanath, more or less, stresses the same content that has been visualised by Indian ancient Indian thinkers. Today, our Constitution is federal in nature but with a strong unitary character, i.e., giving more powers to the Centre. Furthermore, one finds that decentralisation of powers between various states and the Centre were viewed to have political control over other states so that they could be protected during natural calamities and war.

The relevance of political realism in the writings of Yogi Adityanath form four main tenets. the first is the deduction of difficult questions about international politics arising from the conflictual nature of politics. The second is the recognition of the relationship between individuals and the state. The third, to a certain extent, is the acceptance of historical optimism and its persistent belief in the perfectibility of man through spiritualism and scientific temper. And the fourth is the connection between morality and political action despite the inherent complexity of the nation on the one hand and focussing on human knowledge, nationality and reasoning on the other.

Basically, in international and national politics there are two different schools of political thought, viz, idealism and realism. Yogi Adityanath belongs to the second school because realism in international and national politics does not signify the Platonic doctrine which emphasises abstract reasoning. Yogi Adityanath is more focussed on the issue of national integration and unity of the nation through its culture which has played a unique role in the conduct of national identity. He believed that a nation could be secured "where there is good law there is good arms and where there is good arms there is good law." This statement was earlier articulated by Kautilya and many centuries later on by Nicolo Machiavelli. What does it mean? A state's prosperity lies in the welfare and protection of the people for which even the ruler had to adopt the harshest of measures. Today, in India, normal conditions have deteriorated badly. Hence, Yogi Adityanath wants to introduce the Gujarat model to improve the safety of the people. This aspect has been dealt with in detail elsewhere.

The basic assumption of real politics has given rise to various conflicts—external and internal. Therefore, the on-going strife can be contained by good and coercive laws as the situations demand and also that political realism accepts for its guide the permanence and ubiquity of the struggle for power. In other words, both means and end become important to achieve national and international objectives.

Political realism has given rise to competition and conflict. Realists consider the principal actor is the state which is more concerned with its own powers. There lies difference between the approach of national and international politics. National politics basically focuses on authority and law and international politics is an area without justice and concentrate more on potential conflict among states. Not all realists deny the presence of ethics in international relations. But, in reality, the realists lay emphasis on the supreme value to successful political action based on prudence. They have the ability to judge the correct situation from various given options on the basis of political consequences. The ancient political thinker, Thucydides, saw politics through moral questions. To him so far as relations among states are concerned, power can be influenced by the norms of justice. One cannot deny that taken in this sense, Yogi Adityanath's political writings do play an important role in determining the political behaviour of states.

Laying down the realist theory is marked by certain characteristics:

1. The first characteristic that influences realism is human nature. Even Thucydides and Kautilya and, later on, Yogi Adityanath believe that considerations of right and wrong have never turned people aside from the opportunities of aggrandisement offered by superior strength.
2. Realists consider anarchy as the primary determinant of national and international political outcomes. Generally, anarchy leads to a situation in which power has the overriding role in shaping interstate relations.
3. As anarchy prevails in a nation, security becomes the central issue. To acquire security, states tend to increase power and wars are fought to prevent competing states from becoming militarily stronger.

Where can one place Yogi Adityanath in shaping the national and international order? One can say that he believes that in the conduct of the state's affairs morality and power are important. But they work in their own spheres. In ancient times, Cicero had developed the idea of a natural moral law that was applicable to both domestic and international politics. His ideas were further carried by St. Augustine and St. Thomas Aquinas. So can we may say that Yogi Adityanath believes in the doctrine of separation of politics from ethics. In terms of national identity and development, power becomes important and all means are justified to achieve certain political ends. It does not mean spiritualism in the form of morality has no role in cultivating the culture of a country. This is also important as it reflects the nation's spirit and all the culturally developed countries are today major powers. Therefore, it could be said that culture and political processes are the inherent strength of a nation. In other words, a strong cultural and political power could play a more dominant role in national and international politics. Seen from this perspective, one cannot deny that all the attributes that are essential to political realism are well presented in Yogi Adityanath's writings.

In recent years, Kenneth N. Waltz reformulated political realism with his scientific temper approach. Distancing himself from the philosophical discussion of human nature, he came up with a theory which was focussed on microeconomics. He argued that "states in the international system are like firms in a domestic economy and have the same core interest, i.e., to survive." Realists aim at the fundamental interest of each state which revolves around security and hence concentrate on the distribution of power. Hence, "states do not willingly place themselves in situations of increased dependence. In a self-help system, consideration of security subordinates economic gain to political interest."[48]

In a sense, Yogi Adityanath does not believe on increased economic dependence on any state. For a state to grow, he believes in the slogan "sabka sath, sabka vikas". It would then result in good governance that could be properly delivered by political leaders or parties. This would also enable political leaders to fulfil their political aspirations and help the country in the growth of Indian culture that could bind diverse groups of people into one single entity. Hence, to say that a realist does not give much attention to ethics or spiritualism would be a wrong assumption. Yogi Adityanath has proved that both spiritualism and political realism can go side by side if one does not enter the other's area. If there is a clash between them, the nation will definitely suffer. But his focus on its age-old spiritualistic traditions have kept alive the real potential of political realism even in modern times.

NOTES

1. Sri Aurobindo Birth Centenary Library, 14: 409.
2. *The Times of India*, 5 September 2017.
3. Ibid.
4. Ibid.
5. E. Lezotte, *Spirituality and Social Work, Focus of Course*, December 2010, p. 2.
6. Ibid.
7. M. K. Hellwig, "A History of the Concept of Faith," in J. M. Lee (ed.) *Handbook of Faith*, Birmingham Al-Religious Education Press, 1990, pp. 3-23.
8. J. W. Fowler, *Stages of Faith, The Psychology of Human Development and the Quest for Meaning*, San Francisco, Harper and Row, 1981, p. 321.
9. Ibid, p. xiii.
10. Ibid, p. 24.
11. P. Love and D. Talbot, "Defining Spiritual Development: A Missing Consideration for Student Affairs", *NASPA Journal*, 37, 1999, pp. 361-76.
12. J. Smith (ed.), *Dictionary of Religion*, San Francisco, Harper Collins, 1995, p. 893.
13. Ibid, p. 905.
14. R. C. Solomon, *Spirituality for the Skeptic. The Thoughtful Love of Life*, Oxford Scholarship.
15. J. Mahan, "Religion and Media", *Religion Compass* 6(1), 2012, pp. 14-25.
16. Schuurmans–Stekhoven, "Measuring Spirituality as Personal Belief in Supernatural Forces: Is the Character Strength Inventory—Spirituality Subscribes a Belief, Reliable and Valid Measure," *Implicit Religion*, 17(2), 2014, pp. 211-222.
17. Sabinet, "Secular Spirituality vs Secular Dualism: Towards Post-Secular Holism as Model for a National Theology, http://reference.safinet.coza/sa_publication_article/hervorm-V62-4-58.
18. Ibid.

19. Van der Veer, "Social Research, An International Quality," *Spirituality in Modern Society*, 76 (4): 1097-1120.
20. Ibid.
21. J. Newman, *Religion and Technology: A Study in the Philosophy of Culture, West Post, CT*: Praegar Pub., 1997, pp. 110-111.
22. Ibid.
23. See Aurobindo, *Essay on Gita.*
24. Sri Aurobindo Birth Centenary Library, 14: 427.
25. *Rig Veda*, X-121-2.
26. Aurobindo, *The Foundation of Indian Culture*, Centenary Volume 14, p. 260.
27. Sankaracharya, *Geeta Bhasaya*, Gorakhpur, 1960, pp. 11, 48.
28. http://www.himavanti.org/himavanti-I/nath-Sampradaya-hatha-yoga-kundali-and-kriya-yoga.
29. See *The Complete Works of Swami Vivekananda*, 2:385-88, 6:16-17, 137-38.
30. Swami Sivananda, *All About Hinduism*, published by Divine Life Society, Tehri Garhwal, Uttarakhand, 1999, p. 77.
31. Ibid, p. 78.
32. See note 29, Works, I, III.
33. www.inuth.com
34. www.inuth.com
35. A. C. Bose, In *Hymns from the Vedas, Yajurveda*, Bombay, Asia Publishing House, 1966, p. 301.
36. K. Bharadwaja, *A Philosophical Study of the Concept of Vishnu in the Puranas*, New Delhi, Pitamber Pub. Company, 1981, pp. 361-62.
37. Sri Aurobindo, *The Foundation of Indian Culture*, New York, Sri Aurobindo Library, 1953, p. 243.
38. Yogi Adityanath, 'Culture is Soul of Nation, Not Religion', *The Times of India*, 5 September 2017.
39. Ibid.
40. Ibid.
41. Kautilya, *Arthasastra*, Book I, Chapter XIII, 23, p. 22.
42. M. K. V. Rao, *Studies in Kautilya*, Munshi Ram Manohar Lal, Oriental Publication, Delhi, 1958, pp. 2, 3.
43. L. N. Rangarajan, *The Arthashastra*, Penguim Books, Delhi, 1992, p. 31.
44. A. A. Athale, 'An Enigma that is India: A Holistic View of National Security,' *Strategic Analysis*, March 1989, p. 1398.
45. G. Tanham, 'Indian Strategic Thoughts', in Kanti Bajpai *et al* (eds.) *Security India*, New Delhi, 1996, p. 32.
46. S. Cohen, *The Idea of Pakistan*; Brooking Institute Press. 1984, p. 67.
47. B. Stein, *A History of India*, Oxford, Blackwell Publication, 1998, p. 78.
48. K. N.Wattz, *The Theory of International Relations*, Boston, MA, McGraw, Hill, 1979, p. 93.

3

DEBACLE OF CONGRESS PARTY

The national integration and territorial sovereignty of a country are essential elements of its security. In the process of nation building, it is important to examine the role of various political parties. If one studies the history of the national movement in India, it was found that the policies and ideologies of these parties had to pass through various processes in shaping its destiny. At one particular stage, the goal of all these parties was to fight colonialism and imperialism. In other words, the struggle was against the oppressive rule of the British government. It is true, as stated above, that the goal of all parties was the same but they adopted different approaches to attain national independence. Hence, it becomes important to re-examine the then dominant role of the parties in the integration of the nation to fight against a common enemy. The author restricts this chapter to the role played by the Congress, Muslim League, Bharatiya Janata Party (BJP) and the Communist Party of India. The important question was whether these political parties worked for the country's national interest or protected their own. It is interesting here to note the comment made by Yogi Adityanath that when politics serves the well-being of the people, the nation is united in one single mainstream. But when politics is used to serve the selfish interests of a particular political party, it poses a danger to national culture, spiritualism and integrity.

How does Yogi Adityanath see the role of the Congress since its inception? In its initial period after its formation, one cannot minimise the role of the Congress party in the struggle for freedom. But in this process, the mistakes committed by the party were so grave that Yogi Adityanath feels that instead of promoting national interests, a double standard was adopted to promote its own ideology and this had harmed the nation before and after the Second World War. As India approached independence, the rivalry and selfish interests of the party became apparent because it started promoting its own interests at the cost of national integrity. This narrow-mindedness of its political leadership made it more arrogant and the purpose was one, i.e., party dominance over other national parties, though when India got independence we opted for democracy and the parliamentary form of government. Under this, our Constitution was federal but unitary in nature, i.e., focus was on decentralisation of power but with a strong Centre. In due course, the basic federal structure was weakened because of the interference by the then ruling Congress party. The dual approach of the Congress can, as visualised by Yogi Adityanath, be seen in the political and economic spheres. Let us examine these aspects separately when the Congress was at the helm of national affairs. The author here divides the political aspirations of the Congress party into various phases and how it ultimately became the cause of the decline in national politics.

Establishment of Indian National Congress

It is accepted by everyone that the foundation of the Indian National Congress in 1885 was the culmination of a process of national awakening. It emphasised the need for an all-India organisation. Enlightened imperialists like A. O. Hume, William Wedderburn, George Yule, Alfred Webb and Henry Cotton tried to keep the Indian National Congress as a "loyal and innocuous" organisation in the beginning. But they had a hidden agenda. On the one hand, they did not try to harm the British interests and on the other, they worked for a secular and democratic national movement to spread political awareness among the masses, to form the headquarters of the movement on an all-India leadership basis and to propagate an anti-colonial nationalist ideology.

Before independence, Indian historians had studied and analysed the history of the national movement in the wake of the political and economic development that surfaced within the Indian framework. To them, the development of the national movement was attributed to the growth of communalism in India. Bipan Chandra, Mridula Mukerjee, Aditya Mukherjee, Sucheta Mahajan and K. N. Pannikar reveal that communalism as an ideology consisted of three basic elements. The first was common secular interests, i.e., common political, economic, social and cultural interests. From this, arose the notion of socio-political communities based on religion. These different communities were led by their own leaders.[1] The second element of communal ideology rests on the notion of a multi-religious society in India having their own social, cultural, economic and political interests.[2] The third element of the so-called communalism was seen in terms of the interest of the followers of different religions or communities which were mutually incompatible, antagonistic and hostile to each other.[3]

The pertinent question that becomes important is why historians had claimed that the growth of communalism began in the 19th century and not earlier when Islam made its presence in Hindustan. In one of his articles, "Alapsankyak Tustikaran Aur Esske Nateja" Balbir K. Punj says one has to rethink about Hindu-Muslim relations which started almost 1300 years ago. The induction of Islam as a religion began with the invasion of Muhammad bin Kasim in A.D. 712 when he conquered Sindh. In the process of expansion of Muslim rule in India by subsequent rulers, Hindus were forced to accept Islam as their religion. During various battles fought by Hindu and Muslim rulers, the victorious Muslim rulers indulged in brutal murder, loot, rape and religious conversion. This aspect has also been highlighted by Muslim historians.

Historians have explained Indian history as a Hindu-Muslim conflict and that Hindus felt that the medieval Muslim rulers were anti- Hindu and tyrannized them to accept their suzerainty. But at the same time, there also existed distinct Hindu and Muslim cultures. One can recall the growing impact of Sufism and the Bhakti movement of the respective communities. Since Muslim rulers had their origin in foreign soil, they tried to glorify their tradition and culture. If one reads history, there are good examples of the rise and fall of empires. This happened also in the case of Muslim rule in India. The seeds of dissension started with the rise of Shivaji and Guru Gobind Singh. Once again, we saw the growth of Hindu patriotism and glory. When Aurangzeb, was in power one also saw an era of hatred between Hindus and Muslims. After his death, Hindu's ascendancy was on the rise while that of the Muslim community declined as a political power in the 19th century. The question then arises why historians did not accept this era as an era of communalism?

It was during the Mughal period that the European powers made their presence in India. Initially, the process was slow but in due course their presence grew larger. Of all the European powers, the British Crown was the predominant one in India. Still then, there were native Indian rulers under Maratha-Sikh-Jat Rajput leadership who vehemently opposed the British rule. In the famous Anglo-Maratha war, the Marathas were defeated by the British forces but Hindus and Muslims jointly stood firmly against them. Thus, Yogi Adityanath has said that in the Indian War of Independence (1857) there was a new awareness among the people to fight for their identity and integrity. He further clarifies that these historians do not connect themselves to the idea of War of India's Independence. Moreover, from 1857 till India achieved freedom they looked at history from different perspectives and in the process overlooked the nationalistic spirit and pride of Indian leaders.

Balbir K. Punj has rightly pointed out that in India's War of Independence the majority of the Hindu rulers stood behind Bahadur Shah II and efforts were made to establish him as the king again. As soon as he ascended the throne, the first step he took was to ban cow slaughter. This did not last long as the fighting spirit of the masses was crushed in 1857. From thence onward, one sees major changes in the Indian political system. In order to promote the imperialistic design, the British followed the policy of "divide and rule." John Stratchey wrote in 1888 that the existence of two opposite Hindu-Muslim-religions acted as an obstacle in promoting the British interest. But the British government fully exploited the growing internal dissension among the masses. This internal dissension had its roots in society and British policy was to prevent any kind of national unification in India because it had other commitments in Europe. As such, the British government treated Hindus, Muslims and Sikhs as separate entities. It was said that Indian society was fractured, exclusive and had antagonistic based religious communities. The British used religion as a mobilising factor to promote their self interest by widening the gap within Indian society

Thus, from here onwards, one can consider this rise of so-called communalism was due to the British policy towards different communities. It was a clear departure from the politics of the pre-1857 period. This modern communalism was based on people's politics and greatly inspired the nationalist spirit of the people. Once Nehru in 1936 said "one must never forget that communalism in India is a latter day phenomenon which has grown before our eyes."[4]

It is also relevant to figure out that similar ideologies in the form of fascism, Nazism and racism, were developed by the parties in Europe to promote the spirit of nationalism among the masses so that a nation could be united into a single political entity. There are some critics who have tried to equate the emergence of different Indian communities with fascism or Nazism. But there was a difference in their respective approach. In Europe, these ideologies were the result of political consolidation of the state by compulsory military service. It, thereby, created the concept of levee-en-masses. This was necessary as all European nations wanted stability and security and this was also made possible by famous French slogan, "liberty equality and fraternity."

With the growth of industrialisation and science and technology in the 18th and 19th centuries, history was reinterpreted by political and economic thinkers as the struggle between the haves and the have-nots. The purpose was to transform society and to minimise the gap between the privileged and unprivileged classes. Hence, the masses took to the revolutionary method which was violent in nature. But, in the case of India, as Yogi Adityanath sees it, the rise of Hindu and Muslim communities was the outcome of the British policy of colonialism and imperialism. Thus, there was a need for a strong united front to fight the common enemy.

The ideology and programmes of the Congress from 1885 to 1947 can be divided into three phases:

First Phase: In the initial stages, it could be said that from 1885 to 1905 the vision of the Indian National Congress was obscure and confused. The period could be referred to as a period of moderate politics. The followers were Dadabhai Naoroji, P. N. Mehta, D. E. Wacha, W. C. Banerjee, S. N. Banerjee and Gopal Krishna Gokhale. They believed in constitutional methods to resolve the national crisis through the policy of protest, prayer and petition. These nationalists were critical of British economic policy but failed to expose the true nature of British imperialism. Hence, their objective of developing national awakening among the masses failed as the movement was confined to the educated middle class and elite population.

Second Phase (1905-1919): During this phase, one saw the rise of a new group within the Indian National Congress. Leaders like Bal Gangadhar Tilak, Lala Lajpat Rai, Bipin Chandra Pal, M. A. Jinnah, and Aurobindo Ghosh were not satisfied with the ideology of these moderate Congressmen. Hence, they opposed them and a new era of extremism was seen in the history of national integration of India. The rise of extremism could be attributed to the overall deteriorating economic condition of India under British rule. The extremists favoured the idea of Swaraj, that is, complete independence from British rule. Tilak even remarked that "Swaraj is my birth right and I shall have it." Aurobindo Ghosh said political freedom is the life breath of a nation. The revolutionaries advocated a boycott of foreign goods and promoted the use of swadeshi goods. Promoting swadeshi goods would generate more jobs. Soon, it was realised that an economic boycott could be a powerful instrument against the oppressive rule of the British government. Hence, these extremists turned their attention towards villages for social work. Besides this, they also used religious revivalism for mass contact. Tilak started the Ganapati festival in 1893 and Shivaji festival in 1895. But the movement could only attract urban centres and failed to reach the rural areas. The narrow social base and internal dissension within group to take appropriate steps to fight British rule became a destabilising factor in Indian national politics.

Third Phase (1919-1947): The dream of Purna Swaraj or complete independence under Mahatma Gandhi became the focal point against British rule. An effort was made to eradicate the British empire from Indian soil. The method adopted by Gandhi was a non-violent one which would be discussed later. On the other hand, fear and hatred cultures were developed among the Hindu and Muslim masses by the British rulers. As a result, it gave rise to such parties like the Muslim League, Hindu Mahasabha and Rashtriya Swayamsevak Sangh (RSS) who had their own agenda to fight colonialism and imperialism and to free India from the clutches of British rule.

With the rise of Hindu and Muslim parties one witnessed the politics of hatred and fear psychosis among these communities. The British government used the Muslim community as a means to sustain its existence in India. As a result Muslims became more isolated from the national mainstream. It is said that they had the support of the British government. The first step towards the division of India can be traced to the demand of a separate election mandal in 1906. In the same year, under the leadership of Shia Imam, the Agha Khan met Lord Minto. The main demand was for a separate Muslim election mandal. Lord Minto agreed to this demand and it was included in the Mall-Minto reforms in 1909.

On the basis of these conditions, the Congress made an agreement with Muslims to involve them in the national independence struggle. Again, in 1927, under the leadership of Mohammad Ali Jinnah, a meeting took place. Four demands were presented. In place of a separate election mandal, Jinnah wanted reservation for joint election areas. These were:

- Separation of Sindh from Mumbai province.
- To increase province of western boundary and Baluchistan by giving them the status of complete province.

- In Punjab and Bengal on demographic ratio, representation should be given to Muslim majority provinces.
- In Central Vidhan mandal there should be at least one-third Muslims.

This kind of politics acted as a barrier to promote nationalism. Throughout the 1930s, the interests of both parties clashed at regular intervals. The year 1937 was important because election was held. Both the Muslim League and Hindu Mahasabha fought on liberal communal lines but the performances were negligible. Soon both of them realised that they had to remodel their strategy by resorting to more militant mass-based politics. The focus was on mass movement and cadre-based politics. At that time, the Congress was the only party that succeeded in appeasing the Muslim people. Hence, Jawahar Lal Nehru took the initiative for a massive campaign to work with the Muslims. This campaign is known as the Muslim Mass Contact Programme. Till, 1937, the Congress had permitted Hindu-Muslim communities to work together within the Congress organisation. Soon, under Left pressure, the Congress took a drastic step by not accommodating these communities in the 1934 and 1937 elections.

Here special mention has to be made of how Muslim leader Mohammed Ali Jinnah looked at Congress mass politics. He left the party and instead of going into political oblivion turned to liberal communal politics. Beside him, there were other Hindu leaders like Surendranath Banerjee, Bipin Chandra Pal, Tej Bahadur Sapru and C. Sankaran Nair who left the party.

So far as Jinnah was concerned, his approach towards independence was not acceptable by other sections of society. He organised the Muslim League in 1924 and worked for the betterment of Muslim rights and interests. His politics was based on the idea that "Muslims should organise themselves, stand united and should press every reasonable point for the protection of their community."[5]

Soon Jinnah was isolated from the main current of nationalism because the Congress then had organised a huge mass movement in 1930 and worked for more radical socio-economic programmes.

Being a man of action, Jinnah once again revived the Muslim League in 1936. Throughout 1936, he spoke of nationalism and Hindu-Muslim cooperation. At the same time, he asked Muslims to organise themselves separately. The Muslim demands were protection and promotion of Urdu language and script and adoption of such measures suitable to the general conditions of Muslims. In the 1937 election, Jinnah had to opt for mass politics. It was based on the semi-feudal and semi loyalist social base of the Muslim League. His slogan was 'Islam is in danger' and the danger arises from Hindu Raj. He felt that the Congress wanted not independence from British rule but a Hindu Raj with British cooperation. He also felt that the Congress would dominate Muslims and would be the cause of the destruction of Islam in India. In the 1939 Second Round Table Conference, for the first time the word 'Pakistan' came into existence. In March 1940, Jinnah told the students at Aligarh, "Mr. Gandhi's hope is to subjugate the Muslim under a Hinduraj."[6] Again, at Aligarh, in March 1941 he spoke, "Pakistan is not only a practicable goal but the only goal if you want to save Islam from complete annihilation in this country."[7] The Muslim community targeted such nationalist Muslims like Maulana Abdul Kalam Azad and regarded him as a traitor to Islam and a mercenary of the Hindus. During 1945-47, the radical Muslim community indulged in religious fanaticism and even had to resort to physical attack. Religion was used as propaganda to secure their interests. The slogan was 'Vote for Islam' and even proposed that Pakistan would be ruled under the Sharia.

These kinds of incidents, as Yogi Adityanath sees them, hampered the growth of nationalism in India. In order to promote national interest and work for the integration of the nation, the Hindu Mahasabha and the RSS came to the forefront to see how the Hindu community could assert its role in nation building. This aspect has been discussed fully in a chapter ahead.

Yogi Adityanath says that the antagonistic behaviour of two different communities put the Congress in a dilemma. The message was clear that the Indian nationalists had failed to wage a common mass ideological, political and economic struggle against the rising tide of British imperialism. Hence, the Congress had to pay a heavy price. The Congress failed to negotiate with other national parties and as a consequence it lost the opportunity to evolve a viable and effective long-term strategy to combat the evil of communalism.

Economic Policy of Indian National Congress

A re-examination of the Congress's economic policy leads to one important conclusion that the party could not ignore the trend that was shaping the world economy. Since India was the product of a colonial state and the Congress, in the words of John McGuire,[8] it was partially a by product of the emerging world economy. The Congress was in a dilemma on how to protect the interests of diverse social groups when the entire world was influenced by the Western pattern of economic growth. To some extent, the Congress party tried to balance the global economic trend and mood of the masses by cultivating consensus within the party.

The basic philosophy of the economic policy of the Congress centred on the term 'development' so that it could modernise the backward society. But, at this point, the Indian dominant elite and policy-makers favoured a self-reliant economy and a powerful state.[9] It was also a stage when the bourgeois class supported the Congress for attaining an interventionist state. This was done by them to develop an indigenous bourgeois class.[10]

Before the Second World War, economic development, as pushed by the Congress, became a source of major conflict. In the 1930s, the major conflict on economic development was not between the socialists and the capitalists but between the Gandhians and the socialists. In 1931, the Karachi resolution that was adopted called for an international state that could preserve the economic rights of the people. This was a Congress Left-centred approach. But later on, the Congress also adopted the Gandhian ethos of economic strategy. As such swadeshi, or self-reliance, became a major theme of the Indian National Congress. But the balance tilted in favour of a socialistic pattern of economy. In 1938, the National Planning Committee was formed under the chairmanship of Nehru. It was laid down that the solution to the problem lay in the adoption of socialism. The leadership also felt that since a good economy was a precondition for good democratic politics, the economic well-being of social groups would consolidate the role of the Congress in Indian politics. But in reality, when India became independent, the Congress party had to face pressures arising from different political parties.

Partition of India

The partition of India was on religious and ideological lines. On 14 and 15 August 1947, Pakistan and India emerged as independent countries. The important question was why did the Congress accept partition. Yogi Adityanath feels that partition was the most unfortunate event. It has serious implications on Indian national politics. It exposed the Congress approach of handling the situation. Instead of uniting Muslims and Hindus under one banner, the Congress succumbed to Muslim pressure. Hence, Muslims and Hindus drifted apart. This was a clear indication that the problem would be more serious in the future. It is important to note that soon after partition, hatred among these two communities was so serious that a member of the Hindu Mahasabha did not hesitate to kill Mahatma Gandhi. A new chapter began in the history of Indo-Pakistan relations, built on the theme of hatred, antagonism and fear. Today, Yogi Adityanath says that the problems that India faces is the outcome of the diverse antagonistic approach of Muslims and Hindus and the Congress could not play the role of a balancer in uniting them.

After independence, India adopted a Constitution borrowed from 26 or 27 countries. On the one hand, the Congress party, the most dominant party, the policy was not to succumb to the influence of colonialism, imperialism and communism. But in real terms India was reeling under colonialism in the form of "constitutional colonialism" and even today we do not have our own Constitution. This had a great impact on the working pattern of states within the constitutional framework. Soon, the federal structure of India was affected to such an extent that the popularity graph of the Congress was on the decline. It would be rather interesting to note the comment made by Yogi Adityanath. Yogi Adityanath said that the word "secular" was the "biggest lie" that has been told since Independence and has damaged the country. The BJP leader also said that "distorting history was no less a crime than sedition," and claimed that the word "Paki" was the biggest insult" used in Europe.[11] On November 15, 1948, when the newly-independent dominion of India was in the midst of a heated debate in the Constituent Assembly on the nature of the Constitution, Prof. K. T. Shah made an intervention demanding the inclusion of the word "secular" in the preamble, "Sir, I beg to move, that in clause (1) of article 1, after the words 'shall be' the words 'Secular, Federalist, Socialist' be included. The amended article or clause shall read as follows: 'India shall be a Secular, Federalist, Socialist, Union of States'," he said. In the ensuing discourse, while the members agreed on the nature of the Indian state adhering to secular principles and the word 'secular' was dropped from the preamble. It made an appearance though, about three decades later, when the Indira Gandhi-led government included it in the document as part of the 42nd Amendment of the Constitution.[12]

In the decades that followed, secularism in the Indian Constitution has been appreciated by some but has come under criticism by several others who have repeatedly pointed out to the foreign origins of the words, its inapplicability in the Indian context and the problematic ways in which it has been applied in India. "Independent government implemented secularism mostly by refusing to recognise the religious pasts of Indian nationalism, whether Hindu or Muslim, and at the same time (inconsistently) by retaining Muslim 'personal law," writes historian Ronald Inden in his work, "Imagining India."[13]

The word "secularism" is known to have originated in late medieval Europe. "Secularism, the theory that governments ought to have no religious connection, nor indeed anything to do with matters of religious belief or ritual, is manifestly a Western intervention, specifically a product of the Protestant Reformation and the Enlightenment," writes historian lan Copland. Thereafter, secularism as the ideal theoretical basis of nation-states was utilised in lands outside the European continent such as the United States and Turkey. The majority of the makers of modern India, shaped as they were by European thoughts and practices, were ardent supporters of secularism as well. Foremost among them was the first prime minister of the country, Jawaharlal Nehru. For him, having a secular state was a crucial mark of modernity. "We have only done something which every country does, except for a few misguided and backward countries," he said in the Constituent Assembly debates.[14]

Making clear his stance on the State following the spirit of secularism, while avoiding its inclusion in the Preamble, Ambedkar said "what should be the policy of the State, how the society should be organised in its social and economic side are matters which must be decided by the people themselves according to time and circumstances. It cannot be laid down in the Constitution itself because that is destroying democracy altogether." Consequently, the Constituent Assembly adopted Articles 25, 26 and 27 of the Constitution with the intention of furthering secularism. Though not formally inserted in the document, secularism was definitely embedded in the constitutional philosophy.[15]

The word secular was inducted in the 42nd amendment. This 20–page- long detailed document gave unprecedented powers to Parliament. Almost all parts of the Constitution, including the Preamble, were changed with this amendment. Thereafter, the description of India in the Preamble was changed from "sovereign, democratic republic' to a sovereign, socialist, secular, democratic republic."[16]

Responding to a question on communalism and secularism at a function organised by the Dainik Jagran group in Raipur, Adityanath said, "Mera maana hai ki azadi ke baad Bharat mein sabse bada jhooth dharmnirpeksh shabd hai. Nagrikon ke saath Bharat ke logon ke saath...un logon ko maafi maangni chahiye, inhone shabd ko janm aur yeh jo istemaal karte hai...koi vyavastha dharmnirpeksh nahin ho sakti. Rajneetik vyavstha panthnirpeksi ho sakti hai. Agar koi humse kahega ki shasan us upasna vidhi se chalni chahiye, toh nahin chal sakti. UP ke ander dekhna to 22 crore logon ko dekhna hoga. Mein in logon ke suraksha ke prati, unki bhavaon ke prati javabdeh hoon. Lekin ek samuday ka dushikaran karne ke liye bhi nahin baita hoon. Panthnirpeksh ho lekin dharmnispekh nahin ho saka" (I believe that the word secular is the biggest lie since Independence. Those that have given birth to this lie and those who use it should apologise to the people and this country. No system can be secular. Political system can be sect-neutral. If someone were to say that government has to be run by one way of prayer, that is not possible. In UP, I have to look at 22 crore people and I am answerable for their security and their feelings. But I am not sitting here to ruin one community either. You can be sect-neutral but not secular.[17] The BJP regards itself as a distinct party and rejects the idea of secularism. It perceives it as only pseudo-secularism because it is promoted by opportunistic political parties for the appeasement of minorities in order to secure their votes.

Global Pressure on Congress

Global developments also influenced India's national politics. After 1945, the world saw the emergence of two dominant hostile powers with their own ideologies. They were known as superpowers. The aim of the USA and the USSR were the same; to promote neo-colonialism. How did India cope with this kind of international power politics? If India, under the Congress party, had accepted the suzerainty of the USA or the USSR, it would have gone against the nationalistic spirit of the people. The Congress then came up with the policy of non-alignment, a concept that was based on development rather than joining any power bloc. The policy of non-alignment then became the cornerstone of our foreign policy. On this pretext, the Indian government tried to solve internal and external problems. But mounting domestic compulsions forced the Congress party to adopt the socialistic pattern in order to nurture the Indian economy. This kind of politics was against the spirit of non-alignment and India had to pay the price. The Sino-Indian war of 1962 was a bad experience for us as the country was badly humiliated by China and India had to surrender a major chunk of its territory to China. Here, what is important to note how many non-aligned countries supported India is during the Sino-Indian war.. It was only five or six countries and the others questioned the relevance of the non-aligned approach adopted by the Congress in addressing national and international problems.

Overall, it was a clear indication and Yogi Adityanath firmly believed that Nehru had a vision of one-party domination in the Indian political system and other national parties like the Jana Sangh, Swatantra party, Communist party and Muslim League could not match the personality of Nehru. This was quite visible from the elections held at for Parliament and in the states. The Nehru legacy of hegemonist domination of the party, in fact, led the party towards the "cult of dynasty" and was very much against the spirit of our national cultural growth. Moreover, the shift in economic policy too affected the people of India.[18]

What was the outcome of the Congress policy of integrating India into one single entity? It failed in its mission. The popularity graph of the Congress declined. Its political journey can be divided into three time frames. It started first with the Indian National Congress after independence. After Nehru and Shastri's death there was a revolt within the party and eventually Indira Gandhi emerged as the party leader. This dynastic legacy continued till the death of Rajiv Gandhi in 1991. There was a political interregnum between 1992 and 1997 when the party was not led by any member of the Nehru-Gandhi family. Let us discuss in brief the role of the Congress party and its consequent effects on Indian national politics.

Indian National Congress (1952-1968)

Political Development: Elections are, no doubt, an indication of the rise or decline of any party. In the very first general election held in 1952, the Jawaharlal Nehru-led party won a landslide victory at the Centre and in most states. This paved the way for a Nehruvian era of a single party dominance. Rajni Kothari in his book "Politics in India" defines the one-party dominant system as "a competitive party system but one in which the competing parts play dissimilar roles and one which consists of parties of pressure and parties of consensus."[19] What does it mean? The parties of pressure work within the margin of pressure which comprises opposition parties and the party of consensus works within the framework of the ruling consensus. Seen against this framework, the Congress party was then the ruling party of consensus and, therefore, the dominant party as it was seen from the electoral victories in the 1952 and 1962 Lok Sabha elections. Further, Rajni Kothari stated that while the Congress gained in strength, Nehru was also responsible for weakening the party by concentrating power in his own hands and believed that he alone could hold the country together.[20]

The general election of 1967 under the leadership of Indira Gandhi proved Rajni Kothari's argument correct as the Congress party had to face internal dissensions and factionalism. It lost not only more than 100 parliamentary seats but there was a 4 per cent decline in the popular vote. It also lost eight state elections thereafter. There is no denying that Nehru's strong leadership created insecurity among his party members. It harmed the image of the Congress party.

The Congress party's counterpart, the Jan Sangh, then focussed mainly on political issues such as the reunification of the country while the Congress relied more on an appeasement policy towards Pakistan and the Muslim minority in India and reconsidered the Indian state on a unitary basis. It favoured traditional culture rather than favouring orthodoxy in Indian politics. Instead of aggressive modernisation as postulated by Nehru, it regarded Indian culture as the main foundation of Indian life and accepted the necessity of adaptation in the prevailing situation. Hence, seen against this perspective, the Jan Sangh's first election manifesto in 1951 criticised the Congress government for trying to become "a carbon-copy of the West" and ignoring "the best in Indian life and ideals." Instead, the Jan Sangh was more concerned with the revival of Bharatiya culture and revitalisation of true Bharatiya nationalism on the basis of such adjustments as may be necessary to make India truly modern, progressive and powerful. As such, one finds complete compatibility of political positions between the Jan Sangh and, later, the Bharatiya Janata Party because the idea of Hindu nationalism is completely embedded in a vision of a politically strong India.

The lack of consensus within the Congress party indicated the first sign of the moral decline in it and the loss of public support. This has been well documented in the chart I.

Chart I
Lok Sabha Election: Performance of Congress Party

Year	*Total Seats*	*Seats Won*	*Vote Share (in %)*	*Gain/loss (Vote Share)*
1952	401	364	45.0	-
1957	403	371	47.8	+2.8
1962	494	361	44.7	-3.1
1967	520	283	40.8	-3.9

Source: Election Commission of India

Economic Development: During Nehru's era, the Congress policy moved in two different directions, i.e., the development of the state and experiment of democracy. It was an attempt to provide a platform to accommodate the demands of new classes within a democratic framework. The Congress was already in a process to develop a self-reliant modern economy. It sought an interventionist state which could play an active role in the development process. Yogi Adityanath's statement of the dual character of the Congress was also seen in its economic policy. The contradiction was quite visible in the sense that, on the one hand, it wanted the involvement of all social classes in the growth of the economy and on the other hand Nehru adopted a socialist pattern of economy. This was against the spirit of non-alignment, a policy that was adapted to keep India aloof from global power politics.

Nehru's experiment with Soviet centralized planning was focused on development which occupied the centrestage of economic development. On 21 December, 1954 he stated in the Lok Sabha that the objective of "our economic policy should be based on a socialistic pattern of society."[21] Later, at the Avadi session of the AICC in 1955, the socialistic pattern of society became the party objective and the aim was to create a mixed economy, a mixed polity and a mixed society.[22] This was also necessary for the Congress as Nehru had to counter the Jan Sangh and the Swatantra party for their pro-liberal and market-oriented approach.

Hence, a contradiction was bound to occur within the Congress itself. There were three basic streams of thought. These were the Gandhian philosophy of sarvodaya, the socialist pattern which focused on heavy industrialization and Sardar Patel's and Rajendra Prasad's approach based on private capital and market economy.[23]

Though planned development was a crucial part of the legitimate ideology of the Congress, planning as a domain outside policy became an essential instrument of "patronage politics."[24] The patronage politics enabled it to bargain with various social strata in rural and urban areas for political support. Furthermore, the patronage politics and distribution of resources made it difficult for other parties to cope with the Congress aspiration. It had far-reaching consequences. First, the Congress had developed one-party domination and, second, it countered the opposition parties electorally despite being a multi-party system. Nehru's dominance was also based on the social and ideological consensus on development policy. Being a party of consensus, the Congress tried to mobilize diverse social constituencies. Hence, at one level it was ruled by a single political party but inside it was the politics of coalition. Dualism in Congress policy, as Yogi Adityanath states, was seen in economic spheres. It damaged the Congress image. After the demise of Nehru, Congress policies and strategies entered an era of crisis that the nation is facing till now. Thus, the past Nehruvian period was seen as a traditional phase when one saw a shift from the old model to a new era in the formula of economic policy.

It is true that the basic issue of the BJP's economic programmes was quite visible in the Jan Sangh's early policy formulation. It was in favour of decentralization of power at the village level. It even promoted the ideas of defence industries to be owned by the state. It was then not in favour of large-scale industries. Shyama Prasad Mookerjee acknowledged the necessity of an integrated design of development focussed on "large, medium and small industries" and said that "sanctity of private property will be taken care and private enterprise will be given an adequate opportunity but not at the cost of national welfare." Furthermore, in the 1950s and the 1960s, the Jan Sangh opposed Nehru's idea of land cooperatives on the basis that it was similar to communist collectivization. What the Jan Sangh was propagating was the idea of a revival of the spirit of swadeshi. It even proclaimed that foreign trade should be regulated in the interest of self sufficiency and swadeshi.

Congress (1969-1991)

After the death of Prime Minister Lal Bahadur Shastri, Indira Gandhi was elevated as the next Prime Minister of India in 1966. Soon, the internal struggle for power began and it resulted in a vertical split within the party. The majority of the members supported Indira Gandhi. In the 1971 general election, the Congress won on the slogan of 'Garibi Hatao."

But at the same time, Indira Gandhi destroyed the second-tier leadership in the party and at state levels. Instead, she appointed leaders who had no political base and were completely loyal to her. Soon its effect was seen in the 1972 election when the Congress party lost several by-elections and simultaneously faced internal problems like inflation due to war with Pakistan, drought in some parts of the country and the 1973 oil crisis. Moreover, Indira Gandhi's low popularity graph was also related to the verdict of the Allahabad High Court on electoral malpractices. This led to the declaration of emergency in 1975. Complete centralization of power in her hands and the role of her son, Sanjay Gandhi, dealt a severe blow on the party structure.

The general election in 1977 saw, for the first time, the unification of opposition parties by forming the Janata party against the oppressive rule of the Congress. Though the Janata party won the election in 1977, differences sharpened among the coalition parties. Again it brought the Congress party to power in the 1980. From then onwards till her death, Indira tried to introduce many political and economic measures. It was clear that the people started questioning the credibility of the party. After her assassination in 1984, Rajiv Gandhi won the election on the sympathy wave. The party was criticized for the Bofors deal and almost lost its political pre-eminence and single-party dominance in the 1989 general elections.

Though the Congress party returned to power with a clear-cut mandate between 1979-1988 and still was the largest political party between 1989 and 1996, its organizational leadership was slowly met with severe criticism. This affected the general election as can be seen from the chart II.

Chart II
Lok Sabha Election: Performance of Congress Party

Year	*Total Seats*	*Seats Won*	*Vote Share (in %)*	*Gain/loss (Vote Share)*
1971	518	362	43.7	+2.9
1977	543	154	34.5	-9.2
1980	543	353	42.7	+8.2
1984	543	415	48.1	+5.9
1989	543	197	39.5	-0.6
1991	543	244	36.4	-3.1

Source: Election Commission of India

For the first time, it was seen that in 1992 and in 1996 the Congress president was not from the Nehru-Gandhi family. The party also suffered because of Mandal-Mandir politics, market reforms and growth of identity-based regional parties and the Hindutva-based BJP. In the 1996 general election, the mandate was against the Congress and three year later the BJP won 182 seats and emerged as the single largest party. It formed an alliance under the National Democratic Alliance (NDA) and formed the first right-wing government with Atal Bihari Vajpayee as Prime Minister.

In order to check the rising tide of the BJP, the Congress had no other option but to invite Sonia Gandhi to steer the party back into the reckoning . This was the third phase of Congress Party politics and it was able to form the government again in 2004.

Economic Development

Economic policy under Indira Gandhi underwent drastic changes due to external pressure. One saw American and World Bank intervention in the overall development of the nation. The key pillars of Nehru's policy of self-reliant growth and social transformation through the expansion of heavy industries in the public sector and land reforms and cooperative reorganization in agriculture were virtually overturned.[25]

In mid-1960, India witnessed one of the worst economic crises. Devaluation of the rupee, drought and Western interference became national problems. There was sharp criticism not only from the opposition but also from within the Congress. The economic crisis led to a sharp decline of the popular vote for it. Moreover, centre-state relations were strained because of the politics of realignment of political and ideological forces. As a result, in eight states there were non-Congress governments. Moreover, the problem of unemployment and poverty, industrial stagnation, price inflation and privileges provided to the rich class isolated the masses from the political system. These factors led to unrest and discontent in the political system. As such, Indira Gandhi failed to integrate the nation because it was difficult for her to arrive at a nationwide consensus on major economic policies.

The deteriorating situation within the Congress ranks compelled Indira Gandhi to present an economic package in the form of a Ten-Point Programme. It was another effort of the Congress to go for radical and socialistic reforms and policies. The objective was political, that is, how to regain its lost popularity. Indira Gandhi did it by distributing loans, food and subsidies to backward deprived sections of society. The Congress, then, took one step further when it embarked on a policy of nationalism in key sectors of the economy like banks, general insurance, coal mines, Indian iron and steel companies and 46 textile mills. With this, she tried the politics of populism. Further, the Monopoly Restructure and Trade Practices (MRTP) and Foreign Exchange Regulation Act (FERA) were introduced to check excessive remittance of profits from abroad. With these kinds of measures, Indira Gandhi tried to project herself as a socialist and a radical and opposing parties as reactionaries and supporters of capitalism.

It was seen that during the 1970s, because of the Congress policy, there was a shift of loyalty in the business class to the Janata party and religious groups were activated by the Jan Sangh's ideology. This led to a coalition of various parties that formed the government in 1977. But it did not last because of differences within the Janata party.

The return of Indira Gandhi (1980-84) to national politics signalled the centralization of Indian politics. It was the "Indira system to authoritarian democracy".[26] An attempt was made to bring back two isolated groups—the business class and religious groups.

In this way, more attention was focused on liberalization and a pragmatic Hindu agenda. Thus, there was a major shift in her policy from secularism and socialism to Hindu chauvinism and pro-business classes. The slogan was 'garibi hatao' and anti-poverty. This kind of pragmatic approach in solving the nation's problems led to a shift in policy from state to market economy. Soon, Indira Gandhi announced a 20-point programme.

To some critics, it was a case of "old wine in a new bottle" as 14 out of 20 points of 1975 were repeated in the new programme.[27] The purpose behind the reforms was political rather than economic. Politics, thus, under her regime became one of survival rather than development.

The policy of pro-liberalization and market reforms were further carried by her successors—Rajiv Gandhi, Narasimha Rao and Manmohan Singh. Rajiv Gandhi, as Prime Minister, accelerated the pace of liberalization in 1985. The objective was to take India into the 21st century as an advanced industrial country. His policy was attacked not only by his party but also by the communist parties and the powerful trade unions. Charges were also levelled against him for the purchase of Bofors guns. Furthermore, the BJP criticized Rajiv Gandhi's economic policies for going on "a vast borrowing spree both externally and internally in the name of liberalization."

After the disintegration of the Soviet Union, India, like other countries went for market reforms. Yogi Adityanath says that the new economic policy of former Prime Minister Manmohan Singh, tried to bring economic colonialism. During his regime, the impact was quite visible in that the poor became poorer and a country cannot be a wealthy nation if it is confined to some rich business classes. Baldev Raj Nayar, in his article "The Limits of Economic Nationalism: Economic Policy Reforms under the BJP," says that "BJP considers itself distinctive in economic affairs. It rejects the development model followed by the Congress party, whether the earlier one of Nehru's or the recent one since 1991 of Narasimha Rao's economic policy which drastically shifted the emphasis from the state to the market, allegedly at the behest of the international financial institutions. More broadly, the BJP rejects both communism and capitalism because of their foreign origin. According to BJP, it renders them out of harmony with India's own cultural traditions. It opts forthrightly instead for an organist model of a well-integrated economy and society that supposedly draws upon India's own indigenous traditions. A key feature of its economic programme is swadeshi which can be translated as economic nationalism."

Congress, 1998 onwards

The Lok Sabha election in 2004 was fought mainly between the NDA led by Atal Bihari Vajpayee and the United Progressive Alliance (UPA) led by Sonia Gandhi. Though the NDA had performed well, it still lost the election and the UPA, under Manmohan Singh, was voted to power. The leadership was not concentrated in a single person. Instead, the Manmohan Singh-Sonia-Rahul troika worked for five years and again in the 2009 national election the Congress was able to retain power by capturing 200 seats on its own. The opportunity given to the Congress by the people in 2009 was lost somewhere. The UPA II government was faced with numerous scams, high inflation and unemployment rates and price rise which became the cause of its decline in the 2014 election. There were two main reasons for the Congress decline. The first was an anti-incumbency wave against the Congress and the second factor revolved around Narendra Modi's magical spell which propelled the BJP back to power in Delhi. This can be seen from the chart III.

Chart III
Lok Sabha Election: Performance of Congress Party

Year	*Total Seats*	*Seat Won*	*Vote Share (in %)*	*Gain/loss (Vote Share)*
1998	543	141	25.8	-3
1999	**543**	**114**	**28.3**	**+2.5**
2004	**543**	**145**	**26.5**	**-1.9**
2009	**543**	**206**	**28.6**	**+2.1**
2014	**543**	**44**	**19.5**	**-9.1**

Source : Election Commission of India

From the above analysis, it is clear that the deterioration started during the period of Nehru and escalated during the Indira Gandhi rule. It had far-reaching consequences during the Sonia-Rahul period because the problems prevailing then were not addressed properly. Yogi Adityanath says the fault lies within the party structure and duality of approach in tackling the political and economic problems which affected the common masses to such an extent that the nationalist sentiment of the country was on the wane. Yogi Adityanath blamed the Congress for the ills plaguing the country, and accused the opposition party of "dividing" people and playing appeasement politics. He said the Sonia Gandhi-led party was responsible for "mismanagement" in the country and that the BJP-led NDA government is working to tackle problems and take the country on the path of development. Addressing a convention of BJP workers at the Balbir Singh Juneja Indoor Stadium, Adityanath accused the Congress of playing with the sentiments of the people and dividing them on the basis of caste, region and language for its vested interests. Further, he said that the Congress practised politics of appeasement for political gain and gave birth to the scourge of terrorism, naxalism and separatism. The country is still paying the price. If the Congress leadership had discharged its duties properly, the country would not have been grappling with starvation and lack of health facilities. If anyone is responsible for the country's mismanagement, it is the 55-year rule of the Congress. On the other hand, the "BJP works without discrimination on the basis of religion, caste and creed. We consider the entire country a family." He said 'Ram Rajya' is considered the best model of good governance in the entire world where there is no fear, discrimination, pain and starvation.

The general election of 2014 under the able leadership of Narendra Modi brought a new political discourse which promised to usher in a new India, free of the Congress. The BJP with its rightist politics outlasted the Congress ideological dual approach based on a right-centre-left approach. As a consequence, the Congress lost not only the Lok Sabha election of 2014 but also paved the way for the BJP to form governments in Uttar Pradesh, Uttarakhand, Punjab, Manipur and Gujarat in March, 2017. The electorate of Uttar Pradesh and Uttarakhand gave the BJP one of the biggest state election mandates in independent India. The BJP has now extended its political reach and rule in 21 states. This has turned the tide against the Congress and indicated the rise of the party as a dominant player in uniting the masses into one single stream. Adityanath praised the prime minister for launching a slew of welfare schemes and said their benefits are reaching the people of the country.[28] The people ask what Prime Minister Modi has done in four years and when will 'achhe din' come? We should tell them that "we gave electricity to the poor who did not have a power connection even after 70 years of Independence. The poor who had never seen a bank now have bank accounts. It's 'achhe din' for them."

Though there are problems but given sufficient time, the author is hopeful the BJP will be able to resolve most of those faced by the common people to bring back the past glory and respectability of India. This is the only underlying factor in recent and coming years that the nation can be brought under a single national mainstream.

NOTES

1. Bipan Chandra, Mridula Mukerjee, Aditya Mukerjee, Sucheta Mahajan, K. N. Pannikar, *India's Struggle for Independence*, Penguin Books, 1989, p. 398.
2. Ibid.
3. Ibid, p. 399.
4. See Bipan Chandra, *Communalism in Modern India*, New Delhi, 1987.
5. Stanley Wolpert, *Jinnah of Pakistan*, New York, 1984, p. 26.
6. M. A. Jinnah, *Speeches and Writings*, ed. by Jamit-ud-din, vol. I, Lahore, 1960, pp. 69-70, 72-73.
7. Ibid, p. 127.
8. John McGuire, 'The World Economy and the Colonial State and the Establishment of the Indian National Congress', in Mike Shepherdson and Colan Immunes (eds.), *The Indian National Congress and the Political Economy of Indian 1885*, Avebury, 1988, p. 51.
9. Lloyd Rudolph and Sussane H. Rudolph, *In Pursuit of Lakshmi. The Political Economy of the Indian State*, Chicago, University of Chicago Press, 1987, p. 21.
10. Ibid.
11. *Indian Express*, 14 February 2018.
12. Ibid, 27 December 2017.
13. Ibid.
14. Ibid.
15. Ibid.
16. Ibid.

17. Ibid, 14 February 2017.
18. Pravin Rai and Sanjay Kumar, 'The Decline of the Congress Party in Indian Politics,' *Economic and Political Weekly*, vol. 52, No. 12, March 2017, p. 2.
19. Ibid.
20. See Bipin Chandra, 'The Indian Capitalist Class and Imperialism before 1947,' in Bipan Chandra (ed.) *Imperialism and Nationalism in India*, Vikas Publications, Delhi, 1979.
21. Lok Sabha Debates, vol. VII, no. 26, 21 December, 1954, p. 11773.
22. Rajni Kothari, *Democratic Polity and Social Change in India: Crisis and Opportunities*, New Delhi, Allied Publishers, 1976, p. 52.
23. Stanley Kochanek, *Business and Politics in India*, Berkeley, University of California Press, 1974, pp. 77-78.
24. Slivart Corbridge & John Harris, *Reinventing India, Liberalization, Hindu Nationalism and Popular Democracy*, Cambridge, p. 57.
25. Francini Frankel, *Indian Political Economy, 1947-77, the Gradual Revolution, 1978*, Oxford University Press, Delhi, p. 247.
26. Corbridge & Harris, op.cit, p. 68.
27. *Hindustan Times*, 15 July, 1982.
28. *Indian Express*, 14 February 2018.

4

DUAL CHARACTER OF INDIAN COMMUNISM

In one of his articles "To understand the Dual Character of Communism," Yogi Adityanath has vehemently criticized the nature and functioning of Indian Communists. Today, it is the most corrupt party as its ideology has become an ideology of convenience rather than going to the roots in solving national problems. The method adopted by them is to transform Indian society through revolutionary violence. He says through violence the communists want to change the mindset of the Indian people. National culture has no meaning to them and religion is like opium. With this kind of character, the communists have tried to influence the Indian way of life. Indian society, after independence, tried to solve its national problems by promoting the social and economic order in such a way that the true Indian nationalistic spirit and sentiment could be defended. But, the Communists work with a contrary approach that is detrimental to national integration. In fact, the Communist ideology in India is an imported one which believes in violent expansion. Hence, Yogi Adityanath forcibly points out that in order to establish their hold on Indian soil they follow an old theory "to speak one lie hundred times it becomes true." On this theory, the Communists are very eager to spread their wings throughout India. As stated above, excessive violence becomes the means to achieve the desired goal. Yogi Adityanath portrays a negative picture of

Communists because instead of providing a solution to problems, they have been aggravated. It had led to various political-socio-economic issues making things more complex that is detrimental to the democratic structure of the Indian political system. Today, the whole of India, as Yogi Adityanath says, is engulfed in naxalism. It has not only affected India but also its neighbour, Nepal. The problems were fully exploited by these Communists and in their effort they had the support of those who tried to destabilise the country. What was the Communist ideology in general and its implications in India? Any analysis of the study demands a holistic view of the problem. The proper treatment of the subject would be done only when one examines its emergence and its role in the Second World War.

British Rule in India

It would be important to examine the necessity of Communist ideology in India. There is no doubt that Indian communists were basically influenced by Marxism. In his article "British Rule in India," Marx chose to focus exclusively on India. He has described India as, politically and geographically, an Italy of Asiatic dimensions." He later compared her socially to Ireland, where she formed a "strange combination of Italy and Ireland, of world of voluptuousness and of a world of woes, as anticipated in the ancient tradition of the religion of Hindustan."[1] Marx perceived perpetual state of invasion and fragmentation leading to Company Raj of the British East India Company that outstripped all other calamities by collapsing the fundamental structure of Indian society. Thus, he saw this misery as "essentially different and infinitely more intensive kind than all Hindustan had to suffer before."[2] Later, Marx said that "the whole administration of India by the British was to destabilise and still remain so today."

For Marx, the Indian village community had several features that imbued it with changelessness. Members tilled their own plots but the village was held in common. The individual had no property but only possessions.[3] The communities were isolated and self-sustaining. Its members were engaged in farming and small-scale industry but primarily it was meant for the community's needs. The "domestic union of agriculture and manufacturing pursuits[4] inhibited the development of the division of labour brought through exchange. Instead there was "unalterable decision of labour[5] produced by a caste system that fixed an individual occupation through hereditary and a community that provided the individual with an unchanging market. The unconsolidated nature of these scattered communities made them vulnerable to foreign invasion.

Thus, Britain, in Marx's view, had a dual vision in India. One was destructive, i.e., annihilation of the old Asiatic society and the other was regenerating, providing for industrial revolution in Britain. The emphasis was on the material foundations of Western society in Asia. So far, the destructive side had been mainly visible nevertheless the work of regeneration was also done.

Equally important was the inevitable consequences of industrial capitalist exploitation of India. In order to develop the Indian market, it was essential to secure the transformation of India into a reproductive country. This made necessary the development of railways, roads and irrigation and this was only the beginning at the time when Marx wrote. Thus "modern hereditary and division of labour were decisive impediments to Indian progress and Indian power."[6]

What does it mean to Marx? He saw imperialism in India as a force capable of emancipating the Indian people and carrying them along the path to socialism. He was clear in his perception that imperialism would lead to new material conditions conducive to the Indian environment. This could be possible by Indians' successful revolt or by the victory of the industrial working class in Britain in accordance with the liberation of the Indian people. Marx's analysis of the Indian situation up to middle of the 19th century was based on three factors. These were (1) the destructive role of British rule in India, uprooting the old society; (2) the regenerative role of British rule in India in the period of free trade capitalism laying down the material premises for the future new society; and (3) the consequent practical conclusion of the necessity of a political transformation whereby the Indian people should free themselves from imperialistic rule in order to build a new society.

Thus, Marx commented that in India the struggle of the workers and peasants should support each other. Their struggle should merge in a mighty torrent that will sweep away feudalism and the indirect rule of imperialism. The affairs will be splendid and it would be even more splendid if the enemy's peasants in military uniforms, come out in support of the revolution. Though the Indian revolution took place in 1857, Marx lamented the absence of a centralised coordination among diverse groups that led to their defeat. Both the Communists and the Naxalite movement, as Yogi Adityanath sees them, relies on the philosophy of Marx's theory of revolution which had hampered Indian growth as a nation.

Criticism of Marx

Marx's early characterisation of Indian society has met with criticism. Sumita Ghosh has pointed out that the Indian village was "not a proprietary but an administrative unit." He further remarked that "trade between the urban areas and external commerce were considerable.[7] Indian society was clearly not devoid of a system of production founded in exchange and therefore a division of labour. It is thus, this "universalism" that made some post-colonial historians see Marxist theory as a "mode of production" narrative. But perhaps, we can see both the elements of the universal and the neglect of the particular in Marxism thought as it relates to India. This, according to Yogi Adityanath, was fully exploited by the Indian Communists and later on by the Naxalites.

The Development of Communist Movement in India

For the world largest democracy, India has a long and complicated relationship with Marxist ideology. Ideology is a high-minded idealism opposed to the selfish and petty scrambling for power that others see as the content of politics.[8] But, seen in this perspective, ideology is aimed at uniting group identities and positive goals for them. Perhaps, it was Lenin who first projected that there can be no revolution without adherence to violence as the means to change Indian society and projected the teaching that without revolutionary ideology there can be no revolution. Hence, the Indian communists had a definite positive ideology that could serve their goals. It would be more interesting to examine the history of the Communist movement in India and then relate it with the nationalist movement in India. The author has dealt in detail on the national movement in an earlier chapter. But, here efforts will be made to see how far the communists were influenced by the Indian national movement.

The history of the Communist movement in India can be traced back to the Bolshevik revolution in Soviet Russia against the oppressive rule of the Czar. Ultimately, in 1917, the Russian Socialist Revolution defeated Czarist power. With the collapse of the Czar, the revolutionaries tried to bring changes in the social structure by the active participation of the people. S. G. Sardesai opines, "the Russian revolution opened up a new horizon before the toiling people all over the world for the abolition of capitalist and landlord exploitation. By freeing all countries under Czarist rule, it also blazed a new path for the struggles of subject countries for national independence and self determination.[9] The cause was good but it could not be sustained for long.

Even before World War I, Indian revolutionaries like Madame Cama, Rana Shyamji Krishna Verma, Hardayal and others were supported by progressive, socialist and labour movements in Europe and America and thus we find some traces of the revolutionary activities of Madame Cama, Rana Shyamji, Krishna Verma, Hardayal, etc.[10] Later, Nalini Bhushan Das Gupta, Virendra Nath Chattopadhya and M. N. Roy participated in revolutionary activities abroad. Though the Communist movement was anti-imperialist, they were hesitant to resort to violence as a means of ushering in a new society. The problems faced by the people during British rule were poverty, ignorance and degradation of the masses. Similarly, Indian society was marked by a series of divisions and cleavages of race, religion, caste and language which posed major obstacles in the way of realisation of full nationhood. Moreover, there was wide gap between the living conditions of the rural and urban masses. On the other hand, the princely states were patronized and created by the British rulers. It provided a model of extreme poverty and ignorance of the common people for the princely order. Thus M. R. Masani wrote that "the Indian Maharajas, the big feudal landlords and the rising industrialists stood like lofty mountain peaks above the plains of poverty."[11] The idea of contradiction between the princely states and the poor by the historians of the early communist movement was to figure out class disparities so that the people could muster support for their cause. The British oppressive policy brought urban and rural unrest in India. It had more impact on rural India. As such, unrests and uprisings began in Punjab, UP, Malabar and other parts of India. To counter it, the national leaders called for a protest, hartal and countrywide non-cooperation movement which got unprecedented response from the masses. They opposed the administrative measures of the British government in India and as a result discontentment prevailed among the people as they came to know that the real intention of the British government was to divide Indian society. The British supported feudalism and destruction of the self-sufficient village community that were designed to create social support in Indian society for them. The Indian communists fully supported the system of exploitation and, hence, the problem was similar to the British plan of divide and rule.

Emergence of the Communist Party and Rule

The Communist Party of India was formed on 17 October, 1920 at Tashkent with M. N. Roy, Evelyn Roy, Abani Mukherjee, Tirumal Acharya, Rosa Fingove, Muhammad Ali and Muhammad Shafiq as its members. It is one of the oldest communist parties in Asia. This study will be confined to those policies and ideas that led Yogi Adityanath to ponder over the issue of the growing influence of Naxalism in recent times. But any study of the role of communist ideology on India's revolutionary activities would be incomplete without studying the development of the nationalist movement in India.

The Communists had already prepared themselves to work for the cause of the workers and peasantry even before the Communist Party of India had come into existence in 1925. However, one saw that the Communist movement in India drew its inspiration and actual strength from: (i) the socialist state in the USSR; (ii) the radicalisation of the Indian national movement as represented by the Indian National Congress; and (iii) the class consciousness and organisations of the labouring masses. The formation of the Communist Party in India was in accordance with the revolutionary class ideology propounded by Marx and Lenin. Lenin, in his words, asserted that insurrection by Indian masses against colonialism had an important role to play in the anti-imperialist movement and capitalism in the world.

The Communist Party of India laid much importance on the trade union movement which led to a countrywide strike of all textile workers. The strike hampered production and created a crisis in industrial sectors. The British government ordered the arrest of important leaders of the Communist Party and even declared the party illegal. A vacuum was created and filled in 1934 when the Congress Socialist Party was formed within the parent organisation. The leading members were Jayaprakash Narayan, M. R. Masani and others. The members of the Congress Socialist Party were influenced by Marxist thinking. But in many ways, the socialists and the communists differed. Socialist thought as understood by the Communists was not to support the bourgeois-led freedom movement and was seen to prevent the application of the principle of Marxism to the Indian situation.[12]

The idealisation of the national movement in India was the first before and especially after World War I increasing began to draw the masses into the movement. Mahatma Gandhi played an important role in mobilising peasant support for the Indian National Congress. In the words of Masani, these socialists, despite their allegiance to Marxism, were deeply influenced by Gandhism. In the meanwhile, the peasant movement had arisen in India and some of the revolutionaries turned violent. Intervening in the peasant uprisings, Gandhi applied his unique weapon of Satyagraha. On the other hand, Lenin, being head of the only communist nation after the October Revolution, had under fully exploited such measures so as to fulfil the need to conduct a global revolution. He had studied two streams of peasant movements, one moved with terrorism to failure and another moved in non-violence to success. Comparing these two different methods, Lenin came to the conclusion that it would be extremely wrong in many of the Oriental countries to solve the agrarian problems according to pure communist principles.[13]

The communist concept of eradication of the bourgeoisie through armed revolution, as done by Lenin in Russia, cannot be applied everywhere irrespective of tangible veracities existing in society. Lenin described Gandhi as a revolutionary. Gandhi's revolution was not limited to the political element but was also against the traditional element like groupism, sectarianism, casteism, provincialism and all such narrow 'issues' creating discord and hatred among the people. It was a revolution to get freedom for the production and reproduction of real life for all the people. In this way, Gandhi was a true revolutionary according to the materialist concept of history.

So far as the policies of the CPI were concerned, it gained more significance in the political set up after 1939 when the Second World War broke out. The CPI leadership then declared that it was an "imperialist war."[14] The alliance of the Soviet Union with the Allied Powers, they declared, was a "People War" and, therefore, India should cooperate with the British government.[15] Because of this, the CPI also supported the British cause for participation in World War II.

On August 9, 1942, when Mahatma Gandhi launched the Quit India movement in order to attain independence through non-violence, the Communists not only opposed it but also all other Congress activities against the British. Later on 24 July, 1942, the ban on the CPI by the British government was lifted so that it could function as a legal party after a decade. The Congress opposition to the Muslim League's demand for a separate state for the Muslims was seen by P. C. Joshi, the Secretary General of the CPI, as "sectarian arrogance."[16]

A major change occurred in CPI policies in 1945 when the British government conducted elections for the Provisional Assemblies and the party decided to participate in them. During the 1940s, the country witnessed serious internal problems like workers' strike, communal riots between the Hindus and Muslims, revolt in the navy, etc. The CPI, then, visualised that because of these developments, the time was ripe for the party to launch a revolution. The leader of the revolutionary wing of the CPI was B. T. Ranadive who supported the revolutionary course. It stated that India had not attained independence and British rule was replaced by a new and far more effective colonialism in the form of Anglo-American imperialism. In view of this, he urged that the party must give up its pro-Congress stand as propagated by P. C. Joshi and use the strikes to transform them into revolutionary action in order to attack Congress policies. As a result, P. C. Joshi was replaced by B. T. Ranadive as the Secretary General.

Developments after Independence

India's independence in 1947 found the Indian Communists unprepared and confused. The most conservative British political element in India believed that India was unfit for unification and would collapse as soon as the protection of law, order and civilisation had been withdrawn. The Communists blended this British distrust with a crude adaption of Mao-Tse-Tung's peasant war strategy. They sought a Yenan of their own from which to move towards New Delhi. But in doing so, they overlooked the fact that Mao did not march to Nanking until after 20 years of trial and error and in this process he had consolidated the most powerful communist party outside the Soviet Union.

While formulating new policies for the party, Ranadive stressed on two factors: (i) workers in the urban areas and (ii) Telangana peasant insurrection. The Communist-led movement in Telangana was essentially a nationalist movement against princely rule in the state. Anyhow, Ranadive's stress was upon the struggle in the cities rather than in the country side. He said that revolution, led by the proletariat in the cities, would be based on the Russian model. After the successful operations in cities, the struggle would spill over to the villages where they would get the support of the peasants. In this way, he propagated a "two class alliance for launching a revolution in India, based on workers and poor peasants. Ranadive failed in his effort. He was soon replaced by R. Rajeswara Rao as Secretary General of CPI. Rao argued that the revolutionary activities against the government must be based on an agrarian armed uprising. In this way, he followed the "Chinese model" of revolutionary struggle. Before we take up this issue and challenges in the form of naxalism as perceived by Yogi Adityanath, it is necessary to assess the aggressive designs of China.

The Role of China

External Factors: China got independence in 1949 after an intensive internal struggle between the Communists and Koumintang forces led by Mao-Tse Tung and Chiang Kai Shek, respectively. Soon, China was on its mission to settle scores with those countries with which it shared boundaries. With regard to India, as Yogi Adityanath says, China was following a dual policy. On the one hand, it was trying to consolidate its position by supporting the communists in their struggle. On the other hand, China was playing her Asian card. It was against Nehru's vision that visualised that both the countries becoming independent would be a world force. But Nehru was wrong in his assessment. China's aggressive designs became clear when it forcibly captured Tibet which till now is under Chinese subjugation. From the beginning, as Yogi Adityanath claims, China was always trying to create population dis-balance so that it can destroy the basic culture and race of Tibet. China's endless interests in the Tibetan Autonomous Region (TAR) are well known. It feels that Tibet fits into China's sense of nationalism and in geo-political terms, it has served as a strong wall of defence from Europe and the rest of Asia. For almost 60 years, China has tried to increase its area of influence and at the same time ignored environmental consequences by constructing railway lines in Tibet. More recently, in spite of environmental degradation, it has constructed a massive hydropower project on the Brahmaputra in TAR in November 2014. Besides this, it has also undertaken several infrastructure and mining projects within the resource rich region. China realises that in order to sustain its economic growth, it ought to tap the Tibetan resources. This explains why China is aggressively pushing for integration of the TAR with the mainland.

Tibet, however, continues to be one of China's restive provinces. The Chinese government forcibly tries to integrate the region so that its security can be enhanced. In the enhancement of its security, China will not hesitate to take oppressive measures if raised at any moment. Yogi Adityanath asks what is the real concern of China towards Tibet? The real intention is subjugation to justify its national interests. In this direction, it can go to any extent. The world is well aware of the 15th and 16th March 2008 event when Tibetans were peacefully protesting for their rightful demand and China brutally suppressed their peaceful movement. The impact was severe not only in Lhasa but all the people of Tibet had to suffer. Further, he says that in this incident there were more than 150 civilian casualties. For Communist China, this is not a big incident because it is part of its policy that whoever opposes it will be punished. In world history, massive massacres of this kind have taken place only in China where more than six crore people have died during the cultural revolution in 1967. In such a revolution, not only soldiers but common people, intellectuals, students, writers, artists, peasants, traders, scientists, labourers, etc., were brutally murdered. The world still does not know how many people were sacrificed for not following Communist ideology. It shows that violence is the basic approach in realising the communist goal. Whether it is physical or language or thought, the method is not by peaceful means but by coercion and indeed by destruction and eliminating rivals. Yogi Adityanath also admits that under communism there is no political freedom. The moral and spiritual aspects of life that are inherent in every human being are not only ignored but it also deprives basic norms and values that are essential for any country's culture.

Internal Factors: The Communists in India, actively supported by China, have taken full advantage of the ancient tradition of a larger Hindu society and divisive politics. Chinese influence has been so strong that Yogi Adityanath says that it has given rise to such internal problems like naxalism that has covered most parts of India. A movement can be successful if it has a strong organisation. In this context, later on, we have seen that the Indian communists have indulged in the politics of convenience which kept them aloof from basic human problems. Hence, the Communist organisation had to work according to its plan keeping in view the space factor and hampered the aspirations of the common masses.

To understand its common interests over the decade, one has to understand its dynamics of change and the changing nature of the naxal movement. The characteristic feature of the movement is its disorganised character which led to some interesting formulations, quite uncommon in the history of organisation of movement.[17] Historically, socio-political movements, whether extremist, revolutionary or peaceful, operated through organisations which are known as movement organisation. The movement organisations are mostly characterised as loosely structured, decentralised and prone to political challenges and counter cultural practices.

Since independence we have seen the growth of many communist parties based on the principles enunciated by Marx, Lenin and Mao. Yogi Adityanath says that these groups had influenced the functioning of the naxal movement from time to time.

Communist Party of India (CPI)

The Communist Party of India is one of the oldest Communist parties in Asia. Much work has been done on its policies, personalities and growth in the early period. The study on CPI is focused on the objective that is related to the growth of the communist movement. The CPI became more important during the Second World War by declaring it as an "imperialist war." With the Soviet Union joining the Allied powers to defeat the Axis powers, it declared that it was a 'People's War' and, hence India should cooperate with the British government. This had led Yogi Adityanath to comment that communists in fact had no ideology of their own to counter British rule in India.

After independence, in 1951, the CPI came out with a programme for the party. It declared that "India is the last biggest dependent semi-colonial country in Asia…." It said that the Indian government was "a government of landlords and princes and reactionary……" It pointed out that "the Indian economy, India's foreign policy, the Indian armed forces were all under the control of British imperialism." The key part of our independence is still left in the hands of British imperialism. India also had to face the danger of US imperialism. It advocated self-determination for all nationalities in India, abolition of landlordism without compensation, protection of national industry against foreign competition, withdrawal of India from the British Commonwealth of nations, nationalisation of all factories, banks, plantations, shipping and mining owned by the British in India and an independent foreign policy.[18] When the programme referred to the teaching of Marx, Engels, Lenin and Stalin, it ignored the teaching of Mao-Tse-Tung who had developed and enriched Marxism-Leninism. No Communist party in Asia and elsewhere could ignore Mao-Tse-Tung. Later, the CPI and the CPI-M turned out to be "inveterate enemies of all that Mao represented."[19]

Communist Party of India-Marxist (CPI (M))

The communists, during World War II and the independence movement, did not realise that nationalism was a stronger driving force than economic ideology. Thus, they were isolated from nationalist forces during the freedom movement. The wave of anti-communism during the 1962 Sino-Indian conflict clearly indicated the predominance of nationalism over economic ideology.

The split in the CPI in 1964 and the resultant founding of the CPI (M) was also due to the Sino-Soviet ideological rift in the international communist movement. More important than this was the CPI support to the Indian government on the Sino-Indian border clashes. Moreover, critics often observe that the CPI's support in the 1962 war was also due to Nehru's respect for communist ideology and he was described as "Marxist by intellectual conviction." Speaking at Muzzarfarpur on 3 April 1949 and at Bilaspur on 18 December 1951, Nehru asserted that he had "no quarrel with the fundamental principles of communism." As a result, a group, comprising three leading leftists, Jyoti Basu, P. Sundaryya and H. K. S. Surjeet resigned from the Central Secretariat. On March 9, 1963, the Chinese Communist Party criticised the policy of the CPI. An article was published as an editorial in *Peking Daily* entitled 'A Mirror for Revisionists.'[20] It criticised the party for replacing the theory of the class struggle with the slogan of class collaboration: socialism by bourgeoisie socialism; defending the bourgeois and landlords; giving unconditional support to Nehru's government in its policies towards United States hegemony and playing the anti-Chinese card.

The resignation of these three important leaders was the first demonstration against the revisionist and anti-Chinese policies of the CPI. On April 11, 1964, when the National Council called its session at Delhi, every effort were made to expel S. A. Dange, the Chairman of the CPI. The anti-Dange group demanded he should vacate the chair. Dange outrightedly rejected the demand. As a protest, 32 members of the party under the leadership of Namboodiripad walked out.[21] As a result, seven members were expelled and 25 suspended from the party on April 14, 1964.[22]

The dissatisfied group called a meeting at Tenali from July 7 to 11, 1964 and Jyoti Basu declared that "we are the Communist Party of India and we do not recognise Dange's group as the CPI."[23] The split was complete and a new Communist party emerged in India, which was named "The Communist Party of India (Marxist) or CPI(M).

After 40 years of rule, the CPI(M) supported the United Progressive Alliance (UPA) led by the Congress party in 2004. It is quite debatable whether the Congress had any distinct ideology but it got support of the landed and capitalist classes, Muslims and other minorities who feared the BJP's programme of Hinduism. Till 2008, the Left supported the UPA government in Parliament without joining it. The CPM then withdrew its support to the government on the issue of the US-India agreement on nuclear cooperation and an increasingly close strategic relations with the United States. It shows the CPI (M) ideology was one of convenience. In this sense, Yogi Adityanath made it quite clear that a borrowed ideology was not conducive to Indian conditions in the long run.

From 2006, compromises with the neo-liberal development model opened up a serious rift between the CPM and sections of its social base though the Left won the election by a big margin by capturing 234 of 294 seats in the State Assembly. But soon in Singur and Nandigram, violence triggered an anti-Left Front movement which reached its peak in 2011 when the CPM won only 40 Assembly seats.

Singur and Nandigram were important in Communist history because of the failure of the CPM's economic development strategy for West Bengal. Singur was the area chosen by the Tatas, on the invitation of the government, to construct a manufacturing plant for their new Nano car. The government did not consult the affected peasants and the local government had to face stiff opposition. The thrust for industrialisation took an ugly turn in Nandigram in 2007 when some land was acquired for an Indonesian company to construct a chemical lab. In March 2005, fourteen unarmed villagers in Nandigram were shot dead by the police. The situation became out of control as it escalated into an open revolt by the peasants, supported by armed Maoists and the Trinamul Congress.

In the light of the poor functioning of the CPI (M), it led to the growth of other communist parties with no proper ideologies of their own. The nature and role of these parties are mentioned below.

Communist Party of India (Marxist-Leninist) CPI (M-L)

The CPI (M) decision to participate in parliamentary democracy was met with severe criticism from the more radical group under the leadership of Charu Mazumdar. The new party, the CPI (ML), was more popularly known as Naxalites. It was based on the ideology propagated by Mao-Tse-Tung and was formed on April 22, 1969.

In its first political resolution, the CPI (ML) said the principal contradiction in India at present was between feudalism and the masses of peasantry. The Indian revolution at this stage was called "the People's Democratic Revolution." It gave preference to democracy under a centralised guidance rather than formal discipline. The main content was the agrarian revolution and the abolition of feudalism in the countryside. To destroy feudalism, the Indian people will have to fight a protracted struggle against the USA and Soviet imperialism. The main aim of the CPI (ML) was to organise the peasantry and advance towards seizure of power through an armed struggle. To fulfil this task, the revolutionary Communist Party must focus on Mao's theory of People's War which was the only means of a weak revolutionary force to wage war against a more powerful enemy. The basic tactics of struggle of the revolutionary peasantry led by the working class was guerrilla warfare.

Communist Party of India (Marxist-Leninist) Liberation CPI (M-L) L

The growth of the CPI (M-L) Liberation dates back to 1974. It became mostly active in Indian politics after the post-emergency phase of 1977. The Party Central Committee (PCC) in order to unite the splintered groups which owed their origin to the CPI (M-L) called a meeting in 1981. But it could not yield any positive results. During 1982, the Indian People's Front (IPF) was formed in Delhi. It became the party's open political platform which took keen interest in day-to-day politics. During the same period, the Third Party Congress took place at Giridih in Bihar where the issue of participation in elections was undertaken. This change in the outlook of the CPI (ML) Liberation group, which, according to Bhatia, considers itself the inheritor of the CPI (ML) legacy; its political line has change dramatically from that of the original CPI (ML).[24]

The CPI (ML) Liberation, though functioning overground within the parliamentary democratic set up, has not completely disbanded the path of armed rebellion. The party does not rule out the possibility that under a set of exceptional national and international circumstances, the balance of social and political forces may even permit a relatively peaceful transfer of central power to a revolutionary force. But in a country where democratic institutions are based on essentially fragile and narrow foundations and where even small victories and partial reforms can only be achieved and maintained on the strength of mass militancy, the party of the proletariat must prepare itself for winning the ultimate decisive victory in an armed revolution. A people's democratic front and a people's army, therefore, remain the two most fundamental weapons of revolution in the arsenal of the party.[25]

People's War Group (PWG)

If today, naxalism is considered as the greatest internal security problem and the naxals claim to be running a parallel government, its credit goes mostly to the PWG. Though popularly known as PWG, its official nomenclature is Communist Party of India-Marxist-Leninist (People's War) "the CPI (ML) (People's War) was formed on Lenin's birth anniversary on April 22, 1980."[26] Kondapalli Seetharamaiah was the founding father of the PWG and was later expelled from the group.

The PWG has declared that India is a vast "semi-colonial and semi-feudal" country, with about 80 per cent of the population residing in its villages. It is ruled by the big-bourgeoisie landlord classes which are subordinate to imperialism. In India, there is a marked contradiction between the alliance of imperialism and feudalism on the one hand, and the broad masses of the population, on the other. The ultimate aim of the party is the liberation of the Indian people from all exploitation and the creation of socialism and communism in India. People's War is based on "armed agrarian revolution" which is the only way to obtain a people's democracy. In this way, the PWG rejected the prevailing parliamentary democratic system of India.

The difference between the CPI (ML) Liberation and PWG became quite clear from the ongoing organisational, strategic and tactical conflicts going on within the CPI (ML). So far as the CPI (ML) Liberation was concerned, it focussed on the cause of peasants, while the PWG wanted the party to be a platform for peasants, workers, tribals and other weaker sections of society. Furthermore, on the one hand, the CPI (ML) Liberation wanted to build up a political front focused on the struggle of peasants, while, on the other hand, the PWG focused on mass organisation instead of any democratic front. For a considerable period after its birth, the PWG's activities were limited to Andhra Pradesh while the base of the CPI (ML) Liberation was in Bihar.

It was during this period that another organisation came into existence on January 1, 1982. It was the named the CPI (ML) Party Unity. It came into existence due to a merger between the CPI (ML) Organisation and Central Committees. Hereafter, Bihar remained a strong battleground of the naxal operation and most of the clashes were between the CPI (ML) Party Unity and CPI (ML) Liberation.

While these developments were taking place in August 1998, Party Unity merged with the PWG and the group came to be known as People's War. With this merger, the PWG became stronger in influencing naxal activities in Bihar and in other areas. As a result, the CPI (ML) Liberation almost lost control over most of its territories and supporters to the PWG and the MCC. The PWG, during the same period, registered its presence outside Andhra Pradesh and gradually gained strongholds in Bihar, Odisha, Madhya Pradesh, Jharkhand, Chhattisgarh and Maharashtra.

With the formation of People's War, there was also a tactical change in several aspects of the naxal movement. For a new democratic revolution, there were two important aspects: the "agrarian revolution" and "fight for nationality." It showed the amount of organisational change witnessed by the Naxal movement in all these years. In 1967, it started as an "agrarian revolution" with the purpose of following the parliamentary form of government but the question of 'nationality' was never raised. In the eyes of People' War, the Indian people were weighed down by three big mountains: feudalism, imperialism and bureaucracy and all these were to be overthrown in the present stage of the New Democratic Revolution (NDR).

However, during the 1990s, the growth of the militarisation became the main feature of the PWG. The formation of the People's Guerrilla Army (PGA), Special Guerrilla Squads, Permanent Action Team (PAT) and Special Action Team (SAT) were the major features of PWG activities for quite some time before it merged with the MCC to form the CPI (Maoist).

Maoist Communist Centre (MCC)

The Maoist Communist Centre (MCC) is the next important group of the Naxal movement. Conventionally speaking, it was never a part of the CPI (ML). "The MCC, while supporting the Naxalbari struggle, did not join the CPI (ML) because of some tactical differences and on the question of party formation.[27] The MCC was formed on October 20, 1969, although at that time it was known as Dakshin Desh. It was in 1975 that the party renamed itself as the Maoist Communist Centre. In 2003, it merged with the Revolutionary Communist Centre of India—Maoists (RCCI-M)—to form the Maoist Communist Centre-India (MCC-I).

Right from the beginning, the MCC resorted to armed struggle as the main form of resistance and waged protracted guerrilla warfare as its central task. The then prevailing economic and political conditions of India led to the concept of Mao-Tse-Tung's philosophy of war, i.e., to establish a powerful people's army and establish a dependable strong and self-sufficient base area in the rural areas to constantly consolidate and expand the people's army and the base area and gradually encircle the urban areas from the rural areas by liberating these areas and finally capture the cities and establish the state system and political authority of the people themselves by decisively destroying the state power of the reactionaries.[28]

The main front organisations of the group are Nav Jawan Pratirodh Sangarsh Manch, Krantikari Budhijivi Sangh, Krantikari Sanskriti, Krantikari Chhatra League, Communist Yuva League, Nari Mukti Sangh and Mazdoor Mukti Sangh.

Communist Party of India (Maoist)

The naxal movement in India reached another phase of organisational transformation with the merger of two of the principal armed organisations, namely, the People's War and the Maoist Communist Centre of India. It resulted in the formation of the Communist Party of India (Maoist). "The formation of the unified CPI (Maoist) is a new milestone in the history of the revolutionary communist movement of India. A unified Maoist party based on Marxism-Leninism is a long delayed and highly cherished need of the revolutionary minded and oppressed people of the country, including all the ranks and the Maoist forces of South Asia. Now, this long aspired desire and dream have been transformed into a reality.[29] The new group claimed direct linkage with the CPI (ML) formed by Charu Mazumdar of Naxalbari fame and decided to give him the status of the founder along with the Late Kanhaiya Chatterjee, founder of the MCC (I).

The aim of the CPI (Maoist) is to establish a Compact Revolutionary Zone (CRZ) which will stretch from Nepal to Bihar, Andhra Pradesh and beyond. The ultimate aim is to capture power through a protracted armed struggle by overthrowing the semi-colonial, semi-feudal system under the neo-colonial form of indirect rule, exploitation and control. In this process, the CPI (Maoists) "had to seek to unite all genuine Maoist groups that remain outside this unified party."[30] Thus, Yogi Adityanath says that the history of the naxal movement is the history of a contagious process of organisational conflict, splits and mergers. The movement now aims to have its presence in all parts of the country.

Anomalies in Indian Communism

According to Bipan Chandra, the existence of opposing strands within the Communist movement and the split in 1964 were discerned by him.[31] He perceived the tendency of the three in the sense of "Right," "Left" and "Centre" in the Communist movement. The "Right" more or less correctly perceived the existing and emerging reality and argues in terms of the logic of the policies structured in 1951 and moved towards cooperation with Nehru. The "Left," while objecting to such kind of cooperation, reconciled to a militant anti-government approach accepting the promises of 1951 as the given reality. The "Centre" at the same time adopted a radical opportunist stance towards the government. It simultaneously tried to break out from this and thus gave rise to a host of anomalies.[32] In the words of Yogi Adityanath, with such divisions in the party diverted from the main objective led to the problems that India is facing today.

Later, when the CPI (M) was formed, Satya Narain Singh, a leading Naxalite from Bihar wrote that "this was the party of the proletariat and represents the true aspirations and policies of its revolutionary class. It gives preference to ideological and political building rather than organisational structure. In terms of armed struggle, it was a rural based party with emphasis on developing bases in the countryside rather than in cities and towns."[33] The differences of the parties among themselves boosted the morale of the Naxalite movement. To subdue the movement, the parties believed in the policy of annihilation which was seen as a higher form of class struggle.

In due course, as Yogi Adityanath perceives it, these anomalies within the Communist parties led to a complete failure of communism in India. Right from the beginning, they failed to assess the real need of Indian society, economy, politics, power structure, political parties, role of the caste system, prevailing ideologies both at the popular and elite levels and social strata and groups or even the class structure.

The results were seen in the recent election in West Bengal, Kerala and Tripura. Yogi Adityanath played an active role in minimising and uprooting the communist base from the people. He invoked the idea of a "Sanatan Hindu Rashtra' recalling Adi Shankaracharya's movement to revive Hinduism and described "communism as a foreign ideology" implanted in Kerala. "When the country's religion and culture was threatened by foreign invaders, Shankaracharya launched the movement for the protection of the Hindu religion. Today, the time has come to replicate the Shankaracharya's movement and Hindu culture must be protected and preserved in Kerala."[34]

Yogi Adityanath exhorted people to ponder on how a "foreign ideology gained ground in Kerala and Hindu traditions were in danger. "The Hindu religion has strong roots in Kerala and history speaks about it." Known for his unabashed espousal of Hindutva, Adityanath alleged that the Left has turned the state into a hub of "jihadi terrorism," a matter of concern for the entire nation.

He assured the party cadres in Kerala not to be intimidated by "red terror' as the entire Uttar Pradesh and the country at large had to fight for its safety. "The red will turn saffron soon (Kerala ki dharti jald kesariya hogi."[35] He said the BJP and RSS workers had been killed by Communists while fighting to protect Hindu culture and religion. "Party cadres have fought for the Hindu religion and the sacrifices will not go waste."

It was in the election in Tripura that Yogi Adityanath's political career got a big boost. Soon after it became clear that the Bharatiya Janata Party (BJP) government was all set to breach the Left citadel in Tripura, Yogi Adityanath immediately got in touch with Sunil Deodhar, the BJP's Tripura in-charge. Yogi Adityanath, along with Deodhar, and the party's national general secretary, Ram Madhav, was a key element of the party's Tripura plan. Of the three north-eastern states of Tripura, Nagaland and Meghalaya that went to the polls, the BJP got Adityanath to campaign extensively in Tripura alone.

Yogi Adityanath, the head priest of the Gorakhnath Math, belongs to the Nath sect that has a huge following in the north-eastern state. He had strategically launched his poll campaign in Tripura with a visit to Gorakhnath temple at Padmapur on the outskirts of Dharmanagar where he had performed a puja on February 12, 2018. After launching his poll campaign with a puja there, he had gone to attend pujas in Matarbari, Udaipur temple and Gorakhnath temple at Majlishpur in what appeared to be a clever ploy of Hindutva push by the saffron-clad politician in the Left citadel.[36] "Yogiji's Nath sect is influential in the state. Though its followers are not as much in Pakiachhara as they are elsewhere, still it is undeniable that Yogiji's meetings helped the BJP.

People listened to him both as a politician and as a mahant of a sect that commands a decent following in Tripura. Interestingly, the BJP has put on a good show in the north-eastern states. In Tripura, the BJP rose from zero in 2013 to an impressive 43 out of 59 seats and unseated the 25-year-old Manik Sarkar-led CPM government. The party had shown confidence in the abilities of the Uttar Pradesh CM and he was deputed as the party's trump card to woo followers of the Nath sect and Gorakhnath Peeth as they make up a considerable chunk of voters in the north eastern state.

Later, in a brief interaction with the media, Adityanath emphasised the party's Tripura win and gave credit to Amit Shah's election management skills. PM Modi's appeal and Shah's election management worked wonders. BJP leaders admit that the outcome in Tripura has further increased Yogi's ratings in the BJP that had also used him to campaign extensively in Gujarat, Himachal Pradesh and Kerala along with Tripura, where he had urged the voters to oust the Left government for 'non performance.' Adityanath is also set to campaign in Congress-ruled Karnataka.[37]

Asked if Yogi helped to polarise the situation in Tripura for the BJP, UP BJP general secretary Vijay Bahadur Pathak said, "Yogiji has now been used in most of the elections that the BJP has fought outside

UP. There are subtexts in each victory but the wins are merely showcases that Modiji's leadership and Shah's planning stay unmatched.[38]

NOTES

1. Rajiv Rawat, 'Marx on British Rule in India: Historical, Topical and Contemporary Perspectives,' *Fall*, 2005, Dept. of Geography, New York University, Canada.
2. Karl Marx, 'The British Rule in India', *New York Daily Tribune*, 25 June, 2005.
3. Karl Marx, *A Reader* (ed.) John Elster, Cambridge Press, 1986, p. 190.
4. Karl Marx, *On India*, (ed.) Iqbal Hussain, New Delhi, 2006, p. 14.
5. Ibid, p. xxiv.
6. Karl Marx, 'The Future Results of British Rule in India,' New York, *Daily Tribune*, August 8, 1853.
7. Sumit Kumar Ghosh, 'Marx on India', *Monthly Review*, January, 1984, p. 2.
8. See Raychaudhari, 'Indian Nationalism as Animal Politics,' *Historical Journal*, 22, 3 (1979), pp. 747-63.
9. S. G. Sardesia, 'Why Communists', in Ramdas G. B. Bhatkal (ed.) *Political Alternatives in India*, Bombay, 1967, p. 106.
10. See, G. Adhikari, (ed.) *Documents of Communist Party of India*, vol. 1, New Delhi, 1971, pp. 4-5.
11. M. R. Masani, *The Communist Party of India, A Short History*, London, 1954, p. 15.
12. Bimal Prasad, *A Revolutionary Quest: Selected Writings of Jayaprakash Narayan*, Delhi, 1980, p. xiii.
13. *Comintern Documents*, vol. I (1919-23) p. 84.
14. R. A. Scalapino (ed.), *The Communist Revolutionary in Asia*, Prentice Hall Inc, New Jersey, 1969, pp. 331-32.
15. D. N. Druhe, *Soviet Russia and Indian Communism*, Bookman Associates, New York, 1959, pp. 205-15.
16. S. Ghosh, *Socialism and Communism in India*, Allied Publishers, Bombay, 1971, pp. 317-20.
17. Rajat Kujur, 'Naxal Movement in India: A Profile,' IPCS Research Paper, New Delhi, September 2008, p. 1.
18. Suniti Kumar Ghosh, *Naxalbari: Before and After*, New Age Publishers, Kolkata, 2009, p. 75.
19. Ibid, p. 76.
20. The text is available in *Peking Review*, March 18, 1963.
21. 'The Political Organizational Report' Adopted at the Seventh Congress of the Communist Party of India (Marxist) held from October 31 to November 7, 1964, at Calcutta.

22. Ibid.
23. *Asian Recorder*, vol. XIV, no. 19, May 6-12, 1964, p. 5810.
24. Bela Bhatia, op.cit.
25. A party document of CPI (ML) Liberation titled 'The General Programme', quoted by Rajat Kujur, op.cit, p. 6.
26. *30 years of Naxalbari: An Undated Maoist Literature,* Vanguard Publications, p. 30.
27. Ibid, p. 36.
28. *Red Star*, Special Issue, p. 20. quoted in Alok Banerjee's *Inside MCC Country* dated June 2003.
29. Ganapathy, in an interview given on the occasion of the formation of CPI (Maoist), *People's March*, vol. 5, no. 11-12, November-December, 2004.
30. 'Maoist Influenced Revolutionary Organization in India' available at http.//www.mass line info//India/Indian group.html.
31. Ajay Ghosh, quoted in Bipan Chandra, *A Paradigm in Crisis: the 1955-56 Debate in the Communist Party of India*, (Unpublished mimeograph, n.d.), p. 5.
32. Ibid.
33. See J. C. Johari, *Naxalite Politics in India*, Delhi, 1972, p. 49.
34. *The Times of India*, 5 October 2017.
35. Ibid.
36. *Hindustan Times*, 4 March 2018.
37. Ibid.
38. Ibid.

5

NEPAL IN THE THROES OF COMMUNISM

Nepal is a Hindu state and for centuries it has been culturally and spiritually close to India. It has been well established by Yogi Adityanath that since ancient times Nepal has been an undisturbed, effective and controlled Hindu rastra. He is well known for the support of a Hindu Nepali State. In an interview in 2007 he said that the "unifying force in Nepal, like the soul that unites the bodies, is the Hindu King and Hindu Culture."[1] After his appointment as Chief Minister of Uttar Pradesh, Yogi Adityanath has created waves in the Indian media because, unlike other Chief Ministers, he has more stronger opinions about Nepal than others since independence. Historically, Adityanath and his Math have rendered great support to the Hindu kings of Nepal. To him, the Nepal king is the king of the world's Hindu population. Even today, the Hindu Mahasabha and Rashtriya Swayamsevak Sangh (RSS) demand the restoration of kingship in Nepal.[2]

Yogi Adityanath, the Chief Minister of Uttar Pradesh, says that India shares a long border with Nepal. Geographically, Nepal is a paradox in itself. The boundaries of Nepal stretch from east to west to somewhat 550 miles and from north to south to 120 miles. The state has accommodated more than 2 crore people. It is surrounded by Tibet-China in the north, Uttarakhand, Uttar Pradesh and Bihar in the south, the Mechi river in the east and the Mahakali river in the west. This is Nepal that we see today.[3]

In Nepal, there are many Vedic and Buddhist followers who have been absorbed into its main national stream. It is true that Islam and Christianity have also influenced the behaviour of the Nepali people in medieval and modern periods but still Nepal is a Hindu-dominated state. The social life of Nepal shows that still people worship Rama, Krishna, Buddha, Ganesh, Hanuman, Bhimsen, Durga and Tara. At the same time, festivals like Vijay Dashami, Janamashtami, Ram Navami, Nag Panchami, Lakshmi Puja, Buddha Jayanti and Basant Panchami are celebrated with great pomp and show.

Further elaborating, Yogi Adityanath says that geographically and culturally, Nepal was a part of Hindustan. The territory between the Himalayas and Vindhyachal was a part of ancient Aryavrat. It was an abode of Shiva, Parvati Sindhi and the father of Sita. Major rivers like the Sindhi and Brahmaputra start from there. At every corner in Nepal, one finds temples of Hindu deities, Buddhism and sites associated with Sindhi yogis. It remained for many years the centre of Hindu religion, culture and civilisation. As such, the bonding between India and Nepal has been great from the historical, cultural, linguistic, religious, social cohesion and blood relationship perspectives.[4]

Even before independence, Yogi Adityanath and his Gorakhnath Math had enjoyed a special connection with Hindu-majority Nepal and its erstwhile royal family. When former King Gyanendra organised a Virat Hindu Mahasammelan in Nepal in October 2016, Yogi Adityanath was also invited. Being situated on the Indo-Nepal border, the Math also has an age-old bonding with the temples of the Himalayan state. The erstwhile royal family of Nepal are Gorkhas who trace their origin to Guru Gorakshnath, the founder of the Nath monastic movement in the Himalayan belt.

Geographically, Nepal has been divided into three parts. The first part covers the high snow-clad mountains, the second part is full of trees and the third part comprises the Madhesis. In all, as Yogi Adityanath says, different ethnic groups are settled in Nepal.

In spite of having different living styles, language and regional imbalance there is one unifying factor that binds the people of Nepal and that is culture. Nepal's culture has a close affinity with Indian culture.

Yogi Adityanath claims that according to one research survey, in the 4th century, during the reign of Digvijay Samundragupta, Nepal was in an evolving state between Kumaun and Assam. In the 5th century, it extended up to Karnali. Even Yuang Chang, a Chinese a traveller, says that Nepal's boundaries were between the Teesta and Sakhika. In the 14th century, its boundaries were reduced and confined up to the Bhagwati. It was during the rule of King Prithvinarayan Shah in 1746 that the country was unified into one single entity and hence modern Nepal emerged as an independent entity.

Nepali history shows that the Gorakhpur temple had deep historical ties with Nepal's erstwhile royal family. Prithvi Narayan Shah received the blessings of the mahant of the temple before he waged wars and extended his empire. He was responsible for creating a new larger Nepal. According to Pt. Gauri Shankar Hira Chandra Ojha, after the attack by Allauddin on Chittor, a branch of the Maharana family moved to the Himalayas where the members of the royal family established their rule in Nepal. It is here that the young Prithvi Narayan Shah was not only able to acquire the Mahayogi Gorakhnath philosophy of life but also got the blessings of being a digvijay king. Prithvi Narayan Shah's entire life was spent in waging war and defeating foes and consolidating his empire. At the same time, Christians had made their dent in Nepal. Britain wanted to bring Nepal under its influence. But the king expelled all the Christians from the land. It was also seen that, during his reign in Nepal literature, religion and culture were developed extensively. Yogi Adityanath claims that it would not be wrong to give credit to him for the creation of a larger Nepal. He was the first propounder of a Hindutva Nepali State.[5]

After Prithvi Narayan Shah's death in 1775, Nepal was in a state of chaos and confusion. The reason was the active interest of Britain in Asia. But, under the able leadership of, Bhim Sena Thapa, Nepal prevented the British from extending its influence. In the later part of the 18th century, Nepal witnessed many political assassinations. In such a political upheaval, Jung Bahadur Rana succeeding in suppressing the oppressive rule. In due course, he became the Prime Minister and General of Nepal. The Rana dynasty ruled the state for almost 104 years.

It was during this period, that the then king, Tribhuvan Vir Vikram Shah Dev, with the support of the people overthrew the Rana dynasty. Soon, Nepal got the much-needed political support of India when democracy was introduced in Nepal. From there onwards, in the history of Nepal, a new era started where there was proper coordination between the monarchy and the democracy. Moreover, historically, Yogi Adityanath claims that Nepal was deeply connected with India's political system. The Indian political leaders, from time to time, have asserted Nepali role in its political set-up and helped India in the freedom struggle, national security and protecting the frontiers during difficult times. However, the collapse of the monarchical system in Nepal in recent years and the coming of Maoists to power led to the establishment of a secular and federal democratic state. To Yogi Adityanath, this kind of secularism and sidelining the king had great repercussions in Nepali politics. The Maoist takeover comes at such a crucial time when Nepal is going through a phase of prolonged transition and instability. As such India's pro-federal republican and secular constitution's longevity had become a subject of great concern and speculation in Nepal. At the same time, Mao's ideology infiltrated in the minds of the people and later on gave rise to insurgency in Nepal. Yogi Adityanath had always opposed this kind of political and violent developments that could hamper the growth of the state.

For the first time, Nepal tried to introduce democratic procedures in 1950. In 1951, an Interim Constitution was formed which remained effective for eight years. In 1959, Nepal opted for a Western-style parliamentary democracy. But in the long run it failed. Declaring parliamentary democracy a failure eighteen months later, King Mahendra dismissed the Koirala government and promulgated a new constitution on December 16, 1962. The new constitution was based on a party-less panchayat system. Nepal remained under the monarchy but it was under the shadow of democracy. This lasted for nearly twenty-eight years. It came to an end in 1990 through a democratic movement. The 1990 constitution reinstalled constitutional monarchy in the country and it became a semi-constitutional monarchy.[6]

Gyanendra succeeded as the monarch after the royal massacre of 2001 in which King Birendra and his family members were killed. After that, the 1990 constitution was replaced by the Interim Constitution promulgated in January 2007. The basic objective of the Interim Constitution was to provide a set of rules and regulations for the government of the country till it was replaced by a permanent constitution.[7] The salient features of the Interim Constitution were a constraint on the powers of the king, an outline of the Constituent Assembly's basic structure and a strong executive. In short, the Interim Constitution provided a suitable framework for the conduct of elections.

First Constituent Assembly Election-2008

The Interim Constitution laid down a suitable framework to conduct elections. During the pre-election period, the Election Commission (EC) had acted as a national body responsible for holding the Constituent Assembly elections. The Commission had also been able to maintain transparency while generating a positive relationship with all political actors. To initiate the process of election smoothly, election rules and a code of conduct were issued by the Election Commission.[8] The Election Commission had to face a stiff challenge in certain areas like Lamjung, Banke and Madhesi in the Terai where complaints were raised by the Maoists.

Causes of the Failure of Constituent Assembly

The termination of the Constituent Assembly of Nepal in May 2012 was a disappointing affair to a promising process that began with the People's War from 1996 to 2006, the Comprehensive Peace Agreement (CPA), the 2008 Constituent Assembly election, the formation of the Constituent Assembly, proclamation of the republic and abolition of the monarchy. The Maoists might well have expected that the Communist Party of Nepal (Unified Marxist-Leninist) and Nepali Congress (NC) would pitch their tents on the side of the status quo and prevent the writing of a progressive constitution that would assure a truly federal democratic republic of Nepal. The central objective of the Constituent Assembly was to draft a new constitution for Nepal and adopt it through due process. The Interim Constitution of Nepal itself provided applicable adoptive procedures.[9]

The main declaration by the Prime Minister which brought an end to the Constituent Assembly on May 28, 2012 has been one of the most hampering events in the setup of the constituent building process. The collapse of the Constituent Assembly without making the constitution meant that the job of writing a new constitution, as promised by the Interim Constitution of 2007, had become uncertain.[10] There were several factors responsible for the failure of the Constituent Assembly. These were inter and intra party conflicts, the politics of power sharing, unstable government, ideological conflict and attendance issues.

Second Constituent Assembly Election-2013

After the expiry of the Constituent Assembly on May 28, 2012, the then government announced the election of the Second Constituent Assembly. The task of preparing the new constituent which was entrusted to the first Constituent Assembly failed to reach an agreement on various key issues. Therefore, the Supreme Court did not extend its mandate any further. It was marked by the dissolution of the Constituent Assembly, failure to agree on the formation of a new Constituent Assembly and lack of consensus among political parties. Hence, a High-Level Political Committee (HLPC) in March 2013 was set up. The purpose was to hold the 2013 Constituent Assembly elections.

During the Constituent Assembly election 2013, there were 112 observers present in Nepal. The Election Commission too played an active role by inviting special guests and members of embassies based in Kathmandu. Chief Election Commissioners from SAARC countries and governments, officials as well as parliamentarians from Australia, Japan and the UK were also invited.[11]

As compared to 2008, it was a defeat for the Maoists, who went down from being the single largest party to the third largest party. This time the Nepali Congress and the Communist Party of Nepal (Unified Marxist Leninist) shared the lead with the Congress Party ahead with a slight margin.[12] It was a surprise for Puspa Kamal Dahal-Prachanda's Unified Communist Party of Nepal (Maoist) which could secure only 80 seats in both first-past-the-post and in the proportional representation system, as compared to the 2008 elections where it had a majority of 229 seats.

Maoist Insurgency in Nepal

It is strange to see what went wrong in the history of Nepal. Why did people opt for Maoist insurrection to recreate a new Nepal? The central question is why has Maoism continued to inspire violent revolution even after Mao-Tse-Tung's death. Almost four decades have passed but Mao-Tse-Tung still continues to inspire violence in South Asia. From it, there emerge three compelling reasons for the existence of Maoism in South Asia. First, it employss tactically effective methods. Second, it springs from political organisations that are prone to extremist schisms. Third, it targets populations that have not tasted the fruit of political and economic development.[13]

Historically, in Nepal, violence had played a major role in its politics because of internal and external pressures. First, in 1846, the Kot massacre that led to the establishment of the Rana dynasty which destroyed the powers of the king and second in June 2001, the royal palace massacre that in due course ended monarchy rule in 2008. Maoism in Nepal was inspired by the Naxalite movement in West Bengal. Unlike India, the Maoists have been largely successful in toppling the national government and have effective control over 80 per cent of the country. Its recent success did not come through military action alone but required coordination and compromise with Nepal's other political parties.

Yogi Adityanath says that Nepal is not a piece of land but a geocultural concept. Today, Nepal has become victim of communist and Maoist ideologies. Nepal is in a political crisis because of Maoist terrorism and they are trying their best to crush its national identity. The pertinent question that is often raised by Yogi Adityanath is why did Nepal opt for Maoism and not any other form of radical change? Perhaps the reason could be the Chinese ideological influence in certain sections of the Nepali population. It is important to mention here that Mohan Bikram Singh joined the Communist Party of Nepal (CPN)[14] and by 1957 had elevated his political status. He built a strong communist organisation. Like other communist parties in South Asia, the CPN went through a series of splits following the Sino-Soviet break in the 1960s and further splintered with the establishment of panchayat rule under King Mahendra.

Mohan Bikram Singh demanded elections for a constitutional assembly. He established a radical Maoist party in the middle of the 1960s that was broken into a number of fractions. He established his own party, the Communist Party of Nepal (Masal). He opposed the democracy that was created in 1991 and even called for a constitutional assembly but then mellowed. He, then, later on decided to participate in the elections of 1994. In doing so, he abandoned his district to a more extreme Maoist organisation that capitalised on an impoverished population.[15] Deepak Thapa describes this as 'hope in a radical solution" and a function of poverty rather than a consequence of Maoist ideology.[16]

The party that learnt much from Bikram Singh was the CPN (M). It launched its "People War" in 1996. It was led by Prachanda and Baburam Bhattarai. The movement succeeded in expanding its core areas in western Nepal to cover 80 per cent of the country. The CPM (M) is similar to its contemporaries in India in its birth from a fissiparous communist party to its mobilisation of impoverished rural people frustrated by the workings of democracy. It was more inspired by radical methods to change their social political and economic fortunes. It would be of interest to discuss the impact of the Maoist ideology in Indo-Nepal relations.

Indo-Nepal Relations

Before discussing the Maoist influence in India, it is also essential to discuss Indo-Nepal relations since 1947. Both the countries have strong cultural bonds and history. A sizeable section of the Indian population lives in Nepal and vice versa. Then, there is the Indo-Nepal Treaty of Peace and Friendship (1950) that grants the nationals of India and Nepal with national treatment as far as certain industrial, economic and commercial activities are concerned. It is generally said that this treaty is based on the Himalayan frontier policy of India. It was fundamentally a policy pursued by the British colonial rule.[17]

Indo-Nepal relations have to be seen in the context of developments in their respective neighbourhoods. The problem became serious with the emergence of China as a Communist state in 1949 and its later annexation of Tibet. Yogi Adityanath believes that right from the beginning, the Chinese policy was to create a population imbalance so that the basic caste and culture could be crushed. For the last 60 years, from a strategic viewpoint, China has constructed s railway line that connects Lhasa. The world saw on 15 and 16 March, 2008 such incidents of Tibetan civilians who were peacefully demonstrating for their demands before the Communist Chinese government being brutally massacred. This is not a big incident as Yogi Adityanath sees it. Looking back into the pages of world history, one finds that maximum killings had occurred elsewhere in China in which more than six crore people were killed. Those killed were common civilians, intellectuals, students, writers, artists, peasants, businessmen, scientists, labourers, etc.

Such incidents in Tibet and fear of communist expansion in Nepal were aimed to deter any kind of foreign aggression. More important was that the Indo-Nepalese Friendship Treaty ensured that Nepal would not take international action or defence-oriented policies without consultation with the Indian government. In 1949, India and Nepal signed an agreement on the recruitment of Nepali Gorkhas in the Indian army. Some of the other measures taken by both the countries were setting up of check posts on the border and joint monitoring and patrolling of the border by the Nepalese and

Indian security forces. India also sent military missions to assist Nepal in the reorganisation of its armed forces. India's major concern was the growing power of Communist China and Nepal, then played an active role to keep China away from internal politics because instability would have affected not only India's security but make it easier for Chinese presence in the region in a big way.

As decades passed, Nepal began to assert a more dominant position in South Asian politics by trying to balance India and China. In this course, Communist China succeeding in influencing the national politics of Nepal and a new chapter emerged in regional power politics in the form of close China-Nepal relations. The Chinese opportunists took full advantage by playing the Maoist card and now it is estimated by critics that China was involved in instigating insurgency in Nepal which has great repercussions in India. This is a setback for India. As Yogi Adityanath comments, without monarchy, it has affected religious, social, cultural and political relations between India and Nepal.

This kind of political development is beyond India's tolerance because by virtue, Nepal is a Hindu rastra and ruled by a Hindu king. Neither the communists nor the Islamic terrorists could disrupt normal life. Along with this, Christian missionaries also failed to convert the majority of the Hindu population into Christianity. Troubled Nepal has not only affected its sovereignty and territorial integrity but also become a cause for serious concern to Indian security planners.

On 18 May, 2006, an effort was made to change Nepal from a Hindu State to a secular state and on 28 May 2008 a declaration was made to develop Nepal as a Republic. On 30 May 2008, the Maoists threatened to develop Nepal as a Communist Republic. These developments have not only affected India's security but its 1950 Treaty of Peace and Friendship is in the doldrums. It further helped China to play a more active role in Nepal by encouraging insurgent activities that India is now facing. Yogi Adityanath is right in saying that the Maoists are trying to spread their wings from Pashupati to Tirupati. In fact, today it has engulfed the whole of India.

The Maoist movement began in Nepal in the early 1970s in the context of the Chinese cultural revolution and the rise of the naxal revolt in India. The Nepalese Maoists were preoccupied with the internal ideological and leadership differences. Most of them still believed that their armed struggle should be waged even on the basis of Marxist-Leninist-Maoist ideas. The present leaders of the Maoist movement are ready to accept the real situation in Nepal. Since the Communist Maoists are better educated their leadership has the ability to read the Nepali mind. On the other hand, the present leadership in Nepal learned from the mistakes committed by the communist movement and as a result tried to evolve a synthesis of the ideal and the real principles in the classical Marxist sense. Explaining his approach to a "people's war," Prachanda said:

> "...We must also learn war by waging war. The intellectual's instinctive tendency is that we have to learn all these things, we should read everything...and then we can make war. These kinds of tendencies were there right from the beginning. But, we said, no. This is not Maoism. This is not Marxism. This is not dialectical materialism...the issues are of learning through war itself."[18]

Again in 2011, he added:

> "In our opinion, the real key to rapid development of the People's War is the fusion between the science of proletarian revolution on the one hand and the needs and fighting spirit of the Nepalese people on the other."[19]

The insurgents are engaged in violent activities in 68 of the 75 districts of the country. Their influence varies between moderate and extreme. For instance, in the districts of Ropla, Rukum, Jajarkot, Salyen, Pyuthan and Kalikot in mid-western Nepal, the government presence is limited to the district headquarters with the rest of the district under Maoist control. The Nepalese Home Minister had designated these districts as sensitive Class A'. Dolakha, Ramechha, Sindhuli, Karvepalanchowk, Sindhupalchowk, Gorkha, Dang, Surkhet and Achham districts are classified as "Sensitive Class B" while "17 sensitive Class C" districts are Khotang, Okhaldhunga, Udaypur, Makwanpur, Lalitpur, Nuwakot, Dhading, Tanahu, Lamjung, Parbat, Baglung, Gulmi, Arghakhachi, Bardiya, Dailekh, Jumla and Dopla.

Implications in India

Yogi Adityanath says that the naxalites, with the support of their Nepalese counterparts, had planned a "Red Corridor," beginning from the border with Nepal and extending up to Kerala. Naxalism has become so serious an issue that many states of India have been affected. According to him, in May 2004, it was limited to six states covering 56 districts. In 2008, the number increased to 15 states and more than 300 districts. Today, more than 250 districts across 20 states are affected by naxal activities. Actually, it was in August 2001 that the idea of establishing a Compact Revolutionary Zone (CRZ) or Red Corridor came into existence. It extends from the forest tracts of Adilabad (Andhra Pradesh) to Nepal traversing the forest areas of Maharashtra, Chhattisgarh, Jharkhand, Bihar and Nepal. The notion of a Red Corridor seems to have grown among Maoist cadres between 2001 and 2012 in both India and Nepal. The zone is seen as a prologue to the further expansion of Maoism in the subcontinent.

The strategic aim is to have a continuous stretch of territory under Maoist influence and control with the ultimate goal to liberate the entire zone. Once achieved, the CRZ will virtually drive a wedge through the vital areas of the country and would help to establish linkages with other Maoist groups in South Asia, including the Communist Party of Nepal-Maoist and the Communist Party of Bhutan-Maoist (CPB-M).[20]

The important question is what are the implications of the Red Corridor or CRZ? The impact can be seen as follows:

a) **Free Movement:** Naxal cadres would be able to move freely throughout the CRZ including crossing over to Nepal. The following regions are reportedly being used by (CPN(M) cadres:

   1. **Uttarakhand:** Rauthi, Jhulaghat, Garbygang, Dharchula, Gologad, Baluakot, Sirkha and Banbassa.
   2. **Uttar Pradesh:** Tuthibari, Nautanwa, Sonauli and jungle tracks in Pilibhit, Kheri, Bahraich, Balrampur, Gorakhpur and Maharajgang districts along the Indo-Nepal border.

3. **Bihar:** Haraiya, Raxaul, Mahuwa, Dhobini, Sikta, Bhasatlan and Mahadevnath.
4. **West Bengal:** Kalimpong, Siliguri and Darjeeling districts.

b) **Sanctuaries:** Depending on the role of state security forces, Maoist cadres can establish safe havens and hideouts for operations, training and medical aid and thus evade prosecution and contact with security forces. CPN-M cadres are reported to have taken shelter in:

1. **Uttarakhand:** Pithoragarh, Dharchula, Jhulaghat, Tanakpur and Banbassa.
2. **Uttar Pradesh:** Thutibari, Nichloul, Nautanwa, Dhenera, Baoghekhana, Bankati, Sampuran Nagar, Gorakhpur, Varanasi, Kanpur and Lucknow.
3. **Bihar:** Narkatiyagang, Ramnagar, Valmikinagar, Ghorshan, Chhauradano, Bhastolan, Gardi, Sirsamu and Sonbarsa.
4. **West Bengal:** Bijanbai, Mirik, Sukhiya, Pokhri, Manebhangan, Darjeeling, Siliguri and New Jalpaiguri.

c) **Training:** The Naxalite-affected areas are underdeveloped and forested, safe and thus offer places to set up training camps. It has been reported that some Maoists may have been trained in West Champaran and Aurangabad districts of Bihar and Palamu and Kodarma districts of Jharkhand. Reports also indicate that there are training camps in Ropla district of Nepal.

Focus on Urban Centres

Yogi Adityanath believes that the Maoist influence is so grave that after consolidating themselves in rural areas they will definitely concentrate on urban centres. This is clear from Maoist propaganda. The communists are working in those areas where there is lack of governance. In January 2009, the Central Committee of Maoists formed a five-member "Urban Sub Committee" and was entrusted with the task of preparing an urban perspective document. The new strategy focuses on a six-stage approach called SAARC—survey, awareness, agitation, recruitment, resistance and control. As far as urban areas are concerned, the Maoists have completed the stage of surveying, i.e., identifying target groups and political areas of discontent. Now they are in the process of implementing the second and third stages of their strategy. The process will take time as is evident from their strategy of protracted warfare.

The strategy and tactics adopted at the Ninth Congress of 2001 explains the importance of the urban perspective within the tactics of the Indian revolution in the following manner. "Work in the urban areas has a special importance in our revolutionary work…in our revolution, which follows the line of protracted people's war, the liberation of urban areas will be possible only in the last stage of revolution. From the beginning we will have to concentrate on the organisation of the working class. Moreover, on the basis of revolutionary workers movement we will be able to mobilise millions of urban oppressed masses and build a struggle against imperialism and feudalism, struggle in support of the agrarian revolution and struggle for democratic rights...We should not forget the dialectical relationship between the development of the urban movement and the development of the people's war. In the absence of the strong revolutionary urban movement, and of the people for struggle will face difficulties."[21]

According to the census of 2001, 27.8 per cent of India's population now lives in towns and cities. Most of this urban population is situated in large cities. The centre of the economy has also moved away from the rural areas. In 1950-51, 56 per cent of the national income came from agriculture and today less than 25 per cent comes from agriculture. Today, most of the country's production is from the industrial and service sectors which are mainly based in towns and cities. The urban share in the Gross Domestic Product is, thus, almost 60 per cent.

India's urban population, size, proportion and economic development, today are much higher than what was there in China at the time of the revolution. China, then, had only about 10 per cent of its production coming from industries and only 11 per cent of people living in urban areas. To the naxalites, it means that India's urban areas would have to play a relatively more important role in the revolution than in the cities played during the Chinese revolution.[22]

Since 1947, four major metropolitan cities had dominated the process of urbanisation in the country. These are Kolkata, Mumbai, Delhi and Chennai which were the central hubs of the east, west, north and south. Today, new metropolitan centres like Bengaluru, Hyderabad and Pune are emerging as new centres of urban growth. This change is particularly due to the policies of liberalisation and hence a new pattern of urbanisation has been emerging. Under the liberalisation policies, the main investment is centred around a few areas of the growing urban concentration. The main areas are the following:[23]

Ahmedabad-Pune Corridor. This stretch of the Western Ghats is the main concentration of high industrialisation and urbanisation in the country. It includes four of the 10 cities in the country—Mumbai, Ahmedabad, Pune and Surat—besides two other cities with over 10 lakh population—Vadodara and Nashik. The industries cover engineering, chemicals, textiles, automobiles, telecommunication and electronic goods. The working class is diverse but mostly belong to north India.

Delhi Region

The capital region together with the adjoining areas of Gurgaon and Faridabad in Haryana and Ghaziabad and Noida in UP is a massive urban and industrial zone. The working class here too is diverse but mainly attracts people from North India.

Bengaluru

This has for some time been a centre of many major public sector establishments, besides textiles and silk weaving, electronics and computer software and hardware are the main industries with Bengaluru being the software capital of India.

Chennai

Greater Chennai has become the industrial centre for the entire south. It has a very diverse range of industries—automobiles, textiles, chemicals, petroleum products, electronics, etc.

Coimbatore Eroden Belt

This is the area of the latest growing urbanisation in the country. The principal industries are centred around textile mills, power looms, knitwear, etc.

Hyderabad

This is also a fast-growing urban centre. The new investments are mainly in electronic and information technology.

Hence, the Maoists' united front strategy involves the building and strengthening of the worker-peasant alliance, on the one hand, and the building of unity between the working class and other urban sections and classes, on the other.

It is clear from the naxalite urban perspective that they have diverted their attention towards urban populations and cities. But this perspective is a long-drawn plan where time has no place because the objective could be achieved in one or 10 or 50 years. They wait till their objectives are accomplished. With this kind of peculiar picture of India, divisive forces are trying to create more problems rather than solving them.

The casualties in both India and Nepal are severe. Yogi Adityanath says that during the last decade one saw more than 15,000 civilian and more than 6,000 army personnel killed. According to February 2016 data released by the Government of India, the details of naxalite attacks in the last few years are as follows:

2010

In the year 2010 alone, there were 11 major attacks by naxalites in various parts of the country. Following the Centre's all-out offensive against them by deploying paramilitary forces in 2009 against Naxalite groups in five states, termed as "Operation Green Hunt" by the media, there has been an increase in the number of attacks starting with the Silda camp in West Bengal where 24 paramilitary personnel were killed.

Total incidents: 2212
Total civilians killed: 626
Total security forces killed: 27

2011

Chhattisgarh was the focal state when it came to Naxalite incidents in this year. On 21 July, Maoist rebels in the state blew up a bridge, killing four people and wounding five others. The attack happened when the Congress party chief of the state, Nandkumar Patel, was returning from a party function.

Total incidents: 1931
Total civilians killed: 275
Total security forces killed: 128

2012

In mid-March, Maoist rebels kidnapped two Italians in Odisha. They later released one, while the Government of Orissa negotiated the release of the second. Another hostage situation arose in the same year when an MLA of Laxmipur constituency (Odisha), Jhin Hikaka, was abducted by the Maoists and kept captive for 33 days. They had demanded the release of 30 Maoist cadres in exchange for the freedom of the MLA.

Total incidents: 146
Total security forces killed: 104

2013

In one of the biggest Naxal ambushes in Darbha valley in Sukma, Chhattisgarh, around 24 Indian National Congress leaders including former state minister Mahendra Kumar and the Chhattisgarh Congress chief Nand Karma Patel were killed. The insurgents had attacked a convoy of the Indian National Congress.

Total incidents: 143
Total civilians killed: 159
Total security forces killed: 111.

2014

Two major naxal attacks that rocked the country this year were in Sukma, Chhattisgarh, and Gadchiroli, Maharashtra. Fifteen security personnel and one civilian were killed in Tongpal village, close to the Darbha Ghat area of Sukma district while they were engaged in a road opening exercise in the area. Seven police commandos were killed in a Maoist landmine blast in the forests of Gadchiroli district of Maharashtra.

Total incidents: 155
Total civilians killed: 128
Total Security forces killed: 87.

2015

Attacks in Sukma and the surrounding forest areas have continued to be on the rise year after year. During 2015, thirteen personnel were killed Chhattisgarh alone in ambushes while minor incidents of clashes in several other parts like Dantewada continued to occur.

Total incidents: 118
Total civilians killed: 93
Total security forces killed: 57.

2016

Total incidents: 69
Total civilians killed: 123
Total security forces killed: 66.

Though the number of incidents and the corresponding number of killings of security personnel have fallen drastically, the latest attack in Sukma where the CRPF were ambushed by over 300 naxalites killing 26 and injuring several others, raises doubts on whether the horrors of the red-corridor are beginning to return.

However, the violence perpetrated by the Naxals has declined by 25 per cent in the last three years, notwithstanding occasional reverses suffered by the security forces. Casualties to security forces also dropped by as much as 42 per cent during May 2014-April 2017 as compared to May 2011-April 2014, a Home Ministry official said.[24]

Home Ministry officials also said that currently 90 per cent of Maoist activity was limited to 35 districts though they have a hold over pockets in 68 districts in 10 states.[25] To tackle the menace of left-wing extremism, the Central Government has launched the "National Policy and Action Plan" comprising security, development and ensuring the rights and entitlements of the local communities. Under the plan, as many as 307 fortified police stations were constructed in Naxal-hit areas in the last three years.[26] Besides, 1,391 kilometres of roads were constructed in some of the most difficult areas under the road requirement plan phase-I. A total of 5,412 kilometres of additional roads were approved for construction in nine Naxal-hit areas at a cost of Rs. 11,725 crore. While 2,187 mobile towers were installed for improving telephone connectivity in remote areas, 2,882 more are in the process of installation,[27] modernisation and also upgrading of technology and communication methods to take on the scourge.

The Problem of Madhesis

The Madhesi problem is an internal issue of Nepal. The Indian Government will protect the interests of the one crore Indians living there. The entire Terai along the UP-Nepal border is caught up in violent clashes between the natives and the Madhesis who are Indian and had migrated to Nepal years ago. While many have received Nepali citizenship, the majority of them are still without a nationality. The southern region of Nepal, running along UP, Bihar and West Bengal, is known as Madhes. Madhesis, who constitute 30 per cent of Nepal's population, live in the Terai area. But 40 percent of these Madhesis still do not have citizenship or the right to vote. The Madhesis have alleged that several political and militant organisations have been targeting them and inflicting atrocities to force them to leave Nepal. However, the BJP has been supporting the Madhesis for a long time. Earlier, Yogi Adityanath had actively supported the Madhesi movement in 2007 and 2008. He, then BJP MP from Gorakhpur and Mahant of Gorakshnath Temple, has often been accused of providing logistic support to the movement of the Madhesis against the Nepal government. The idea behind supporting the Madhesis is that they are predominantly Hindus. However, some Indian Muslims and Christians are also among them.

Various political and militant organisations claim that the Nepal government deliberately ignores the Terai area. Large-scale violence has erupted along the areas of Maharajganj and Siddharthnagar. While the Nepal government had invited them for talks, the Senyukti Loktantrik Madhesi Morcha, an umbrella organisation of the

Madhesis, had earlier refused to participate in any meeting convened by Nepal Prime Minister Sushil Koirala.

The Indian Government, however, continues to back the Madhesi cause. In his public address during PM Deuba's visit recently, Narendra Modi said that he would take into account "all sections of society living together and continuing of talking to all sections, and addressing and accommodating the aspiration of Nepali citizens." The constitution will be successfully implemented. It indicated that the Indian Government was asking Kathmandu to consider Madhesi concerns.

India rendered relief when Nepal was facing natural calamities in the form of earthquakes. Following the 2015 earthquakes, the Yogi Math was involved in relief operations and helped in the reconstruction of temples and pagodas in parts of Nepal. Yogi Adityanath himself oversaw the reconstruction work along the border areas.

A large section of people—unorganised though—are fed up with the current chaos and much of the blame is being heaped on the mediation of the Indian Government that pushed Nepal into a radical agenda without directly involving the people. India has acted as a 'factor' some times, but has been unpopular when it has 'over acted'. Yogi Adityanath, given the fact that he represents the seat of Nepal's presiding deity, is not considered an outsider in Nepal in 'religious and cultural terms'. But he has already generated some kind of hope in the future roles of India and Nepal, and he will be judged in Nepal on how he balances his role as head of the Peeth and that of the Chief Minister of a state with substantial clout in Delhi.

NOTES

1. Interview by Prashant Jha, *Nepal Times*, issue no. 365.
2. See Yogi Adityanath, *Hindu Rastra Nepal: Atit and Vartman*, Shri Goraknath Mandir, Gorakhpur, UP, 2006, p. 1.
3. Ibid.
4. Ibid.
5. Ibid.
6. B. C. Upreti, *Nepal: Transition to Democratic Republic State: 2008, Constituent Assembly*, New Delhi, Kalpaz Publications.

7. Ibid.
8. http://www.the researchers.org/publication/EleObser-Mnon Report/Nepal_observation_Report.
9. B. Adhikari, 'Some Initial Comment on the Failed Constitution Building Process', *Studies in Nepal History and Society*, 17 (1), pp. 143-153.
10. M. Chautari, 'Update on the Constituent Assembly,' *Studies in Nepali History and Society*, 14(2), pp. 405-422.
11. EUEOM, Constituent Assembly Election Final Report, 2013.
12. D. Gellner, 'The 2013 Election in Nepal', *Asian Affairs*, 45 (2); 243-261.
13. See Shekhar Adhikari, *Maoist Insurgency in India and Nepal: An Analysis in India Security Interest on Her Neighbourhood*, Pentagon Press, New Delhi, 2015, pp. 208-209.
14. S. Deblieck, 'Why Mao? Maoist Insurgencies in India and Nepal,' *Peace and Conflict and Development, Issues* 9, 2006, p. 16.
15. Thapa and Sajapati, *Kingdom, Under Siege, Nepal Mao's Insurgency, 1996-2003*, p. 67.
16. Ibid, pp. 64, 79.
17. S. Subedi, 'India Nepal and the Maoist Conflict; A Nepalese Perspective,' *Liberal Democracy Nepal Bulletin*, 2005, 1(i); p. 2.
18. S. D. Muni, 'The Maoist Insurgency in Nepal: Origin and Evolution,' *ISAS Working Paper*, No. 116, 28 July 2010, p. 11.
19. Ibid.
20. http://www.wikipedia.org.
21. CPI (Maoist) Urban Perspective Our Work in Urban Area.
22. Ibid.
23. Ibid.
24. *The Times of India*, 11 July 2017.
25. Ibid.
26. Ibid.
27. Ibid.

6

HYDRA-HEADED MONSTER OF TERRORISM

To work for national integration and consolidation of a nation as one unit, India has faced serious challenges in the form of terrorism and separatism. Yogi Adityanath believes that not only India but the entire world is engulfed with this dual crisis. They erupted because of corrupt and incapable political leadership. Yogi Adityanath feels it is the political leadership, despite having sufficient resources and capabilities, that has failed not only to protect Indian citizens but also its religious culture and historical sites that have been made targets. Political leaders under previous regimes were corrupt. They promoted their own selfish interests and India as a nation and Hindu society suffered miserably. Hence, political parties were unable to successfully check the onslaught of terrorism and separatism. The author has divided this chapter into the following parts: (1) Terrorism redefined; (2) The rise of global terrorism; and (3) Bleeding Kashmir.

Terrorism Redefined

The pertinent basic question, then, is what is terrorism? The word 'terrorism' has been derived from the Latin word 'terror'. It is a state of tension amongst the people. Yogi Adityanath defines terrorism in these words: "A terrorist is a person who has been bred specifically to carry out violent activities in the name of a cause which will result in maximisation of death and injuries to the target group. So while you may argue that there are street thugs, rapists, mafia goons, and the like who 'terrorize' people, they all do so as a means for achieving a deterrent end, malevolent as it may be.[1] The Webster New Collegiate Dictionary has defined terrorism as an "acute condition of fear and terrorism as an employment of terror used as a forcible method.[2] The Chambers Twentieth Century Dictionary has explained terrorism as an organised system of intimidation.[3] Brian M. Jenkins believes that terrorism is an act or threat of individual violence or a campaign of violence mainly intended to intimidate.[4] The International Institute for Strategic Studies defines it as the use of violence often against people not directly involved in a conflict by groups operating clandestinely, which generally claim to have high political or religious purposes and believes that creating a climate of terror will assist in the attainment of their goals.[5]

In principle, terrorism has been evolved as the use of violence and threats to intimidate or force people especially for political and religious gain and to restrict a legitimate government to either destabilise it or overthrow it. Terrorism requires a long-term religious and political agenda, formal hierarchical leadership, an established organisation that has vast financial resources, indoctrination cells, media cell to propagate their thoughts and highlight their actions, use of sophisticated means to fight governmental counter-terrorism measures and intimidation of the local civilian population to ensure their passive or active support. Yogi Adityanath says that terrorism has no boundaries and can strike in any part of the world in order to obtain the desired goals.

Factors Behind Terrorism

It is equally important to dwell on those factors that lead to terrorism. Some of these factors are:

1. The first factor emerges from the human psyche of frustration and desperation. When the desired aim or goal is not fulfilled, terrorists opt for violence as a method.
2. The second factor arises from the spiritualistic goal of human beings. It could be laid down as such: "If I die fighting for

God, then I will go to heaven because God wants this act to happen."

3. The third factor is the belief that "my way is the only way."
4. The fourth factor is ignoring human values in order to achieve a goal.
5. The last factor is lack of respect for life itself.

Internal Security Environment

Yogi Adityanath opines that the prevailing internal environment has affected the growth of terrorism in India. The realities in this context is our own Constitution and moreover the diversity of Indian multi-ethnic and multi-religious society has been often been exploited by fundamentalist forces. The absence of adequate employment opportunities and unbalanced development, poverty and growing frustration among the youth lead them to choose the unholy path of violence resulting in the growth of terrorism. There are other factors also that have further accelerated the rise of terrorism. These are:

- uneven socio-economic development.
- demographic displacement causing much social and ethnic tension.
- structure inadequacies in the state apparatus.
- soft approach of earlier governments resulting in lack of clear strategy and policy of internal security.

External Environment

The realities that merit consideration in the existing external environment in India are as follows:

- a hostile nuclear Pakistan with a land border of 3,400 km.
- the unresolved border with China which often adopts an aggressive policy while dealing with our country. It also has the active military and nuclear cooperation of Pakistan.
- a long sea border (7,000 km), prone to smuggling and acts of terrorism.
- a contiguous and porous border with Nepal, Bangladesh, Myanmar and Sri Lanka.

- the growth of Islamic non-state actors who have become a cause of great concern not only to India but to the entire world.

Rise of Global Terrorism

Yogi Adityanath says that the rise of modern terrorism has been more complex and diversified because of ideological, religious and political goals. These terrorist groups often succeed in creating a sense of vulnerability across the world. They gain attention and publicity by sheer acts of violence and by the use of the media to enhance the effectiveness of their violence. They also try to gain the support of similar related groups across the world.

The emergence of modern terrorism with the Islamic threat as its epicentre has serious implications not only for the world but also for India. Yogi Adityanath says that in the last two decades in India, a massive loss of population and wealth has been attributed to terrorism and separatism. More important, he says that Islamic terrorism has been the major cause of concern to Indian security. In one of his articles entitled "Idiot Mujahedeen," he mentions the names of such Islamic organisations like Huji, Indian Mujhadeen, Laskhar-a-Toiba, Jaishe-Mohammed, Deendar Anjuman, etc., as terrorist outfits. They are there to perpetrate more and more violence so that they obtain their objectives.

Islamic or Muslim terror is not a localised Indian phenomenon. Today, there is hardly any part of the world that is not affected by it. One of the major security threats is perceived from the ISIS. Whenever any major event is organised, terror strikes are always in the forefront. Unfortunately, in India, such threats are invariably linked to Islamic terror outfits who target people not only from other faiths but also people of their own faith who are not ready to subscribe to the Islamic religion.

Islamic terror stems from an interpretation of the Islamic faith as contained in the Holy Koran where anyone other than a Muslim is considered an infidel and it is the duty of every Muslim to either convert an infidel to believe in Islam or to destroy him. For them, the only way of life is defined in the Sharia Law where religion is not questioned. There may have sounded logical in the seventh century when it was propagated by the Prophet but today in the 21st century it is certainly irrelevant. Unfortunately, Islam has not only changed with the changing times but seems to have fallen back in the last few decades. Regrettably, there has been no worthwhile opposition to this phenomenon within the Muslim community, both in India and elsewhere. This has resulted in an upper hand for the extremists and those who propagate seventh century Islam.[6]

Today, the Islamic state of Iraq and Syria pose a threat to the entire world. India is no exception. ISIS is backed by thousands of Islamic fighters in Syria and Iraq. A sensational story published in the *Daily Mail*, United Kingdom, revealed the ideological goal of Al-Qaeda and other Pakistani-based terrorist groups to be Ghazwa-e-Hind or 'the final battle in India.' Intelligence reports state that the terror network had made inroads into India, thus sowing the seeds of a final war across the country. One should be aware of the term 'Hind.' What does it mean? On a conceptual basis, Ghazwa-e-Hind is a prophesied battle in which Muslim armies would invade the Indian subcontinent and, if victorious, would establish Islamic law in the region. The term includes both India and Pakistan but anti-Indian Muslims in Pakistan have misled the community in order to create more hatred and violence in India.

Al-Qaeda is another terrorist outfit that aims to turn India into another Syria or Iraq. Indian intelligence agencies have sufficient proof of connections between Al-Qaeda and the Indian Mujahedeen. It was soon found that these two terrorist groups, along with other jihadi groups, have declared war against India. The Al-Qaeda network recently released a video urging Muslims from Delhi, Uttar Pradesh, Bihar, Gujarat and South India to join them for jihad.

Islamic terrorist organisations are out to disturb Indian sentiments. This has affected India's national integrity and now their aims are higher, i.e., the disintegration of India. Hence, that they can attain their targets by means of violence. In the last two decades, there are many instances of such terrorist attacks. Whether it was the 26/11 Mumbai attack, 1993 Mumbai serial blast, 2002 Akshardham Temple attack in Ahmedabad, 2005 Delhi serial blasts,

2006 Mumbai train blasts, 2008 Assam bombing, 2001 Parliament attack in Delhi and the ethnic cleansing of Kashmir Valley in 1990 in which hundreds of thousands had to flee their homes, all these were acts of terrorism. In all these incidents, common people were killed.

The casualties caused by Islamic terrorist groups are well documented in Chart I given below:

Chart I
Fatalities in Terrorist Violence 1988-2017

	Incidents	*Civilians*	*Security Force Personnel*	*Terrorists*	*Total*
1988	390	29	1	1	31
1989	2154	79	13	0	92
1990	3905	862	132	183	1177
1991	3122	594	185	614	1393
1992	4971	859	177	873	1909
1993	4457	1023	216	1328	2567
1994	4484	1012	236	1651	2899
1995	4479	1161	297	1338	2796
1996	4224	1333	376	1194	2903
1997	3004	840	355	1177	2372
1998	2993	877	339	1045	2261
1999	2938	799	555	1184	2538
2000	2835	842	638	1808	3288
2001	3278	1067	590	2850	4507
2002	NA	839	469	1714	3022
2003	NA	658	338	1546	2542
2004	NA	534	325	951	1810
2005	NA	521	218	1000	1739
2006	NA	349	168	599	1116
2007	NA	164	121	492	777
2008	NA	69	90	382	541
2009	NA	55	78	242	375
2010	NA	36	69	270	375
2011	NA	34	30	119	183
2012	NA	16	17	84	117
2013	NA	20	61	100	181
2014	NA	32	51	110	193
2015	NA	20	41	113	174
2016	NA	14	88	165	267
2017	NA	22	22	46	90
Total	**47234**	**14760**	**6296**	**23179**	**44235**

Source: Annual Fatalities in Violence by Terrorist.

Hindu or Saffron Terror

There has been lot of controversy created by the previous governments and social institutions about Hindu or Saffron terror. This was a term coined by S. K. Shinde, the then Home Minister in the UPA-2 government. This was made in reference to the Samjhauta Express and Malegaon blasts. This observation was made for political reasons. He went to the extent of stating that both the BJP and the RSS were running terrorist training camps. The then Home Minister, Shinde was guided by short political gains in order to appease the Muslim community. This is a trait practised by the Congress and like-minded parties like the Samajvadi party for many years and they have done enough damage to the nation. There is no comparison between Islamic terrorism and the so-called Hindu terror. Islamic terrorism is a reality and Hindu terror is only a myth.

Yogi Adityanath says all those who talk about Hindu terror are anti-nationals: "Sanatan dharm is the only religion in India. The rest are followers of different cults and beliefs. There is nothing called secularism in the country. It is the biggest lie in independent India. Everyone has a right to follow their own cult or religion but above them is the nation and one cannot betray the nation by raising their heads in the name of intolerance and Hindu terrorism."[7] "Hinduism is a culture and way of living. This Hindu country has given shelter to Muslims, Zoroastrians, Christians, Jews and so many others. India has given tolerance to the world and we respect all religions. But it does not mean we will allow anyone to call Hindus terrorists," he said in an obvious reference to the ongoing controversy over Kamal Hassan's statement.[8]

Further, Yogi Adityanath said that one cannot impose their religious practices on others. "A Brahmin would remain a Brahmin even if he does not wear vermillion and ponytails." He said that Hinduism teaches religious tolerance but it does not mean that we will remain mute spectators to attacks by others demolishing our religious beliefs. "Lord Ram and Lord Krishna did not want war but they took up weapons to kill demons. We are not cowards and we will also give befitting replies to such demons. Politics and religion are synonyms of each other."[9] "These days people talk about saffron colour. Can they change the colour of sun rays and fire? Art and culture are the soul of development. My government has started this by recreating Treta Yuga Diwali in Ayodhya. Uttar Pradesh will soon emerge as the most progressive state in the country," declared Yogi Adityanath. Earlier, speaking at a VHP function, the Chief Minister reiterated that anyone committing a crime against cows will be punished and go to jail. "Our government is committed to cow protection. We will take stringent measures to protect cows."[10]

In order to established the credibility of Hindu terror, some leaders who have vested interests fail to distinguish between communal riots/clashes and terrorism. Riots or clashes are local phenomena that mostly occur between different communities, particularly Hindus and Muslims. The reason for such riots or clashes would be desecration of a holy place or scripture, eve-teasing, local property dispute or threat of an inter-community marriage. The people involved are mostly local residents of the place except for a few outsiders who try to add more tension. These activities are spontaneous and once the issue is resolved both communities lead a normal life. Most incidents that occurred were not riots. Incidents like the Bhagalpur riot (1989), Mumbai riot (1992), Anti-Urdu riot (1994) in Bengaluru, Gujarat riot (2002), Vadodara riot (2006) and Muzaffarnagar riot (2013) were all clashes between Hindus and Muslims. By any means, they could not be categorised as acts of terrorism.

Even if we examine incidents like the Samjhauta blasts (2007) and the Malegaon blasts (2008), there is sufficient evidence to show it was possibly perpetrated by LeT through its USA-based operative, Arif Quasmani, who funded the operation. So fares the Malegaon case is considered, fingers were pointed to a rightist Hindu organisation but one should not forget that there were nine Muslim activists who were arrested in connection with the blast. Since in both the cases the final verdict has come out. It would be wrong to blame them for unleashing such terror.

Yogi Adityanath's Perception of Global Terrorism

On terrorism, Yogi Adityanath comments that our fight is not for the first time. We had fought in every age and are still fighting. Whether it was the battle of Devasur or the one between Rama and

Ravana or the battle of the Mahabharata or other wars, we always fought for justice, truth and tradition. This has been our ancient Indian tradition of fighting against external and internal foes to maintain harmony in society and by doing so India was preserving its culture and religion.

Yogi Adityanath believes that we would have to come forward to face the grave challenges facing us. But, once again, our weak and cowardly political leadership has shielded terrorists when they targeted Hindu religious and other public places like in Jaipur. These terrorists succeeded in their plan and as a result hundreds of Hindus and civilians were rendered homeless. Yogi calls it a shameful act and wonders how long it will last. Secular parties have done nothing except condemning these acts. The objective of the terrorists is to wipe out Hindus. Yogi questions how long this situation will remain and who will end it? What is their relationship with the Indian motherland? All these questions come to his mind and they remain unanswerable. He further elaborates by stating that unless we know about a disease how can we cure it? Similarly this also applies to terrorism. Unless we are not acquainted with the problem of terrorism, we cannot face its challenge. Is it not true that the society of India has overlooked the massacres of its own brotherhood? Do we have to live under the shadow of the army? If so, for how long? Is this is terrorism? In our country there are such classes that oppose the idea of identifying terrorism with Islam. But Yogi Adityanath says that they are not aware that not only in India but the entire world has become a victim of terrorism in the name of Islam and Allah.

Furthermore, there are other equally good questions raised by Yogi Adityanath. Why are Indians targeted in Afghanistan and Pakistan? Why has it reached the last stage in Bangladesh? Kashmir is no exception. This issue will be treated separately. Why do Muslims in Russian-dominated regions demand separation? Why has Yugoslavia disintegrated? Why does the Muslim world want to end the existence of Israel as a state? Ultimately, whether it is Checheynia, Yugoslavia, Kosava or the valley of Kashmir, the situation is the same. Why is there one cause for all these regions?

And why do all terrorist attacks today have their deep roots in madarssas?

Yogi Adityanath claims that terrorist attacks give rise to a feeling that it is water and not blood that flows in our veins. Hindu society has accepted it as a normal way of life. If this is not true, then why have the killings of innocent Hindus every day not affected us? Is it the weakness of the earlier governments or is it merely to capture the vote bank that these political leaders try to gloss over these incidents? He boldly states that in order to save and preserve our Hindu culture and tradition, we will have to fight against terrorism.

Yogi Adityanath's perception of Islamic terrorism got ample support from the American President Donald Trump, recently. In an address to leaders of more than 50 Muslim majority countries who gathered in Riyadh, Donald Trump maintained that "every nation has an absolute duty to ensure that terrorists find no quarter on their soil."[11] He said further, "drive them out. Drive out the terrorists and extremists...drive them out of this earth."[12] Terrorism, he said, is not a battle between different faiths, different sects or different civilisations. It is a battle between those who seek to obliterate human life and those who seek to protect it. Terrorists do not worship god. They worship death.[13] Trump said all countries must work together to confront the crisis of Islamic extremism and the Islamic terror groups it inspires. Trump also reminded the leaders that "95 per cent of the victims of terrorist attacks are themselves Muslim," although terrorism must not only be measured by the number of dead but by the number of "vanished dream."[14] Larry Pressler, in his book, "Neighbours in Arms" advocated that "Pakistan must be considered a terrorist state. In President Trump's review of Asian policy, the State Department distributed a dozen of his books throughout the various federal agencies. He wrote: "Pakistan should be treated like North Korea—like a rogue state. The only reason Pakistan is not a totally failed state is that countries like China and the United States continue to prop it up with massive amounts of foreign aid. Unless Pakistan changes its ways with respect to terrorism, it should be declared a terrorist state."

Several leading foreign policy experts besides him have

expressed the same feeling. Indeed, the first Bush administration seriously considered doing so in 1992. "Pakistan's leaders have essentially blackmailed us into providing aid for the war on terror with threats to cease assistance in rooting out terrorists in Afghanistan. Meanwhile, we know fully well that Pakistan harbours terrorists, and many military leaders believe that terrorists have infiltrated Pakistan's ranks." Perhaps, President Donald Trump is the first US President to openly attack Pakistan and to identify it as lying about terrorism. Moreover, he said that "the USA has foolishly given Pakistan more than $33 billion aid over the last 15 years and they have given us nothing but lies and deceit. They gave safe haven to the terrorists we hunt in Afghanistan with little help."

Bleeding Kashmir

Yogi Adityanath discusses in detail about the impact of terrorism in the state of Jammu and Kashmir. The 'Paradise on Earth', Kashmir, is today bleeding. The year 2018 marks 29 years of insurgency and terrorism in Kashmir. During this period, Kashmir has metamorphosed in terms of political discourse, the nature of the military, the level of external intervention and perception of possible solutions.

Brief History of Kashmir

Kashmir has a long history with the forced partition. Out of this partition, India and Pakistan emerged as two different independent states. But the partition was not a peaceful one as there was much bloodshed on both sides and the people suffered miserably. Yogi Adityanath believes that this kind of violent activity began with the decline of the Hindu king as the protector of the state. Furthermore, he believes that active support from Pakistan in Kashmir has been the cause of major concern.

Before analyzing the pertinent issues of terrorism in Kashmir, a brief history of the state is essential. The state of Jammu and Kashmir is an integral part of India. It is situated in the northern part of India. It shares borders with Pakistan in the west, China in the north and east and the Indian states of Punjab and Himachal Pradesh in the south. It consists of three district regions—the Kashmir valley, Jammu and Ladakh.

History reveals that Jammu and Kashmir basically has a heterogeneous character—politically, ethnically and religion-wise. This makes it susceptible to exploitation. The composite culture provides inherent potentiality and susceptibility to wage terrorism by any detrimental external power. However, it is surprising to note that of the 64 to 65 per cent of Muslims of the region, 70 per cent belong to the Al Hanfi sect with Sufi culture and only 10 to 15 per cent are Al Hadeen[15] with a fundamentalist outlook. One cannot also overlook their economic deprivation[16] and in due course it attained the dimension of deprivation syndrome. It was gradually seen that the demand for economic rights became persuasive and the government failed to deliver the goods. This economic deprivation syndrome provided a fertile ground for weakening the social fabric susceptible for exploitation by vested interests. Similarly, the political aspirations of the parties could not reconcile to the Kashmir issue, i.e., it is one entity like other states. As a result, they became the target of Pakistan's secessionist propaganda. The isolation syndrome harmed the nation more because it tried to induce its Kashmir population to drift away.

Pakistan and Kashmir

Against this background, one has to examine terrorism in Kashmir. Since its inception, the tribal invasion of Kashmir, aided and assisted by Pakistan forces, was the first case of state-sponsored terrorism against India to wrest Kashmir. It was a demonstration of the use of terrorism by a state as a tool to obtain foreign and security goals. Pakistani forces are waging low-cost war, using irregulars and warlike tribes. The 1965 misadventure of Pakistan was on the 1947-48 line. Pakistan set up a mujahidin force of 1.5 lakh insurgents who were given intensive religious and political indoctrination. The so-called "Razakars" were pushed for sabotage in order to create trouble and incite violence to create the mood for an uprising. Operation Gibraltar was launched by Pakistan President Ayub Khan in the Rann of Kutch as a diversionary measure. The terrorists were well placed with their targets identified in August 1965. Terrorist intentions were clear to capture Srinagar radio station and announce a new government. But it did not go down well with the Pakistani intentions. As result, the Razakars found no favour with the local population. Thus, Pakistan's misconception of further division of India failed miserably.

However, when Pakistani designs of attaining the objective by conventional war failed miserably in 1965, it then thought of "bleeding India by a thousand cuts." This policy was conceived by Gen. Zia-ul-Haq and soon Pakistan embarked on her ambitious design to misguide the population of Jammu and Kashmir by false propaganda in order to win local support. Zia-ul-Haq succeeded in its mission as the international environment favoured him to push his plan forward against India so that Pakistan could gain something which could raise the morale of its political and military decision makers.

Radicalisation of Pakistani Society

Internally, we saw the radicalisation of Pakistan society. It was inspired by the success of the Iranian Islamic Revolution in late 1970 and by the Soviet intervention in Afghanistan in 1979. Pakistan took full advantage of the situation as the USA was compelled to assist Pakistan militarily and economically to fight against the Soviets in Afghanistan. But the American calculations went wrong when the money and resources were used to further bleed India through terrorism. This bred the "culture of violence"[17] in Pakistani society. Another aspect was that Pakistan honoured the acts of these jihadis in Afghanistan, ushering in the "cult of jihadi heroism."

Of all the forms of terrorism, jihadi is the most deadly. The killing by jihadis is considered a sacred act. Jihadis believe that they speak for the Divine. In the 1980s, terrorism commenced with an indigenous flavour with the stated objective of attaining azadi but events proved that it was supported by Pakistan. The Jammu and Kashmir Liberation Front (JKLF) was used to initiate the process that was subsequently exploited by foreign mercenaries. This explains the initial support to the JKLF and its subsequent scuttling by the ISI which needed terrorist tanzeems which were more Islamic, more strident and more dependent on it.

Terrorist Outfits

Terrorism sustained by foreign mercenaries cannot be termed as freedom nor is it indigenous in nature. Had it been indigenous, the JKLF should not have been raised in Peshawar in August 1965 but in the Kashmir Valley. The Pakistanis raised it in Peshawar and used it initially to create an impression that the Muslims had launched an armed struggle in the state to liberate it from India. Once the terrorist violence in the state spread, the marginalisation of the JKLF for not toeing the Pakistani line reveals the design. Pakistan had inducted more powerful Islamic groups and more and more dependent foreign terrorist outfits into the state like the Hizbul Mujahideen, the militant outfits of Jamaat-e-Islamic, LeT, JeM and Al Badar. They were entrusted to enhance the level of violence and liquidate and marginalise all those who were not advocating but desiring the accession of the state of Pakistan. They speak for terrorism and not for an indigenous movement. Major terrorist acts were executed by Pakistan-based foreign terrorists. Moreover, the Muslim faith had a discernible effect in motivating suicide bombers as the faith contains belligerent feature like "kafir" and "jihad."

There are various terrorist organisations operating in Jammu and Kashmir. They have their own objectives. These organisations are:

Proscribed Terrorist Group	*Active Terrorist Group*
Hiz-ul-Mujahideen	Laskar-e-Omar
Harkat-ul-Ansar (presently known as Harkat-ul-Mujahideen)	Laskar-e-Jabbar
Lashkar-e-Toiba	Tehrik-ul-Mujahideen
Jaish-e-Mohammad	Jammu and Kashmir Liberation Front
Al Badra	All Parties Hurriyat Conference
Jamiat-ul-Mujahideen	Mutahide Jehad Council
Harkat-ul-Jehad-al Islamic	
Al Umar Mujahdeen	
Dukhtaran-e-Millat	

Source: South Asia Terrorist Portal available at http://www.satp.org

In the last two years, the situation in Jammu and Kashmir has become worse day by day. The militants have targeted sensitive areas that have disrupted the normal life of common people. In recent months, South Kashmir has become the hotbed of home-grown militants. Intelligence inputs suggest the presence of 200 active militants in the Kashmir Valley comprising 10 districts. Ninety of them are from South Kashmir.[18] Once known for its famous apple orchards, Pulwama, Anantnag, Shopian and Kulgam have seen the escalation of violence between militants and security forces.[19]

South Kashmir was also the focal point of street protests triggered by the alleged rape and murder of two young women in Shopian in May, 2009. The then government dismissed the death as a result of drowning but resentment still lingers among residents. Then there was Burhan Wani, the Hizbul Mujahideen commander, who was killed in an encounter with security forces in 2016. It drew many youngsters of South Kashmir to the fold of militancy. Officials say Wani became a hero and turned out to be an effective recruitment tool for the militants and the number of locals joining militant outfits have been on the rise. Compared to 2013 when 31 youths joined militancy, the number rose to 66 in 2015. In 2016, some 88 youngsters have joined militancy.[20]

The rising dissonance between Kashmiri separatists and terrorists based in the Valley on the one hand and Pakistan-based terrorist commanders and cadres in Kashmir on the other, have led Indian agencies to suspect that the terror masterminds across the country might covertly plan a new terrorist organisation in Jammu and Kashmir with focus on ex-Hizbul Mujahideen commander Zakir Musa.[21] Pakistan might attempt a repeat of its Kashmir strategy of the 1990s when the only terror organisation, the JKLF, was supplanted and eventually replaced by many new outfits by 1993-94. In the case of creating a new terror organisation in Kashmir, Musa spoke of a new anti-separatist, anti-Hizb and anti-Pakistan line. It has been targeted at the Kashmiri youth. He is advocating an Islamist uprising for the freedom of Kashmir. It is true now that these Kashmiri youths have adopted a new technique to challenge government policies. It is stone pelting at the army and police forces. This has made the situation more grave as the Indian government now has not only to deal with the terrorists but also its own people inspired by the militants. As a result, clashes have re-occurred more in recent times and led to many casualties.

On 27 September 2017, the security forces killed Sabzar Bhatt in Tral in South Kashmir. He was seen by many as a successor to Burhan Wani. The news of his death triggered violent protests at least in Pulwama, Shopian, Anantnag, Srinagar, Sopore and Kupwara. A civilian was killed and several others were injured in the protests. A statement from the army's Northern Command said that the encounter was the result of a "relentless operation" by security forces to defeat desperate attempts by Pakistani and Pakistan-sponsored agents to spread terror in the state in the run-up to the holy month of Ramzan.[22] The cumulative fatalities have been amply demonstrated by in Charts II, III, IV and V:

Chart II
Fatalities in Jammu and Kashmir
Fatalities in Terrorist Violence 1988-2018 under UPA

	Incidents	*Civilians*	*Security Forces Personnel*	*Terrorists*	*Total*
1988	390	29	1	1	31
1989	2154	79	13	0	92
1990	3905	862	132	183	1177
1991	3122	594	185	614	1393
1992	4971	859	177	873	1909
1993	4457	1023	216	1328	2567
1994	4484	1012	236	1651	2899
1995	4479	1161	297	1338	2796
1996	4224	1333	376	1194	2903
1997	3004	840	355	1177	2372

Chart III
Fatalities in Jammu and Kashmir Under NDA

	Incidents	*Civilians*	*Security Forces Personnel*	*Terrorists*	*Total*
1998	2993	877	339	1045	2261
1999	2938	799	555	1184	2538
2000	2835	842	638	1808	3288
2001	3278	1067	590	2850	4507
2002	NA	839	469	1714	3022
2003	NA	658	338	1546	2542
2004	NA	534	325	951	1810

Chart IV
Fatalities in Jammu and Kashmir Under UPA

	Incidents	*Civilians*	*Security Forces Personnel*	*Terrorists*	*Total*
2005	NA	521	218	1000	1739
2006	NA	349	168	599	1116
2007	NA	164	121	492	777
2008	NA	69	90	382	541
2009	NA	55	78	242	375
2010	NA	36	69	270	375
2011	NA	34	30	119	183
2012	NA	16	17	84	117
2013	NA	20	61	100	181

Chart V
Fatalities in Jammu and Kashmir Under NDA From 2014 Onwards

	Incidents	*Civilians*	*Security Forces Personnel*	*Terrorists*	*Total*
2014	NA	32	51	110	193
2015	NA	20	41	113	174
2016	NA	14	88	165	267
2017	NA	57	83	218	358
2018	**NA**	**6**	**15**	**26**	**47**

Source: http://www.satp.org/satporgtp/countries/india/states/jandk/data_sheets

State-Sponsored Terror in Kerala

Yogi Adityanath who has led the Bharatiya Janata Party's Jan Suraksha Yatra in Kerala's Kannur raked up the issue of love jihad, Islamic extremism and political violence. The Hindutva leader is the face of the BJP protest today even as the CPI (M) lashed out at the party for attempting to create communal unrest in the state.[23] He said that, "we don't do politics over issues of national security and innocent lives lost in political killings. Jihad is a serious threat to the whole nation and the Kerala government had provided political patronage to such elements. It has done nothing, even though radicalisation has been reported in the state. Women are not safe. The order of the Kerala High Court judgment was a landmark and now the Supreme Court has asked the NIA to probe incidents of love jihad."

Yogi Adityanath further said, "The political killings of BJP and

RSS workers are instances of state-sponsored terror. As many as 120 BJP workers, 84 in Kannur alone, have been killed in the state since 2001 with 14 of them in the Chief Minister's home town since he took over the reins in 2017. The Left parties have no tolerance towards other political parties and this has to stop. Moreover, the people of the state are peace-loving and would not tolerate politics of murder terror. It is against the Indian democracy and the CPI (M) government has always supported such instances. The yatra held a mirror to their deeds. We would stand by our workers."[24]

Rohingyas Linkages with Terrorist Outfits

Over the years, security challenges in Jammu and Kashmir have been serious. On the one hand, security forces are involved in checking militancy in the state and now, the other two parts of the state—Jammu and Ladakh—are faced with a new threat arising from the migration of Rohingyas from Myanmar. Yogi Adityanath said that recently, the Rohingyas have become a subject of serious concern to our national security. In an exclusive interview to a news agency, Adityanath said, "The Indian government has cleared its stand on the Rohingyas. They are from Myanmar in India and not refugees; they are intruders. This is very condemnable and a sad act that some people are showing concern towards them, as in Myanmar many innocent Hindus were killed brutally, and it was also found that they (Rohingyas) have links with terrorist organisations."[25] Jammu and Kashmir, Deputy Chief Minister, Nirmal Singh said that Rohingya Muslims were a threat to security in the state as they were prone to the sinister designs of terrorists in the border state.[26] The Government of India has told the Supreme Court that the illegal entry of Rohingyas will cause a threat to national security. "The illegal influx of Rohingyas, in significant numbers, who have entered Indian territory since 2012-13 and the Central Government has been reported by security agencies and supported by authentic material to indicate linkages of some of the unauthorised Rohingya immigrants with Pakistan-based terror organisations and similar organisations operating in other countries.[27]

In the coming years, it is an indication of a dangerous political trend. Infiltration of terrorists from Pakistan is on the rise. However, the presence of Rohingyas, particularly in the Jammu and Ladakh regions, has alarmed the intelligence agencies and security bodies over their involvement in terror activities. Such fear is justified because of the following events that occurred in recent years.

- Chota Burmi of Rohingya origin was killed along with Pakistani mercenaries in Kashmir in 2015. He is said to have received the patronage of Hafiz Saeed in Pakistan.
- In October 2016, reports emerged that a Rohingya terror group, known as Aqa Mul Mujahideen (AMM), was in touch with terrorist outfits active in the state including Lashkar-e-Toiba (LET) and Jaish-e-Mohammed (JeM) and men belonging to AMM were trained in Pakistan.
- Zakir Musa, the head of Al-Qaeda's offshoot in Kashmir, Ansar Gazawat-ul-Hind, has expressed solidarity with the Rohingyas living in Jammu. In a 10-minute-long audio clip, Zakir Musu warned the Modi government against deporting the Rohingyas from India and called for liberating Kashmir from the leadership of 'cow-worshipping' Hindus.
- In early September, the Mutahida Majlis-e-Ulma (MMU), headed by separatist Mirwaiz Umar Farooq and other religious organisations observed a solidarity day in the Valley for Rohingya settlers.

Terrorism, as we see it today, was basically an attempt made by the Pakistani government to divert the local masses from the government functioning. Communal riots in Anantnag, destruction of Hindu temples and migration of Hindu Pandits were the major pointers. Yogi Adityanath is right when he says that Kashmiri Hindus who left the state earlier have not been re-established even today in Kashmir. This is a pathetic situation where the people are deprived of their fundamental rights.

Yogi Adityanath feels that the people are deprived of their basic natural rights. He was also critical of the role of the state government in the distribution of land to devotees who visit Amaranth temple every year. This is a normal practice that land is distributed to religious-cultural organisations for the conduct of religious activities.

Yogi Adityanath says that there is a liberal attitude of Hindu society as compared to madrassas or kabaristans. One saw the construction of mazars in public places in thousands. In almost every state, in the name of Haj house, public land has been distributed. But never has the Hindu community objected to it and never created obstacles. Yogi Adityanath had questioned the credibility of the earlier political leadership and questioned whether the liberal attitude of the Hindus were because of weakness. These separatist organisations or political parties had always opposed the land distribution of the Amarnath Pilgrimage Board but they must not forget that the money gathered from it were spend in subsidies. But what about the Muslim community? Nobody objected to it because they thought that it was in accordance with Islamic principles. He further said that the fault lies within us that we had not read the barbaric, violent and crude face of Islam. Those who had opposed this are those Muslims who earlier supported the partition of India. In spite of all these, Yogi Adityanath firmly said that if the people of India still ignore the bleeding in Kashmir, then separatist tendencies in India will get more encouragement to play their dirty game in the name of terrorism.

To tackle the terrorist menace in Jammu and Kashmir, Yogi Adityanath says many options have discussed. Some of these options proposed by him are the following:

First, after 1947 we saw the partition of India as a nation. One part came under Indian sovereignty that was known as Jammu and Kashmir and the other known as Azad Kashmir was occupied by Pakistan. For both the countries, there is an international line of control where both had to accept it till the issue was resolved. Some feel that a solution to this crisis can be found through either mutual dialogue or international cooperation where both accept the international line of control and end the problem in a peaceful manner.

But Yogi Adityanath feels that there are certain shortcomings in the options cited above. One is that Jammu and Kashmir has been fully integrated in our federal structure and how to integrate Azad Kashmir as part of India is a serious problem. If any government wants to do it, then the pertinent question is whether there is a need to bring about a basic change in the structure of the Indian Constitution that would be equally acceptable to the judiciary.

Second, Yogi Adityanath says that since independence, Pakistan has shown apprehension and doubts about India's intentions. After the creation of Bangladesh, Pakistan's policy has changed to revenge and Jammu and Kashmir provided the fertile ground to foment trouble and bleed India with a thousand cuts. Will Pakistan accept the reality and work in accordance with Indian wishes.

Third, in the solution of the above-mentioned problem, some experts put forward another option. Those who propagate this view lay emphasis on a public plebiscite and through it know the mood of the people of Jammu and Kashmir. On this basis, the problem can be solved. But to accept this, there are many legal difficulties. For example, as we know Jammu and Kashmir has already been integrated into the Indian federal structure and from time to time on the basis of democratic procedures many Vidhan Sabha and Lok Sabha elections have been held. Furthermore, the established state of Jammu and Kashmir under the first government Sheikh Abdullah and even today the present government in Jammu and Kashmir declared it as part of the Indian federal structure. Hence, today there is no need for a public plebiscite.

Fourth, from the point of resolving the crisis there is another option in which some experts hold the view that Jammu and Kashmir is divided into three divisions. From the population perspective, the major portion is Jammu which is dominated by Hindus and Hindi-speaking people. The second division is the valley of Kashmir which is Muslim dominated and the language is Kashmiri. In this area, minority Hindus have already left the place and in recent years Sikhs have become the target of Islamic terrorism. If this situation is not changed soon, the Kashmir valley will become the abode of Muslims. The third division of Jammu and Kashmir is Ladakh wherein in one district one finds a majority of Buddhists and in another Kargil, Muslims dominate. Here also we have seen the massacre of Buddhist monks. Yogi Adityanath says that in spite of Jammu and Kashmir being a more populous state, the adjustment of seats of the Vidhan Sabha in the Kashmir valley was created at the cost of other parts of Kashmir valley so that India could still have its dominance. Some even suggested that in such a situation for balanced development, all these three divisions could be made independent states. Yogi Adityanath says that this will complicate the problem. If we set aside these problems, the state still will have the problem of Azad Kashmir and it will be easy for Pakistan to operate and carry out its nefarious designs by fomenting more and more trouble. Hence, this cannot be taken for granted as solving the Kashmir problem.

Furthermore, Yogi Adityanath says that in order to solve Muslim extremist and separatist problems, the proposal of independence of Kashmir seems to be unconstitutional and impracticable. From time to time, the Central Government has rejected this claim and instead has had to resort to force to bring peace and stability in the region. The important issue is what will happen if it becomes free. This will not be in Indian interests.

Fifth, Yogi Adityanath talks about the feelings of the common people of Jammu and Kashmir and nationalists who regard it as an integral part of India. The state has an age-old history and geography and hence it should be a part of India. It is logical and appropriate that it should remain a part of India. Otherwise, the situation as he sees it, will be grave as some other states will try to assert their independence in the name of separatism.

Sixth, there are some who propagate the idea of removing Article 370 from the Indian Constitution as a permanent solution to the problem. When it was adopted, it was a temporary arrangement and today it has lost its relevance. Because of this article, the Indian government cannot take any action in spite of the wrongs done to the state of Jammu and Kashmir. Hence, Yogi Adityanath believes this article should be immediately put to an end. The reasons cited by him are as follows:

- Inclusion of people of Jammu and Kashmir into one national mainstream.
- To rehabilitate those minorities who have fled to other states.
- Like other states, people from any state may be allowed to purchase property and settle there.

- To create an environment of population balance so that an atmosphere of peaceful co-existence may prevail.

In the context of the above analysis done by Yogi Adityanath, the author feels that for national unity and integrity, India should stick to the dual policy of dialogue and use of force. Earlier, during the Atal Bihari Vajpayee regime, one saw the government succeed in bringing a faction of the Hizbul Mujahideen to the table for talks. But their leader was killed soon. So was the Hurriyat representative, Abdul Goni Lone, whose son Sajad is a minister in the present coalition government. A mechanism that provides security and enable people to give up arms has not taken root in Kashmir even 29 years after insurgency and terrorism have made the 'Paradise on Earth, Kashmir, a violent and disturbed state. Still one should not lose hope as human beings have two instincts—conflict and cooperation. Sooner or later, once Pakistan is isolated by the international community, one can think of greater chances for positive dialogue for the betterment of people in Kashmir.

NOTES

1. Webster New Collegiate Dictionary, Indian edition, Calcutta, 1983, p. 1193.
2. Chamber Twentieth Century Dictionary, New Delhi, 1973, p. 1393.
3. B. M. Jerkins, 'International Terrorism: A New Mode of Conflict' in Carlton, David and Carlo Scherif (eds.), *International Terrorism and World Security*, London, 1975, p. 13.
4. 'Defining Terrorism: Focussing on the Target', Strategic Comments, 7, 9 (2005). http//:www.iiss.org stratcomsubarchivephp? scID=193.
5. http://www.quorq.com/AHindu_cannot_be_a terrorist_India_is_his_com
6. Saroj Chadha, 'Hindus, Muslims and Terrorism in India', July 8, 2016, http//: hillpost.in2006/07hindus-muslims and terrorism/106818/.html.
7. http://www.indiatimes.com/news/india/up_cm_yogi_adityanath says all.
8. Ibid.
9. Ibid.
10. Ibid.
11. *The Times of India*, 23 May 2017.
12. Ibid.
13. Ibid.

14. Ibid.
15. S. Sahni, *Kashmir Underground*, Har Anand Publications, New Delhi, 1991.
16. Ibid.
17. Tara Kartha, 'Terrorism—a New Face of War,' *World Focus*, No. 241, 2002.
18. *Hindustan Times*, 19 May 2017.
19. Ibid.
20. Ibid.
21. http://www/oneindia.com/india/yogi_adityanath_setsto_lead padayatra.
22. *The Times of India*, 21 May 2017.
23. *Hindustan Times*, 28 May 2017.
24. Ibid.
25. *Financial Express*, 29 September 2017.
26. *Hindustan Times*, 8 December 2017.
27. *Financial Express*, 29 September 2017.

7

THE PROBLEMS OF UTTAR PRADESH

Nelson Mandela once remarked, "It always seems impossible until it is done." This statement is quite true when we look into the past history of the state of Uttar Pradesh. When Yogi Adityanath took charge as head of the state, the tasks were daunting. Critics then often argued how UP could become a frontline state of India in terms of development. But Yogi Adityanath did not show any kind of negativism that could hamper the growth of the state. He seems to be a shrewd politician as he has his own agenda to overcome the obstacles that the state was facing for the last 60 years. By dint of courage and political vision, he was able to change the meaning of Uttar Pradesh for ever when he once claimed that the state meant "unlimited potential." Taken in that sense, the state of Uttar Pradesh has plenty of potential in terms of geography, culture, natural resources, etc. But the problem was that the potential was never fully tapped by previous governments. Hence, UP became a *Bimaru* state and was more dependent on the Centre for its existence. Though it is a landlocked state, it did not have to face external threats. The threats were coming from within society and had its ramifications globally and nationally. The author has discussed in detail all these aspects of the state's development. Hence, for convenience it would be appropriate to divide this chapter into various sections.

Physical Characteristics of Uttar Pradesh

Uttar Pradesh is a land of diversity in terms of geography, culture and religion. Geographically, it is bounded by Uttarakhand and Himachal Pradesh in the north, Haryana in the west, Madhya Pradesh in the south and Bihar in the east. In one sense, the state can be divided into sub-regions: (1) southern hills; and (2) Gangetic plain. It is to be noted here that the only external power that shares its boundaries with India is Nepal. The land is vast land and full of historical monuments, forts, museums, natural beauty, wildlife sanctuaries and religious sites. Moreover, Uttar Pradesh has been referred to as the "Hindi-speaking heartland" of India. It covers 2.41 lakh square kilometres and accounts of 7.3per cent of the total area of the country. Its share in the population of population is 16.16 per cent or 19.95 crore.[1]

Uttar Pradesh is divided into 17 administrative bodies, 71 districts, 212 tehsils and 820 development blocks. There are 52,000 village panchayats covering 1.06 lakh people inhabiting villages.[2] As stated above, the state is situated in the Indo-Gangetic plain and intersected by rivers. In economic terms, it is bifurcated into four regions, viz., western, central, eastern and Bundelkhand. The first three regions fall in the Gangetic plain and Bundelkhand forms part of the southern plateau.

Being a state of full geographical diversity, it has been responsible for different environmental conditions in different regions. Because of such environmental conditions, Yogi Adityanath says that Uttar Pradesh had to suffer a lot and the end result is stagnation in every field as a result of which the overall growth of the state was hampered.

Yogi Adityanath's observation needs further analysis. What are those hurdles that pushed Uttar Pradesh into a state of languish and agony? It seems that from time to time problems emerged that deprived the state of becoming a developed one as compared to other well-established states of India. The author has highlighted the current situation. It has to be examined in the light of various threats emanating from the state that has badly affected its security in terms of national integrity and culture. The threats could be assessed in various ways. Well, one could say, Uttar Pradesh is a vulnerable state because of terrorism and naxalism. It has become the breeding ground of violence. Violence has got ample support from external actors. Some aspects of terrorism and naxalism have been discussed in the earlier chapters. The ongoing problems of terrorism and naxalism have completely crippled the functioning of the Uttar Pradesh government.

Terrorism in Uttar Pradesh

There is no denying the fact that in the last two or three decades the division between two dominant communities in Uttar Pradesh—Hindus and Muslims—has increased progressively. Today, it has become a cause of great concern not for political leaders but also for the common man. It is also true that the previous governments took no active constructive initiatives and tried to bridge the gap between the two communities. On the other hand, they tried to give their own political flavour. Such a situation adversely affected not only the state and the entire nation had to suffer from such terrorist acts.

As discussed earlier, UP is facing the onslaught of Islamic terror. It is not a local phenomenon but the locals are more affected by it. In promoting their interests, these Muslim outfits target people not only from other faiths but Muslim communities are also affected by their radical ideology of perpetrating more and more violence in the state. These Islamic terrorists know no other language except to play with the sentiments of the people either through coercive methods or financial support.

The worsening situation in Uttar Pradesh has also alarmed the new government under Yogi Adityanath. The challenge is big but one should not be pessimistic. Though terrorism cannot be wiped out in a day, months or years, efforts have to be made to minimise its effect so that the state can take developmental measures necessary for the welfare of the people. This will no doubt curb the menace of terrorism.

In the last two decades, Yogi Adityanath found the conditions of eastern Uttar Pradesh, compared to other parts, to be more pitiable. The reason is that Azamgarh has become the epicentre of Islamic terrorism. He says the situation in this district did not deteriorate suddenly but has a long history because of its connectively with terrorist outfits. As a result, today, it has engulfed the whole of Azamgarh. If we read history, this district was known as Aryamgarh. It is more known for great maharishis like Durvasa and Brigu. Yogi Adityanath believes that the cruel ruler Aurangzeb was responsible for the bad condition in Azamgarh. At that time, King Vikram Singh ruled the district. Aurangzeb, with his army and fear made him captive and forced him to accept Islam. The name he gave was Azamshah. Thus, Azamgarh got its name from the converted Hindu king Azamshah. His wife refused to accept Islam and left the place to settle in a nearby village. Yogi Adityanath says that if Vikram Singh has taken a lesson of sacrifice from Maharana Pratap, he could have been remembered even today by the people. But kingdom and his own selfish interests and traditions became more important than the nation. This is the reason the people do not remember him.

Three hundred years ago the mistake committed by the Hindu king is been repeated again by the so-called secular political leaders today. It had repercussions not only in Azamgarh but other districts and localities have become hubs of Islamic terrorism. In 1980, the journey began with Haji Mastan and today we see Abu Salem, Abdul Bashr and others who have made the situation worse not only in Uttar Pradesh but their evil designs have affected India as a nation. One cannot forget Dawood Ibrahim and Abu Salem who were responsible for the Mumbai bomb blasts. Abu Azami also belongs to Azamgarh and was interrogated first under the NADA Act. The list is long as Yogi Adityanath says.

The twenty-first century saw terrorism as the single biggest internal security threat to UP in particular and India in general in terms of violence, area covered and governing complexity amongst the masses. Generally it was found that these terrorists were working in all parts of the state depending upon the acceptability and place. They rose from among the common people and disappeared with relative ease. This made the task of state security complicated. The history of terrorist activities in UP is long. As cited by Yogi Adityanath, the terrorists have no common cause but are fighting a jihadi war against the nation so that the state may become vulnerable and weak thus having a great impact on Indian nationalism.

If one traces the development of terrorism from 2001 to 2009, one can readily come to the conclusion that in most cases the role of Pakistani terrorist groups was to bleed the state in particular and India in general. This Islamic ideology cannot be ignored by true nationalist Hindus. The targets selected were both in urban and rural centres. The terrorist groups that were involved in propagating Islamic ideology and involved in incidents were Jaish-e-Mohammad, Harkat-ul-Ansar, ISI, LeT, Lashkar-e-Toiba, Hizb-ul-Mujahideen, HUJI and others. Though the Uttar Pradesh police have made attempts to curb the terrorist menace, it could not get complete success in wiping them out from our land. Moreover, as the years passed, the situation worsened.

Let us examine the involvement of these terrorist groups in bringing instability to the state from 2010 onwards.

2010

In 2010 there were many cases of serial bomb blasts in various parts of India and the terrorists took shelter in various cities of Uttar Pradesh. Whether they took shelter in Azamgarh, Lucknow, Gorakhpur, Noida or Ghaziabad, they were arrested by the State police and the Anti-Terrorist Squad. It is reported that they were produced in the courts and verdicts are still awaited. In all these cases of bomb blasts, the Indian Mujahedeen and the LeT were behind the scenes. Of all the terrorist activities conducted in 2010, special mention may be made of the effort made by the Maharashtra Anti-Terrorist Squad. It was found that two LeT operatives visited some important places in Uttar Pradesh prior to their arrest. Mirza Himayat Baig and Shaikh Lal Baba Mohammad Hussain were arrested by the Anti-Terrorist Squad (ATS) for their alleged involvement in the German Bakery blast case. They had some maps of the twin cities of Noida and Ghaziabad where they were planning to disturb the normal life of the people. One cannot forget the famous Bhatkal brothers, Riaz and Iqbal, who were involved in the Varanasi bomb explosion. It was said that the planning was done in Pakistan which gave shelter to the militants. There were also many cases of Fake Indian Current Notes (FICN) on the Nepal and India borders. It affected the Indian economy badly.

2011 -2012

The first half of 2011 witnessed no major incident of terrorism or FICN. But in July, the police busted a gang that was involved in the manufacture of fake currency from Bahraich. In September, at least 15 persons were injured in with an improvised explosive device in Agra. Two persons wanted in the Agra blast case were detained by the Anti-Terrorist Squad on September 23, 2011. Again, in Agra, in December a crude bomb was recovered from a roadside eatery in Tehri Bagia but it was defused later.

To check the circulation of FICN, the UP government in 2012 directed banks to be more alert on the safety of ATMs installed on the Indo-Nepal border. Some persons tried to exchange fake currency notes but they were arrested by the respective district police forces. The number of FICN cases swelled in the months of September, October and November. The year 2012 was also important because militants were involved in motivating youth to join terrorist outfits. Similar cases of FICN occurred on September 11, October 3, 6, 7, 14 and November 3, 2012.

2013

Some of the incidents related to terrorist acts in 2013 can be stated as such. In January and April, several persons connected with FICN were arrested. On April 9, a Pakistani national and ISI agent, Mohammed Masroor, was awarded life imprisonment by a local court in Bahraich. Similarly, on April 13, two people, including a Pakistani national, were given life imprisonment by the Sessions Court in Ghaziabad for their role in the 1996 Modinagar blast that claimed 16 lives and left 48 injured.

On June 7, the SSB handed over three Kashmiri militants to Delhi Police. The Anti-Terrorist Squad arrested a suspect, identified as Ahmad Teli, from Lucknow. He was connected with the ISI. On August 20, a CBI team arrested four persons. The identified persons were Rakesh Mishra, Anjani Kumar, Vishvakarma and Pintulal and FICN worth INR 210,000 was recovered them in Basti. Again, two persons, identified as Deepak Mandal of Malda District (West Bengal) and Pawan Kumar Shukla of Nawabganj (Uttar Pradesh) were arrested with FICN worth INR 2.75 lakh from Govindpur colony of Allahabad on September 16. On October 4, the UP Police sounded a high alert across the state with special focus on Varanasi, Faizabad and Mathura on receipt of an intelligence report to guard religious places against possible terror attacks.[3] IM-India operating chief, Yasin Bhatkal, and his key associate, Asadullah Akhtar, reportedly claimed on October 5 that it was their group that had carried out five blasts at Varanasi, Jaunpur, Gorakhpur, Lucknow and Faizabad between 2005 and 2007 and not the HUJI.[4]

2014

The year 2014 opened with the police neutralising an inter-state gang of racketeers involved in the circulation of FICN. Furthermore, police sources stated that the JeM, LeT and IM had made efforts to disturb the peace in the state. On February 25, the NIA arrested two suspects from Manda and Mirzapur for providing explosives for the Patna blasts that targeted BJP prime ministerial candidate, Narendra Modi, on October 27, 2013, in Patna.

On March 26, two suspected Pakistani militants indentified as Murtaza and Owais were arrested by the UP Anti-Terrorist Squad from Gorakhpur. May 28 was important because on that day it was reported that three official websites of the UP Government had been hacked by Pakistani hackers. These websites were www.tajmahal.gov.in, www.agrafort.gov.in and www.fatepursikri.gov.in. In June 2014, security at religious places in Ayodhya, Varanasi and Mathura were enhanced as terror outfits tried to attack them.

There were reports that about six men from Azamgarh who had links with the IM—Dr. Shah Nawaz, Abu Rashid, Khalid Mohammad, Sajid, Mirza Sada Beg, Azia Khan. They were suspected to be involved in numerous attacks between 2005 and 2008 in different parts of the country. Similarly, on July 29, two persons were arrested from Phulpur area of Azamgarh district along with FICN worth INR 47,000.

It was reported that the banned outfit, SIMI, was responsible for sending controversial pictures to some Facebook users in Bareilly that led to communal violence in Meera ki Paith. Furthermore, on August 16, the STF of the UP Police arrested a suspected agent of Pakistan's ISI from Meerut who was passing on important information about the Indian Army to the ISI. On September 5, an IM operative identified as Aiyaz Sheikh was involved in sending e-mails that claimed responsibility for the Jama Masjid and Varanasi blasts in 2010. He was arrested by the Delhi Police Special Cell in Saharanpur. In the same month, later on, a low-intensity blast occurred in a house in Bijnor. It occurred a day before the polls were to be held for the Assembly constituency. There was another achievement of the investigating agency probing the July 10, 2014 bomb blast in Pune. It arrested some suspects belonging to the banned SIMI for the terror act. They were also involved in an explosion at a rented house in Bijnor on September 12. The UP-ATS interrogated five members of SIMI who had escaped from Khandwa district jail in Madhya Pradesh on Oct 1, 2003. They were on their way to Uttarakhand. They were holed up in a rented house in Bijnor but succeeded in escaping. On September 24, the IM planned to carry out a terror strike in Muzaffarnagar in retaliation to communal riots that had taken place in the region. Similarly, the IB warned that groups and supporters of an extremist ideology similar to Al-Qaeda were trying to increase communal tension in Jammu and Kashmir, Maharashtra, Gujarat, Rajasthan, UP, Bihar, Karnataka, Kerala and Delhi. The intelligence report also reiterated that Al-Qaeda chief Ayman-al-Zawahari intended to target commercial centres, tourist destinations, religious places, the aviation sector, railway infrastructure and BJP offices in various states including West Bengal and Assam. Sources in the Central Intelligence Agency stated that Al-Qaeda had announced on October 6 to carry out terrorist activities. It was revealed that AQIS, an Indian wing of Al-Qaeda, had been given the responsibility of Uttar Pradesh.

The terrorists who had escaped from the Jatana area of Bijnor after a low-intensity bomb blast on September 12 were also involved in a bank robbery in Telangana. The purpose behind it was to fund terrorist activities. According to reports, the five SIMI fugitives wanted for the Bijnor blast (September 12) followed the Al-Qaeda training manual that was first implemented by the Al-Qaeda while bombing the US embassy in Kenya in 1998. A trail was set up and the FBI had recovered it from the laptop of an alleged Al-Qaeda operative in Manchester in the United Kingdom. The report added that Al-Qaeda had already announced its intention to revive Islamic terrorism.

2015

The year 2015 was more violent in nature as terrorist activities were conducted in such a way that the common people suffered heavily. There were reports of FICN. The districts identified were Mirzapur, Saunali area in Maharajganj district, Lucknow, Bulandshahr. Sambhal, Gorakhpur, Azamgarh. Allahabad, Gautam Buddha Nagar, Ghaziabad, Kanpur, Bareilly, etc. The transactions were mostly done either through the Nepal border or other parts of India. This kind of nefarious activities had seriously jeopardized the financial condition of the state.

Furthermore, the terrorists were quite active in the first quarter of 2015 in the form of sleeper terror modules, bomb blasts, passing of information by members of the banned SIMI and cyber crime in different parts of Uttar Pradesh. These events mostly occurred in the eastern parts of the state. In April, the Uttar Pradesh Police and SSB were more alert along the U.P.-Nepal border to check the infiltration of anti-nationalists in the garb of earthquake victims from the Himalayan kingdom. In spite of the efforts made by the police department to check infiltration, an LeT operative, Ahmed, sneaked into the state from Nepal in the guise of an earthquake victim on May 7. Irfan Ahmed was also wanted in connection with the Rajdhani Express blast in Kanpur in 1993. Similarly, Mumtaz Mian, booked under POTA, planned to wage war against the nation. He was providing information to Pakistan's ISI from Rampur.

Once again, Azamgarh district was on the radar of the Central Intelligence. In July, Mohammed Sajjid, the most wanted man in the NIA list, was killed in Syria while fighting for the Islamic state. Sajjid was the mastermind behind the serial blasts that occurred in Delhi,

Jaipur and Ahmedabad in 2008. In July 2015, a search was made to find people who had contact with Syria and Iraq. There were also cases of some Nepali citizens crossing the border in Maharajnagar district. It was feared was that they were been used by the ISI for ulterior motives. It was reported that terrorist organisations, after imparting training to youth, would send them across the border through Nepal to create discord in India. Reports were also circulated that the Islamic State might have joined hands with the banned SIMI and other terror outfits, especially Muzaffarnagar, Shamli, Bijnor, Rampur and Azamgarh.

In November 2015, the Uttar Pradesh STF succeeded in arresting Mohammad Kalam. He was suspected to be an agent of Pakistan's ISI and was involved in passing important military information to Pakistani terrorist outfits. He had a fake Aadhaar card with a Bareilly address, a fake voter ID made in West Bengal, a Delhi Metro traveller card, Nepali and Saudi currency and a Pakistani national identity card. There were many similar cases of links with IS, ISI and other terrorist groups to foment trouble in the state and disturb the 2016 peaceful environment.

2016

In 2016, many terrorist incidents occurred that had a close connection with the IS, ISI, Al-Qaeda, Darulb Uloom, Deoband, Indian Mujahideen and others. Their purpose were to instigate youth to plan jihadi assaults within the nation. It was also found that bomb-making literature of Al-Qaeda had become a favourite guidebook for SIMI and IM operatives in the country and by the SIMI men at their hideout in Bijnor. The issue of an IS video threatening to unleash terror in the state made the police department more alert. The 22-minute documentary, mostly in Arabic, shows jihadis who have joined the ISIS threatening to return to avenge the killings of Muslims in India. In this connection, some terrorists were arrested in May 2016 from Deoband in Saharanpur. Their arrests proved that the ISIS and its subsidiaries were trying desperately for a foothold on Indian soil in general and UP in particular. This is a cause of serious concern when one finds young blood turning to the world's top terror outfits. Similarly, the IS released a documentary regarding the life of South Asian jihadis. The video aimed at recruiting more foreign militants and claimed to avenge anti-Muslim communal violence in India.

Like other previous years, there were reported cases of FICN along the Indo-Nepal border. The districts affected were Lucknow, Chandauli, Noida and other parts of UP. Those involved in this had a deep connection with gangs in Singapore, Pakistan, Bangladesh and Nepal.

2017 Onwards

The year 2017 was full of surprises. On the one hand, the election was conducted in Uttar Pradesh. There was widespread speculation that the state would have a hung assembly but the result surprised everybody as the BJP emerged as the single largest majority party. It won the election not on the basis of religion or Hindutva but on the issue of development and change. After few days, Yogi Adityanath was made the Chief Minister so that he could work to improve the economic, social and religious, conditions of the state. But prior to his elevation as Chief Minister, from January to March, there were cases of FICN, terrorist activities, bomb blasts and other nefarious activities that had a great impact on Indian national security. As such, the spirit of nationalism was dampened to a great extent. But no nefarious activities had occurred till now. In 2017, the UP-ATS arrested 13 terrorists and three ISI agents and foiled their nefarious designs. One terrorist was killed during the arrest. On 24 March 2018, the ATS of Uttar Pradesh busted a terror-funding network linked with the Lashkar-e-Toiba and arrested 10 persons from various districts of Uttar Pradesh, Madhya Pradesh and Bihar.[5] The ATS is running a successful de-radicalisation programme to reform 53 individuals who were moving towards terrorism. The terrorist groups are trying to reorganise and release violence in various districts of the state. As part of terrorist policy, these groups are working for the de-radicalisation of Islam so that they can reach those regions discussed above.

Terrorism: A New Challenge for Yogi Adityanath

There is no denying the fact that in the last two or three decades the division between different communities in Uttar Pradesh has increased drastically. The situation is alarming and at the moment there has been no constructive initiative from either side to try to bridge the gap. This kind of development has brought many internal problems that is not good for the state alone but for the entire nation. All the political, social and religious leaders are well aware of problems like political criminalisation, administrative problem, casteism, commercialisation of crime and frequent transfer of officials.

To be more specific, when we compare different religions, one finds that Hinduism is by far the most well-adjusted religion for the changing times. No Hindu scripture, unlike the Koran or that of Christianity, advocates violence or killing of people of other faiths. Yogi Adityanath, a firm supporter of Hindutva, always has in his mind the national and spiritual aspects of Indian society. But oft-repeated violence has disturbed the nationalist mode and style of living of the Indian people. Hence, Yogi Adityanath says that we have to move forward to preserve nationalist culture. By doing so, we are also protecting our national interests too.

When the entire world is trying to find a 'solution' to the menace of terrorism, which has spread its tentacles everywhere, Uttar Pradesh chief minister Yogi Adityanath has come up with an answer. The priest-turned-politician, during an event in Gorakhpur, UP, said that patriotism can counter the menace of terrorism. He added that patriotism could also solve the other two vexing issues plaguing the nation—naxalism and corruption.[6] "The truth is that patriotism can counter the menace of terrorism, naxalism, separatism and corruption," he said. He added that discipline was necessary for making progress: "Modern education and technical knowledge are a must for moving ahead but discipline is equally important. Without it, society will be in danger."[7]

Since Yogi Adityanath is at the helm of State affairs, he will have to approach the problem in a positive manner. He will have to assure society and the state to improve its efficiency and credibility so that the people's dream of a united India becomes true. The state, in the past, has to suffer much on account of terrorism, naxalism and deliberation on division of Uttar Pradesh into many independent states, corruption and unbalanced economic development. While dealing with the two most important problems of terrorism and insurgency, the new government will have to evolve the following effective mechanism:

- to evolve an integrated political military approach. Involvement of political parties is also essential and military action is to be taken only to destroy the political will of the extremists. There is no other alternative, apart from finding a potential solution, along with measures taken to work for equitable economic development and social harmony by developing an integrated strategy;
- to strengthen national and state intelligence agencies. These intelligence agencies must work in coordination which is appropriate, timely and effective at strategic and tactical levels. There is a need of revamping spread investigation branches so that they are better manned and better trained;
- to create national counter-terrorism centres. Terrorism-related attacks are not one single issue. Generally, in the past, there has been lack of trust between the central agencies and the state organs. In Uttar Pradesh and at the Centre, the BJP is the ruling party. It will not be difficult for Yogi Adityanath to come out with political or military solutions to any crisis that disturbs the peace and stability of the state;
- strategy to eliminate the support structure of terrorism. The approach of previous governments to opt for a soft approach could not be a solution now. The present government will have to take stringent measures to eliminate extremist bases, camps, arms and ammunition supply lines and financial funding agencies. This reminds me of Machiavelli's famous dictum "where there are good laws there are good arms" and "where there are good arms there are good laws." It means both must complement each other. In other words, there must be complete cooperation and coordination between the executive and the judiciary; then only the people

will be safe and society will be trouble-ridden. I feel Yogi Adityanath too has to see and work accordingly on these lines. If it happens the state will not suffer but prosper in the coming years. By doing so, Yogi Adityanath will be able to create such a harmonious environment that he will be able to win the hearts and minds of the people.

Naxal Activities in Uttar Pradesh

Today, Yogi Adityanath is facing another crisis in Uttar Pradesh. From time to time he has warned of the evil designs of the Maoist-led naxalite movement. The important issue now is for Uttar Pradesh to be free of the naxalites.

The regions of the Ganga-Vindhya Central Plain and Sonebhadra become important because of naxalite problems. Yogi Adityanath has said that in recent years Gorakhpur has become a victim of naxalite activities.

Palia: The naxalite problem erupted in the year 1968 in Palia area which is a part of Lakhimpur district in Uttar Pradesh. The region is close to the Nepal border. The area is fully covered with dense forests and inhabited by tribals. Earlier, the state policy was to invite poor peasants from eastern Uttar Pradesh to come to Palia and clear the forest and undertake cultivation. But, in reality, the picture was different. The landlords and influential people forcibly occupied large areas of land and deprived the poor peasants of the benefits of their hard work. This gave the naxalites an excellent opportunity to launch their agitation in the region. Even the then Chief Minister, C. B. Gupta, accepted on May 8, 1969, that naxalites were active in some parts of the state because of the injustice committed by some village pradhans in the distribution of gram sabha land. Congressmen and even law makers were responsible for the wrong distribution of land.[8]

The naxalites of Palia region received necessary assistance and shelter from peasants across the border of Nepal. Since most of the peasants were from the eastern districts of UP, they faced the threat of being driven out of Nepal. They felt that they could survive in Nepal only with the help of the naxalites who found them good patrons.[9]

Let us also analyse the importance of the other regions of Uttar Pradesh that became victims of Naxalism. These areas were Ballia, Naugarh, Sonebhadra, Mirzapur and Chandauli.

Ballia: Ballia is one of the eastern districts of Uttar Pradesh. Its boundary touches the state of Bihar. Ballia has Buxar, Bhojpur and Chapra as its neighbouring districts in Bihar and Ghazipur, Deoria, Bhadaoi, Bundelkhand, Gorakhpur and Mau as the surrounding districts of UP. Geography, demography and socio-economic conditions were responsible for the naxalite upsurge in Ballia district.

In real terms, if we look at the developmental measures taken by the state in the 1980s, it was found that the spread of the naxalites was of a more severe nature than that had occurred in the 1960s. Today, in UP, there are eight districts which are affected by the naxalites. The most affected districts are Naugarh, Sonebhadra, Chandauli and Mirzapur. The pertinent question is how these districts became victims of naxalism. The answer to this was the basic problems faced by the local population.

Naugarh: In Naugarh, the small farmers of the eastern district suffered a lot. Though three dams have been constructed, the region is suffering from acute water crisis. The cultivation of cereals and oilseeds is declining and several tree species are also disappearing. Then, there are serious anomalies in land distribution. Moreover, the land records are in extremely poor shape. It has led to large-scale corruption and litigation.

They still have disputes with the forest and revenue departments. In fact, in Uttar Pradesh, mismanagement and corruption in agricultural production is rampant. Here, there are a million cases where people are leasing out their land for cultivation. Seeing this type of cultivation in Uttar Pradesh, absentee landlords tend to support contract farming though it is anti-farmer and it has to be adopted only in a limited way in a well-defined environmental condition.[10]

As per a field survey done by Dr. P. K. Agarwal during 1990-92 and reflected in his book "Land Reform in India" there are approximately 16 per cent share croppers in Uttar Pradesh. Thus, there were about 30.37 lakh unrecorded tenants in Uttar Pradesh out of a total holding of 187.85 (1981). However, from 1981 to 1991, there was an increase in the number of agricultural labourers to the extent of 25 lakh. The problem is a serious one. The reason is partly because the unrecorded share croppers are driven out of their fields and they have no other alternative but to resort to daily labour.[11] These conditions had made the poor people vulnerable. Today, the state of Uttar Pradesh is at a critical juncture. Thus, the naxalites have fully exploited the situation created by the policies of the previous governments, as pointed out by Yogi Adityanath.

Sonebhadra: The main problem of Sonebhadra is related to tribes and their land ownership. The indigenous communities of the region are being displaced frequently in the name of development since independence. The people are struggling for rehabilitation and satisfactory land entitlement and possession. Land disputes between the forest and revenue departments are common. The lack of basic facilities for farmers and a severe scarcity of water are other problems in the rural area.

Besides these problems, there is a clear disparity in Sonebhadra. The district has four assembly segments. Barring Renukoot, where industrial development has generated employment for locals, the remaining three segments remain largely underdeveloped.[12] Ghorawal is another segment where some crushing units operate in the name of industry. It is known for tomato cultivation. But at times, the tomato growers have to throw away huge quantities of their produce when there is a surplus yield. The tomato cultivators are demanding some food processing units that can help in increasing their earnings and avoid wastage of tomatoes but no development initiative has been taken in this regard.[13] To avail better prices and services, the locals have to move either to Mirzapur or Varanasi. Robertsganj, the other assembly segment, is known as the core zone of the Maoist threat. The segment lacks facilities for higher and technical education. Power plants in Obra supply electricity to many parts of the state but the locals reel under a power crisis. The crisis of water is not only limited to neighbouring Obra, Renukoot and

Duddhi; residents of even Robertsganj suffer from various pollution problems caused by industry.[14]

Mirzapur: If we enter Mirzapur, from the Chunar or Aurai sides, one notices that ceramic pottery and carpet industries are on the decline. Chunar had more that 200 ceramic pottery units. But, increasing cost of coal and poor valuation of products has resulted in the closure of the units. Now only a few ceramic pottery units are functional in this area and the major businesses have shifted to Khurja. The carpet belt has also shifted towards weaving of cheap floor coverings like counterpanes of Bhadohi. The brass industry has also lost its glitter after the closure of many units while many have shifted to Moradabad.

Chandauli: In the name of development, Chandauli district has a good network of canals and the biggest railway yard of Asia at Mughalsarai. The district is known as the "rice bowl" but during the long spell of drought from 2002 to 2009, local farmers have been adversely affected. The reason is that most of the canals are charged from the water stored at the dams which have remained dry due to insufficient rain during the drought years. The farmers of these districts from time to time have complained that they do not get proper rates for paddy at the purchasing centres set up by the previous governments. Moreover, paddy bought by the government is often dumped in the open along the roads.[15]

The rough terrain of Nepal adjoining Chandauli have emerged as the "Silk Route" for smuggling hooch to Bihar following a blanket ban imposed on liquor by the Bihar government in April 2016. This fact surfaced after the Chandauli police started an operation in the Naxal-hit Naugrah region of the district. The police unearthed hooch manufacturing units-cum-storage sites in the dense jungles of Naugarh and arrested four persons. Two members was caught in Mughalsarai.[16] Therefore, the people in all the assembly segments of this district want the new government, under Yogi Adityanath, to save the dying industries, generate employment and provide better infrastructure and facilities.

On 9th May, 2017, Yogi Adityanath said that to tackle the menace of naxalism, the state government (UP) would extend all possible cooperation to the Union Government. It included beefing up of security and exchange of intelligence inputs. He further clarified that efforts have been undertaken to take care of the important needs of the police forces, to equip them with latest weaponry, improve communication systems and get more support from the Centre. He also pointed out that the naxalite problem has not only affected some states but was also a bane for the development and economic progress of the country. In naxal-affected areas, he announced projects and schemes for improvement in power supply, construction of roads and improving the public distribution system. Healthcare and education services are in abundance, but taking care of the water problems and creation of jobs will have to be rolled out effectively. He also underlined the urgent need of modernisation and upgrading of technology and communication methods to take on the scourge of the present times.

Law and Order Situation

In spite of growing threats from terrorism and naxalism, the present government has taken certain harsh measures to check their nefarious activities. One cannot deny that fact that Uttar Pradesh is gifted with fertile soil and rivers. But still, it is one of the poorest states in India. Though endowed with "ultimate" potential, it is often paradoxically called the "Ulta Pradesh."[17] It was called "Ulta Pradesh" because certain discrepancies have swept the state and it had failed to qualify as a good performer in establishing state integrity, unity and prosperity. As a result, the state has to suffer heavily because of bad politicisation of society by the previous government.

As soon as he was sworn in as the Chief Minister of Uttar Pradesh, Yogi Adityanath said that the first thing he wanted was to concentrate on the deteriorating law and order situation in the state. The law and order situation was at its lowest and there were riots within a week. As a result, the state became a breeding ground for criminals in the past 12 to 15 years. Yogi Adityanath further elaborated that criminalisation of politics and the politics of criminals took place during all these years. Whereas 450 riots took place during the last three years of the previous regime, no riots had broken out in the last one year.[18] The condition needed to be improved and brought on to right track. He made it clear that no innocent was to be harassed and harsh measures were to be taken against criminals. This kind of adverse situation prevailed in the case of previous governments. The state witnessed anarchy and "goondaraj" during the earlier governments. Elaborating, he says that Uttar Pradesh has been known for goondaraj. He says that the present state was infested with large-scale lawlessness, corruption and dynastic politics. When the grip of the police forces hardened, many criminals withdrew their bail applications and preferred to serve their time in prison. It was seen that in about 1,478 crackdowns in 2017, nearly 3,435 criminals were arrested, 390 injured and 48 shot dead. This kind of harsh step has brought down criminal activities. Simultaneously, one saw casualties of the security forces too. These operations led to injuries to 308 policemen and loss of life of four. There were 188 detentions under NSA and 4,881 criminals were arrested in 1,455 cases under the Uttar Pradesh Gangster Act.[19]

As compared to 2016, in 2017 there has been a sharp decline in heinous crimes. For instance, there was a decline of 5.70 per cent in cases of robbery, 7.35 per cent in cases of murder, 100 per cent in cases of road holdups, 13.21 per cent in cases of ransom, 16.41 per cent in murder and crime against the SC/ST community, 29.73 per cent in cases of arson. Over 2,596 cases have been registered against 1,531 land mafias while 1,922 were arrested under various acts of forcible and illegal possession of property to the tune of Rs. 7.45 crore.[20]

Furthermore, the establishment of Anti-Romeo squads has led to a decline in cases of molestation. In 2017and 2018, the squads did a physical surveillance of more than 27,60,841 people. It showed its result when complaints were registered against 2,068 accused and 12,54,991 were given stern warnings. In the same period, some 2.05 lakh complaints were received by the 1090 Women Power Line. Out of the above-mentioned cases, 77 per cent were successfully resolved. Similarly, on the occasion of International Women's Day 2018, a three-day awareness drive was conducted by district police units.

Over 1,250 encounters have taken place in the state in the last year, but none was found to be fake. In this way, Yogi Adityanath's government tried to give protection to the people. Because of this change, industrialists are coming forward to invest in the state while criminals who were honoured are leaving the state. Yet, the situation was kept in control with whatever little resources that were left by the previous governments. More important was the passing of the UPCOCA Law in the Vidhan Parishad.

Casteism has always played an important role in state politics. Even after independence in 1947, Uttar Pradesh was ruled by high-caste elites with strong economic and political bases. They failed to cater to the needs and demands of the so-called lower castes and ethnic minorities. Hence, these groups organised themselves in the 1970s under socialist leaders. It led to an alignment of political forces on the basis of caste and ethnic identities. As a result, several parties like the Samajwadi Party (SP), Bahujan Samaj Party (BSP) and Janata Dal emerged in Uttar Pradesh. Though they won elections they failed to improve government performance in terms of social and economic growth. When Yogi Adityanath took over as Chief Minister of Uttar Pradesh, he found the coffers empty. There was no funds to pay salaries to government employees. There was anarchy in the state and the youth were restless as a result of which they started committing suicide. Recruitments were banned by the courts and investors were fleeing the state.

Yogi Adityanath vehemently criticised such politics-based ideology like socialism. While criticising the Samajwadi party, he called socialism as an ideology and an illusion that the country did not need.[21] While proving it to be an illusion, he said, "in Germany and Italy, socialism finally resulted in fascism and Nazism."[22] Further, he says that the Samajwadi Party alliance with the Bahujan Samajwadi Party made it look like a circus tiger which survives on jhoothan (leftovers) of others as it is unable to hunt for its prey. It feeds on leftovers and gloats over the fact that it got its share of the prey.[23] Moreover, he said that the Samajwadi Party and Bahujan Samajwadi Party governments had devised policies which promoted corruption and nepotism and were largely driven by caste and communal agenda.

Demographic Indicators

Both the terms are interrelated in terms of socio-economic growth of the state. It is said that one-sixth of the world's population lives in India and one-sixths of India's population live in Uttar Pradesh. Only four other countries of the world—China, the USA, Indonesia and Brazil—have a population more than Uttar Pradesh. The demographic profile of Uttar Pradesh is well documented in Chart I.

Chart I
Demographic Profile of Uttar Pradesh

Year	*Rural Population % of Total Population*	*Urban Population % of Total Population*	*Decadal Growth Rate of Population %*
1951	86.354	13.646	–
1961	87.192	12.808	16.38
1971	86.101	13.899	19.54
1981	82.101	17.834	25.39
1991	80.333	19.667	25.61
2001	79.218	20.782	25.85
2011	77.732	22.268	20.09

Source: Handbook of Statistics of Indian States, RBI, 2015-16

It is a well-established that India's demographic parameters and population stabilisation primarily depend on the changes that could occur in the eight large states, viz., Uttar Pradesh Uttarakhand, Bihar, Jharkhand, Madhya Pradesh, Chhattisgarh, Odisha and Rajasthan that account for about 45.87 per cent.[24] Being the biggest state, UP, with all potential powers, still has a low level of development.

Demographers refer to these changes from a stable population with high fertility and mortality to a new stability in population due to low fertility and morality patterns as demographic transition. It occurs in four stages which are characterised by population growth.[25] They are:

1. In the first stage there is a fall in the death rate and improvement in longevity. This leads to population growth.
2. In the second stage, there is a fall in the birth rate but the fall is less steep than the fall in death rates and consequently there is population growth.
3. In the third stage, death rate plateau and replacement level

of fertility is attained but the population growth continues because of the large size of the population in the reproductive age group.

4. The fourth stage is characterised by a fall in the birth rate below replacement levels and reduction in the proportion of the population in the reproductive age group. As a result, population growth ceases and stabilises.

Different countries of the world have witnessed such a demographic transition at different periods of time. Hence, there were substantial differences in the rate of demographic transition at the time taken to achieve population growth. But it has not occurred in Uttar Pradesh. As a result, it has affected the development of the state. Yogi Adityanath is right when he says that development could be given greater impetus by controlling the rise in population. While addressing a function on World Population Day on 11 July, 2017, he said, "Without population, development will not be visible. So it is necessary that everyone join hands for the welfare of our families."[26] By 2023-24, when the capacity of food production is excepted to touch its peak, there can be still be a food crisis if the population rise is not controlled. He further said that "population stabilisation will ensure all basic facilities for human beings and will also boost development. To keep our families happy and ensure that development reaches the last man, focus on population stabilisation is necessary."[27]

The population explosion will give rise to problems like poverty, employment, health and nutritional status, education, socio-economic development and rural-urban interstate migration.

Poverty

The Directive Principles of State Policy in the Indian Constitution lay down the right of the people regarding poverty and employment. They direct the states to promote and protect the welfare of its people (Article 38-1), to minimise inequalities in income, to provide facilities and opportunities (Article 38-2), to ensure right to an adequate means of livelihood (Article 39-a) and distribution of material resources as best to subserve the common good (Article 39-b) and to raise the level of nutrition and standard of living (Article 47). In this context, it was the primary duty of the state to raise the living standards and work for the elimination of poverty and generate employment. But these problems have become so complex that people had lost confidence in the functioning of the government.

It is well known fact that poverty in India is widespread. A third of the world's poor live in India. The World Bank has estimated that 68 per cent of the population lives on less than U$2 a day. Poverty is also understood as deprivation. Deprivation basically includes basically freedom from want. People are more vulnerable to adverse events that are beyond their control. Poverty, as stated above, endorses all those facilities that could fulfil the minimum requirements of life. It includes food, clothing, housing, education and health facilities. Furthermore, poverty is an indication of a state's failure to provide jobs, dignity and basic rights. In Uttar Pradesh the position is deplorable as the people are unable to get two square meals a day.

If one goes by government records, it shows that for a certain period there has been a decline in the poverty percentage at the state level. It decreased from 57.4 per cent in 1973-74 to 32.8 percent in 2004-2005. During the same period, poverty at the national level too declined from 54.9 per cent to 27.5 per cent. It is true that there has been a substantial decline in the poverty rate but overall the number of poor people remained high. Comparative studies from government sources indicate that the level of poverty was higher among the scheduled castes and other backward categories. Even the agricultural labourers, artisans, and Muslims in urban areas were affected by poverty. When we look at Uttar Pradesh, there is a vast variation in the poverty levels at regional and district levels.

Recently, in a report submitted to the Bharatiya Janata Party (BJP) government in July 2014, the Rangarajan report said that those spending over Rs. 32 a day in rural areas and Rs. 45 in urban areas should not be treated as poor. Further, an earlier report (2011-12) clarifies that persons with an the average monthly per capita expenditure below Rs. 972 in rural areas and Rs. 1,407 in urban areas shall be declared as being below the poverty line.

When we analyse our state—Uttar Pradesh—it is found that deprivation is an important cause of poverty. According to the Economic Survey 2012-13, the literary rate in Uttar Pradesh has increased from 12.02 per cent in 1951 to 56.2 per cent in 2001. It was estimated in 2011 that the provisional literacy rate was 69.72 per cent. It seems that it is a substantial growth but it is well below the all-India average of 64.8 per cent of 2001. Moreover, the attendance of boys and girls is poor in schools. By the end of the 1990s, half the girls from the poorest of 20 per cent of the population were enrolled as compared to 80-90 per cent girls belonging to rich families.

Today, there has been quite an improvement in education with the coming of the Bharatiya Janata Party (BJP) in power in Uttar Pradesh. Basic education has seen an increase in the number of admissions from Classes I to 8. In 1,58,837 schools of the Basic Shiksha Parishad, almost 1,54,22,047 students were enrolled. It was an increase of over 2 lakh from 2017. A total of 1.67 crore students from Class I to Class 8 were issued uniforms, books, sweaters, bags, shoes and socks. In the board examinations for both high and intermediate school, cheating was checked.

For the first time in Uttar Pradesh, 147 meritorious students were felicitated. Yogi Adityanath has announced that the state will promote the earlier launched Beti Bachao Yojana for girls. The purpose was to encourage the value of education among girls. Besides, he also announced that every girl child who completes and passes 10th class shall be given an award of Rs. 10,000. The award was given to every girl who had passed the 2017 state board examinations.[28]

What was the reason for this noble idea of Yogi Adityanath? It could be stated as below:[29]

- One of the main objectives behind offering the reward money to girl students in the state was to promote the value of higher education amongst those girls belonging to the backward and weaker sections of society.
- It is also certain that with the launch of this new scheme, the state government aims to educate the girl child and parents to understand the value of higher education.

- The state government has made an initiative to help in improving the overall pass percentage amongst girl students so that the overall state board results can be improved.

Yogi Adityanath has also launched several schemes for the development of the poor. One such scheme is the Mukhyamantri Free Laptop scheme. Under it, the Uttar Pradesh government will provide laptops to young people who had passed the 12th class board examination in 2017. The scheme was applicable with conditions attached. They were:[30]

- Passing class 12 and entering higher education is compulsory to become eligible for the scheme.
- The eligible candidate needs to pursue his or her higher education from Uttar Pradesh only. In case the student wants to move out of India or Uttar Pradesh then he/she will not be eligible.

Another important scheme was the Mukhyamantri Annapurna Bhojanalaya scheme. The purpose was to provide cheap food. The scheme will provide breakfast, lunch and dinner and each meal will cost Rs. 3 and 5 and 5, respectively. It means that the total cost of food under the scheme will be Rs 13 per day.

There is also the Workers' Children Scheme. The scheme was designed for the children of daily wagers who cannot send their children to school because they cannot afford either food, or pay for their education or do without the extra pairs of working hands. Under it, there are three schemes. These are:[31]

- The scheme will provide a scholarship of Rs. 5,000 per month to children of workers who go to school.
- The school development scheme aims to construct 20 residential schools for children of workers.
- Shaadi Anudan assistance worth Rs. 55,000 for the marriage of two daughters of workers within the same caste and Rs. 61,000 for marriage of two daughters with different castes.

Thus, it can be said that with the launch of the new schemes, the state government aims to improve the level of education in Uttar Pradesh and also educate parents of such students to be familiar with the value of being educated. The modernisation of madrassas was also a key policy initiative of the Yogi government. It made the registration of madrassas compulsory. In order to the bring them at par with other institutions, the government took an important step to introduce mathematics and science as compulsory subjects at the intermediate level. In other words, this is one step towards reducing the level of poverty.

Employment

It is noteworthy that Yogi Adityanath is deeply engrossed in reducing the level of the poverty rate. But the task seems to be a daunting one. Generally, poverty gives rise to unemployment. One has to see the psychological hardship of unemployment which has been associated with social stigma. The reality is that, in terms of state-wise share of employment, it emerges that the national average for the share of employment accounted for 11 percent of the total employment in 2009-10. There are nine major states where this share is greater than the national average: Andhra Pradesh (11.9%), Delhi (24.84%), Gujarat (12.6%), Haryana (12.2%), Kerala (13.5%), Punjab (15.9%), Tamil Nadu (19.6%), West Bengal (18.4%) and UP (11.1%).[32] Though the share of Uttar Pradesh is higher than the national average, it is the lowest among the nine major states.

Uttar Pradesh can be called a developed state only when the problems of poverty and employment are solved. It is passing through a critical stage. It could be improved by a high growth rate and the performance of the government. Employment generation and income expansion are the keys to the development process of our economy. In 2010, the unemployment rate stood at around 8.2 per cent. The employment opportunities declined in the public as well as the private sectors in Uttar Pradesh. There has been a marginal improvement in private sector employment since 2007. It indicated a declining trend in previous governments. This could be seen from the Chart II.

Chart II
Employment in Uttar Pradesh

Year	*Public*	*Private*	*Total*
1991	21.41	5.36	26.77
2001	17.58	4.66	22.24
2002	17.18	4.56	21.74
2003	16.92	4.51	21.43
2004	16.8	4.45	21.35
2005	16.5	4.38	20.88
2006	16.36	4.54	20.9
2007	16.3	4.83	21.3
2008	16.19	4.95	21.14
2009	16.15	5.06	21.21

Source: Annual Plan 2010-11

To generate employment in UP, Yogi Adityanath has launched several schemes. One of the most ambitious ones is the Suryamitra Recruitment Scheme. Under it, the government aims to provides employment to 25,000 youths. These government jobs will be given under UPNEDA 2017. This stands for Uttar Pradesh New and Renewable Energy Development Agency. Employment under UPNEDA will require some skill and hence the National Institute of Solar Energy is in the process of organising a programme for the development of the necessary skills.[33]

For better employment opportunities, Yogi Adityanath instructed his officials to establish skill development centres in every tehsil. Nearly12,000 new seats have been introduced in ITIs. With the help of the Pandit Deen Dayal Upadhyaya Rural Skill Development Scheme, more than 67,000 under-privileged youth are under training. Under the scheme, 32,094 youths got employment. A separate fund of Rs. 1,000 crore was allocated by the government for start-ups. 10 centres were set up and 13 more have been proposed in order to increase the number of start-ups in the state. The policy of one district, one product (ODOR) has been implemented. One district, one product is basically a Japanese business development concept. It came into prominence in 1979. It is aimed at promoting a competitive and stable product from a specific area to push sales and improve the standard of living of the local population.[34]

Under this ODOP scheme, products of every district will be

provided better marketing facilities, technical enhancement, skill, business training and finance at a low rate of interest. A Design Development and Training Centre for the zari industry has been established in Lucknow. Over 1,223 workers have benefitted from the scheme till now. A wood processing and training centre has been set up in Moradabad. Two schemes of Rs. 2,448.20 lakh have been approved. They include monofilament, yarn cluster in Kanpur and carpets in Bhadohi and rug cluster in Sonebhadra.[35]

Another scheme launched by the Chief Minister of Uttar Pradesh was the Mukhyamantri Yojana. It is aimed towards creating self employment opportunities for 25,000 youth in Uttar Pradesh. The scheme will also bring SC and ST youth under the scheme and it will ensure at least 21 per cent of the total 25,000 youth belong to these communities. The Yojana will take into account various schemes launched by Prime Minister Narendra Modi. Basically, these schemes that have been launched by the BJP government at the Centre should be stitched together to create at least 1 lakh 19 thousand employment opportunities in the state.[36]

Urban Development

The Uttar Pradesh Chief Minister has accorded the cities of Mathura-Vrindavan and Ayodhya-Faizabad the status of a municipal corporation. Cities like Lucknow, Allahabad, Kanpur, Varanasi, Jhansi, Moradabad, Saharanpur, Meerut, Rai Bareli, Rampur and Aligarh have been chosen to be transformed into smart cities. In the current year, the smart city project has been allocated Rs. 1,500 crore. The government has set a target to make more than 11 lakh people give up open defection and to achieve this target more than 432,201 toilets have already been constructed. Under the Amrit scheme, in 60 different cities, the government is already working for water supply, green area and open grounds.

Furthermore, the first phase of the Lucknow Metro from Transport Nagar to Charbagh has started. The Ghaziabad Metro network has been broadened. The DPR for Agra, Meerut, Kanpur Metros have been sent to the Central Government for approval. Similarly, DPR work is under progress for Gorakhpur, Varanasi and

Allahabad metros. Rs. 1,692.17 crore have been allocated for the development of Allahabad's Naini-Jhunsi-Phaphamau and Vrindavan, Shuklaganj, Ramnagar, Chunar, Farrukhabad, Mirzapur, Ghazipur and Mathura.

Rural Development

There are many schemes launched by the present government for raising the standard of the rural masses. The government has developed 6.20 lakh homes as against the target set for 8.85 lakh homes. The purpose of the government housing policy was to provide free homes to the homeless. Victims of natural calamities, black fever affected areas, AES/JEE and people of the Vantangia and Musahar communities will benefit from the above scheme. Nearly, 2,697 km of the road network was built under the PM Gram Sadak Yojana. The aim is to extend the road network up to 2750 km. Through MNREGA, 66 lakh labourers were employed. Uttar Pradesh also became the number one state in the sanitation sector with the construction of various toilets across the state under the Swachh Bharat Mission. It is reported that 37,26,445 lakh toilets were constructed in rural areas till now. The number is just double when one compares it with the last year's statistics. There are schemes for women and they have also immensely benefitted by the Ujjwala Yojana.

The Uttar Pradesh Chief Minister has accorded revenue status to 18 Vantangia villages. Soon, 1,625 villages of the Musahar and OBC communities would be integrated with the mainstream. While addressing the public at Chandan Chafi Vantangia village in Maharajganj, Yogi Adityanath said, "The previous government had only divided the people and did nothing for them but even they were deprived of their rights. History says that their ancestors had planned an important role in developing forests but they lived in extreme poverty. They wanted a right government that can give all those amenities which they were deprived of. Their basis issues are schools, electricity, potable water and medical facilities. The present government is working in these directions so that they can lead a comfortable life."

For many years water has been the major problem for people living in urban and rural areas. How to improve the water crisis has become a cause of major concern in Uttar Pradesh. The state government is working in this direction by involving foreign powers to improve the water situation. Israel will be the first major UP partner to work on utility reforms. This will cover drinking water supply in both urban and rural areas. This would be done as part of the MoU signed between the UP Jal Nigam and Israel's ministry of national infrastructure, energy and water resources when Narendra Modi visited Israel in July 2017.

The Israeli authorities will take up the problematic areas to find solutions. In fact, UP will be a kind of test case for India-Israel cooperation. If it succeeds in Uttar Pradesh it can be replicated elsewhere. Though Israeli experts have worked in Tamil Nadu and Gujarat in the field of water use efficiency and desalination, Uttar Pradesh will be the first state where that country will work on multiple issues simultaneously as part of overall water utility reform. Both countries have already decided to set up a "strategic partnership" in water and agriculture to focus on water conservation, waste water treatment and its reuse for agriculture, desalination, water, utility reforms and the cleaning up of the Ganga and other rivers.

Medical Facilities

In 2017, when the Yogi government came to power, medical conditions were in a bad shape. Patients had no access to medicines. There was not enough staff in the hospitals. The first step of Yogi Adityanath was to improve the quality of the resources available to them. It was a positive step that resulted in better medical services. This process has not stopped. In 68 district hospitals and medical colleges, special centres were established for the treatment of malnourished children. Seventy-four such centres are operational. Nearly 1,100 children were treated successfully at these centres.[37]

Recently, the Union Health Minister, J. P. Nadda announced the establishment of eight new medical colleges for Uttar Pradesh. The demand for setting up a virology centre in Gorakhpur would soon be fulfilled for the treatment for Japanese Encephalitis that has claimed the lives of thousands of children in the past few decades and left many persons physically challenged.[38] The financial year 2017-18 saw a major change in the way the government has addressed the Japanese Encephalitis issue by planning to start vaccination in April 2018. This was not possible in previous years as vaccination was done late. Nadda further said that India aimed to eradicate TB by 2025. This is five years before the WHO deadline. Even earlier, as Member of Parliament, Yogi Adityanath had raised the issue of health. He stressed the misconception about tuberculosis. He asked why Azamgarh was lagging behind in the polio campaign. He did not target any particular community. But the misconception was there that the polio campaign was against a community. Citing a Mushahar basti or minority community as an example, one will find a large chunk of TB patients there. Generally, poor people meet private doctors who give them high dosage drugs. The drugs give instant relief. These drugs are costly and as a result the patients stop the treatment midway. But it is important that, as Yogi Adityanath says, they should be made aware of the consequences of such a disease. Related to this kind of disease is proper nutrition.

The state and the Central Government have signed a memorandum of understanding to establish super specialty services in state-run medical colleges in Agra and Kanpur. These colleges will get super-specialty blocks for oncology, neurology, paediatrics, surgery, burn injuries, urology and endocrinology departments. Seen in this perspective, both the state and central governments are doing commendable work. Thus, the "national strategy for 2017-2025 is Detect-Treat-Prevent-Build for TB elimination."[39]

Ailing Power Sector

Yogi Adityanath said that his government received the power department in a very bad condition from the previous government. However, he stressed on the need to improve the condition of the power sector by speedy electrification, setting up of more substations and transformers and enhancing their capacity besides ensuring replacement of defunct transformers within 24 hours in urban areas and within 48 hours in rural pockets.[40]

Accusing the previous government of purchasing power at rates as high as Rs. 8 per unit through dubious deals, Yogi Adityanath said his government had scrapped all such agreements. He claimed that the same electricity could be purchased for Rs. 2-3 per unit. He also distributed free electricity connections to some urban poor. He said that "the way the Indian Prime Minister, Narendra Modi, helped the poor get free LPG connections, the time has come to provide light to every poor person's house by providing them free electricity connections."

To make sure that there is an equal distribution of electricity throughout the state, many decisions were taken. Solar projects of 512 megawatts were completed And 9,050 solar street lights were put up across the state. In addition, 76.2 megawatt solar rooftop projects were also set up. As a matter of fact, the Uttar Pradesh Government has set an ambitious target of generating over 10,000 MW of solar power by 2022. Some 42 MoUs with a total investment of around Rs. 60,000 crore were signed for solar power plants. It shows that the investors have shown a keen interest in solar energy given the huge potential in Uttar Pradesh. Furthermore, the state needs to tap the solar energy potential in areas like Bundelkhand.

In the past, electricity had reached almost 56,000 new villages. The government is also providing 5 KW electricity connections through easy instalments instead of the previous practice of advance payment in full. Nineteen 132 KW power houses, eight 220 KW power houses several of 765 KW have also been started in the PPP mode. A powerhouse of 765 kw has also started in the PPP mode in Hapur. LED light bulbs are being distributed in villages and 16 nagar nigams. It shows there is more trust between the government and power department.

Not only this, recently, private groups have shown a keen interest to invest in the power sector. The conventional power transmission and distribution system saw 42 MoUs, worth Rs. 67,000 crore being signed between the state government and private companies. The Adani Group alone promised an investment of Rs. 4,000 crore for setting up transmission lines and substations in the state. Such investment will definitely improve the heavy demand for power in the country's most populous state. The promised investment will providing round-the-clock power supply across the state by October 2018.

Tourism

Yogi Adityanath says that Uttar Pradesh has immense potential for tourism. His government wants that all the tourist places that have historical significance should be given proper care. He said that "Uttar Pradesh has been a carrier of our ancient cultural heritage. But our young generation has gradually distanced itself from the places of cultural and historical importance. Therefore, our government has formulated schemes for maintenance of places of cultural and historical importance to promote tourism."

Yogi Adityanath places much importance on religious tourism. He said "people used to refrain from taking the name of Ayodhya as it was considered communal. They wore a band of secularism on their eyes." Citing the example of Indonesia, Yogi Adityanath said even after being an Islamic country, people and places there had Sanskrit names and Ramleela was part of the country.[41] Even Ram Manohar Lohia was a socialist and an atheist but he believed that Rama, Krishna and Shiva were central to the country's culture and survival.

Further, Yogi Adityanath said that Uttar Pradesh has all the resources to become a tourist destination. "We need to tap the resources and promote tourism." He even launched the tourist department's portal 'one stop travel solution." The 2017-18 Uttar Pradesh government budget announces "Swadesh Darshan Yojana" with an allocation of Rs 1,240 crore focusing on the Ramayana Circuit (Ayodhya), the Buddhist Circuit (Varanasi) and the Krishna Circuit (Mathura). The budget also provides funds for setting up of the Gita Shodh Sansthan in Mathura and the Krishna Sangrahalaya. Another scheme, Prasad Yojana, with an allocation of Rs. 800 crore, has been proposed for the development of infrastructure facilities in Ayodhya, Varanasi and Mathura.[42]

Yogi Adityanath recently said that Kaushambi has immense tourism potential and was the only district that figured in both the

Ramayana and the Buddhist circuits. He said no development work was carried out in Kaushambi by the previous governments. He laid down foundation stone of development works of around Rs. 300 crore. He also announced that two and four-lane roads would be constructed to connect the district to other holy districts of Uttar Pradesh.

The historical and cultural tourism will not only attract tourists from India but also from foreign countries. Mauritius has shown its willingness to invest as there is much scope in the sphere of religious tourism. Similarly, UMA Hospitality Ventures, Los Angles, led by Indians who belong to Uttar Pradesh, have signed an MoU with the state government for setting up hotels, dharmashalas and homes for the elderly in the religious cities of Ayodhya, Mathura, Varanasi and Allahabad. It would invest some Rs. 500 crore in religious tourism.[43]

The promotion of religious tourism will not only convey a positive message about Uttar Pradesh but will also boost the state revenues. To make this idea a reality, the state government is working towards the branding of the Kumbh Mela. The government is also working to put the Kumbh Mela on an international pedestal. After getting the mega religious fair added to UNESCO's list of 'Intangible Cultural Heritage of Humanity,' the central and the state governments are promoting Kumbh at the global level. It is also an opportunity to improve the image of the state across the globe, Yogi Adityanath said. Expressing concern over the pollution levels of the Ganga, he commented, "Earlier, the forest department was blamed for deforestation but now it has become popular for afforestion and the same time is attracting tourists through eco-tourism."

Recently, the government organised the Deepotsava in Ayodhya, Ramayana in Chitrakoot and Holi in Mathura's Barsana to attract the people's attention towards these religious sites.

Economic Structure

The concept of economic growth and development is important in the context of expansion of national wealth and the average living standards of people. The purpose of development is to enhance the well-being and quality of life of people by providing employment opportunities, increase national income and reduce inequality. Economic development is an increase in living styles, catering of human needs and freedom from oppression. In India, the pace of socio-economic development is slow and it is found that the growth in different states and regions is uneven. The state of Uttar Pradesh is no exception although, in terms of size of the economy, is the third largest after Maharashtra and Tamil Nadu. Being not so developed, Uttar Pradesh is considered as one of the poorest states of India. As the state is rich in natural resources with a sound productive economic agricultural base, it could be an engine of economic growth. The reason is that the state has a diversified potential existence of a very large market. But the problem is that there is not ample opportunities for it to grow in the correct perspective. There are reports that indicate that Uttar Pradesh was the worst performer. Its net state domestic production had decreased from 14.74 per cent to 13.66 per cent in 2006-2007 to 2011-2012. In terms of growth in per capita income, Uttar Pradesh has the second lowest. It was 12,60 per cent in 2006-2007 and declined to 11.71 in 2011-2012.[44]

Seen in this perspective, during the first 25 years of economic planning, the economic growth of Uttar Pradesh was extremely low at around 2 to 2.5 per cent per annum which was hardly above the states per capita income. However, the economic growth rate increased in the fifth plan period and was at par with the national growth in the sixth and seventh plans. But after 1990, the growth performance in Uttar Pradesh declined sharply whereas the national economy had moved to a higher growth path. During the eighth and ninth plans, the growth rate of Uttar Pradesh decelerated markedly and remained around 3 per cent per annum. One of the reasons for the relatively slow economic growth was low plan investments in the state. Being a poor state it was not able to generate much required public savings.

The economic structure could be divided into various sectors like agriculture, industry, manufacturing and services. Broadly, it could be categorised as agricultural and industrial sectors. The development of economic sectors in Uttar Pradesh could be seen from Chart III:

Chart III
Development of Economic Sectors in Uttar Pradesh
(CAGR in percentage)

	1991-93	*1994-96*	*1997-99*	*2000-02*	*2003-05*	*2007-08*	*2009-11*	*2011-15*
GADS AND GDP								
UP	1.49	473	1.32	2.18	5.34	7.69	7.22	5.51
All India	3.37	-66.21	5.48	4.76	7.50	9.44	8.75	21.07
Agriculture Sector								
UP	0.48	2.65	-2.59	27.82	1.29	2.97	2.00	3.17
All India	2.26	1.97	1.79	2.96	4.52	-66.80	4.63	25.45
Industry								
UP	1.22	10.03	1.25	25.56	10.60	11.01	7.07	2.00
All India	1.42	11.68	2.85	4.06	6.57	-88.89	9.20	-31.88
Manufacturing								
UP	8.62	11.37	-3.37	20.09	5.53	14.48	11.78	1.15
All India	0.31	13.12	1.58	4.75	6.86	255.05	10.07	-66.62
Services								
UP	-67.50	4.08	3.53	38.85	5.42	8.77	9.77	7.91
All India	4.85	7.66	243.35	235.20	-65.58	10.21	246.59	-33.78

Source: Handbook of Statistics on Indian Economy, RBI 2015-16 and Handbook Statistics on Indian States, RBI, 2016

Chart III indicates that the performance of service sectors was better than that of agriculture, industry and manufacturing. The average performance of all sectors in Uttar Pradesh declined from 2012 to 2015 and the net result was a sharp reduction in the growth performance of real GSDP.

Agriculture

Agriculture is one the most important sectors of the economy of Uttar Pradesh. Two-thirds of the work force of the state is dependent on agriculture for their livelihood. The state is the largest producer of foodgrains in India and offers diverse agro climatic conditions conducive for agricultural production. In Uttar Pradesh, the major crops are paddy, wheat, sugarcane, potato, mustard, groundnut, gram, pea and lentil. The state exports rice, mangoes, vegetables and potatoes. In the annual budget for 2012 Rs. 4,496 crore was allocated for agriculture and allied activities.

But the problem is the slow pace of structural shift in favour of the non-agricultural sectors. It implies that the agriculture sector remains overcrowded due to the declining size of holdings and the low agricultural income per worker. It increased rural poverty. Today, the need is to reshape its strategy of development to push forward faster growth of non-agricultural activities, both in the urban and the rural areas. Chart IV highlights the performance of agriculture and allied sectors in Uttar Pradesh as against the national economy from the first five year plan to the tenth.

Chart IV
Agriculture and Allied Sector Growth Rate in Plan Periods

Plan	*Agriculture & Allied Sector (%)*		*Overall E1.58conomy (%)*	
	UP	*India*	*UP*	*India*
First Plan (1951-56)	1.86	2.71	2.21	3.60
Second Plan (1956-61)	1.48	3.15	1.75	3.95
Third Plan (1961-66)	(-)0.09	(-) 0.73	1.58	2.32
Third Annual Plan (1966-69)	0.62	4.16	0.32	3.69
Fourth Plan (1969-74)	0.94	2.57	2.23	3.25
Fifth Plan (1974-79)	5.23	3.28	5.70	5.30
Sixth Plan (1980-85)	2.54	2.52	4.11	4.10
Seventh Plan (1985-90)	2.64	3.47	5.70	5.80
Two Annual Plans (1990-92)	5.42	1.01	3.14	2.47
Eighth Plan (1992-97)	2.70	3.90	3.20	6.80
Ninth Plan (1997-2002)	0.80	1.90	2.00	5.60
Tenth Plan (2002-2007)	2.10	1.10	5.30	7.70

Source: Planning Commission, Uttar Pradesh

The agriculture and allied sectors engage more than 65 per cent of the workforce. Most of the workers are below the poverty line. The performance of the agricultural sector is far from satisfactory. It may be observed that the agricultural growth rate of the state economy from the sixth five year plan had dropped drastically. The reasons were attributed to the pressure of population and poverty. The pressure was more on the state and it led to fragmentation of land holdings. Yogi Adityanath blamed the SP and BSP for the bad performances in the agricultural sector. He said that the government will work for the welfare of farmers and youths.

Yogi Adityanath has redeemed crop loans up to Rs. 1 lakh of 86 lakh farmers in his official cabinet meeting. For this, the government made a provision of Rs. 36,000 crore. A payment of about Rs. 27,000 crore was made to sugarcane farmers. To make sure that the farmers benefit the most, the price of good quality sugarcane was fixed at Rs. 325 and that of normal sugarcane was raised to Rs. 315 and finally the rejected sugarcane was to be sold at Rs. 310 per quintal. The state government has focussed on opening new sugar mills. It has earmarked Rs. 273.75 crore for Pipraich sugar mill, Rs. 270 crore for Munderwa sugar mill on the Gorakhpur-Basti border and Rs. 33.35 crore for the Sathiaon sugar mill in Azamgarh district.[45]

While expanding the capacity of sugar mills, Yogi Adityanath said 20 lakh youngsters would be recruited in the next two years as the state would receive an investment of over Rs. 5 lakh crore in the same period. He said that farmers were the priority of his government because their happiness was essential for the growth and development of the state. He blamed the SP and BSP for selling sugar mills at throwaway prices and our government is doing its best to keep all the sugar mills running and ensure payment to farmers in 14 days.[46]

The Uttar Pradesh government has set a target of insuring 50 per cent of the total land cultivated in the state for the next kharif crop. As per Uttar Pradesh agriculture department statistics, around 165.98 lakh hectares of land in the state totalling 68.7 per cent was under cultivation in 2014-15. As on 2010-11, the state had 2.58 crore farmers who produced 439.47 lakh metric tonnes of grains in 2015-16 and 539.19 lakh metric tonnes of grains in 2016-17. The government has instructed all divisional commissioners and district magistrates to ensure insurance for all eligible farmers who have availed loans from banks on a mandatory basis.[47]

The other measures taken by the Yogi government are:

* Setting up of 20 new agricultural science centres in 20 districts with Central Government assistance.
* Allocating Rs. 134.10 crore for establishment of 10 dairy plants in the state.
* Allocating Rs. 35.70 crore for completion of New Green Field milk power plant under construction in Uttar Pradesh.
* Provision of Rs 15.16 crore for subsidy to "Gau Sewa Aayog" for the development of infrastructural facilities in gaushalas.
* Provision of Rs. 200 crore for construction of link roads and Rs. 250 crore for maintenance of these roads to ensure easy transportation of cane by growers to the market place.[48]

Industry

The second largest sector of the economy of Uttar Pradesh is industry. Sugar, vanaspati and cement are the three most important industries in the state. Though there was an improvement in industrial production during previous governments, the state still lacks the requisite level of industrialisation as compared to other states of India. Chart V represents the industrial growth rates during various Five Year Plans in Uttar Pradesh.

Chart V
Industrial Growth Rate in Plan Periods

Plan	*Period*	*Growth (%)*
First Five Year Plan	1951-56	2.3
Second Five Year Plan	1956-61	1.7
Third Five Year Plan	1961-66	5.7
Third Annual Plan	1966-69	1.2
Fourth Five Year Plan	1969-74	1.4
Fifth Five Year Plan	1974-79	0.4
Sixth Five Year Plan	1980-85	11.8
Seventh Five Year Plan	1985-90	10.8
Eighth Five Year Plan	1992-97	4.2
Ninth Five Year Plan	1997-2002	4.3

Source : Uttar Pradesh Five Year Plan 2007-12

Chart V indicates that during the sixth five year plan, the industrial growth of Uttar Pradesh was the highest and was the lowest in the fifth five year plan. The rate of the growth of industry in the recent past has varied between 2 and 6 per cent per annum. There was a significant improvement in the growth and structural change in the factory sector. The chemical and engineering sectors had a higher growth rate than traditional industries such as sugar and textiles.

Seeing the low growth rate in traditional industries, Yogi Adityanath emphasised on the revival of traditional industries. He dedicated a newly-constructed distillery and ethanol plant at Kisan Sahakari Chini Mill at Saithiaon in Azamgarh district. Further, he said that the state government is working for the revival of traditional industries for generation of employment avenues. The distillery has been set up at a cost of Rs. 56 crore and more such industries would be set up.[49] Though the present government is working to uplift traditional industries, the challenges are more daunting. It was seen earlier that poor production efficiency levels was an obstacle to industrial performance.

In 2017, the Uttar Pradesh government approved a new industrial policy that links employment generation with capital investment for sops involving mega projects. Taking a cue from the Central Government's Make in India programme, the policy will also establish a new department called Make in Uttar Pradesh.[50] He said, "we have named our government's new industrial policy as Uttar Pradesh Industrial Investment and Employment Promotion Policy- 2017. Our policy will roll out a red carpet for industrialists and do away with the previous government's red tapism."[51]

The Indian Prime Minister praises Yogi Adityanath because his government had overcome the negativity of the past governments and has shown hope to people with his positive policy. A foundation has been laid to build a new Uttar Pradesh. Progress comes through potential + policy + planning + performance.[52]

Yogi Adityanath has assured industrialists that will face no problems as he would personally monitor the rollout of all the MoUs and remove bottlenecks. Moreover, the improved law and order situation and infrastructure are the basic needs of industry. In 2017, all steps were taken to establish the rule of law in Uttar Pradesh. Earlier, under previous governments, investors used to leave the state but now the criminals are fleeing. Hence, investment in Uttar Pradesh will bring cheer to industry and help the people. The government has set a target of generating four lakh new jobs in the next three years in Uttar Pradesh.

In February 2018, an investment summit was held and well-established investors showed their keen to invest in Uttar Pradesh. Gautam Adani has said his group will invest Rs. 3500 crore in the next five years. Almost 17 per cent of the total population of the country lives in Uttar Pradesh. The development story of the country cannot be written without the state.[53] Mukesh Ambani has said coming to Uttar Pradesh is a patriotic duty because India cannot rise to its full potential without the rise of the 22 crore people of Uttar Pradesh. If Uttar Pradesh starts running, no power can stop India from becoming a global power. This way, the most populated state will become India's most prosperous one.[54] He was at the summit to contribute the maximum for the development of Uttar Pradesh. Jio will invest Rs. 10,000 crore over the next three years. According to Kumaramangalam Birla, Uttar Pradesh districts have grown at a rate of 10.4 per cent which is higher than the national average. He made an investment of Rs. 24,000 crore in Uttar Pradesh and will have 15 manufacturing plants. N. Chandrasekaran, Tata Group Chairman, stated that TCS has a strong presence in the state and they are committed to build a campus for 30,000 employees.[55]

The state government is creating new investment zones in Uttar Pradesh and in this regard work has already been started. Meerut-Muzaffarnagar, Jhansi-Auraiyya, Mughalsarai-Varanasi-Mirzapur, Trans-Ganga, Unnao, Chak, Gangariya city, Lucknow and Saraswati city are being developed as investment zones. Yogi Adityanath said that focussing on Noida alone is not the solution but we need to create more Noidas in Uttar Pradesh. If Uttar Pradesh has to compete with China or North Korea the capital and cost need to be at par.[56]

Development should be in proper order otherwise there will be problems for investors. Better roads and national highways are needed to transform the Uttar Pradesh economy. Nitin Gadkari, Union Minister for Transport and National Highways, said his department would soon begin road projects with Rs. 2 lakh crore in Uttar Pradesh and said that 4000 kilometres of new roads would be made in Uttar Pradesh under the Bharat Mala project. He also emphasised the development of waterways. It would be a game changer for Uttar Pradesh. The ongoing Rs. 54,000 crore Varanasi-Haldia waterway project will transform the economy of Uttar Pradesh.

Defence Corridor

The Central Government had earlier announced the development of two defence corridors. The first is to be built between Chennai and Bengaluru connecting Kattupalli port, Chennai, Tiruchi, Coimbatore and Hosur. The country's second defence equipment manufacturing corridor will be in Uttar Pradesh. It will re-energise 13 production units that had been lifeless in the state for 25 years. The Rs. 20,000-crore defence industrial corridor is the first ever project in parched and torturous Bundelkhand. Yogi Adityanath had personally requested Defence Minister Nirmala Seetharaman to give one of the two defence industrial corridors to Uttar Pradesh. The corridor would be set up along both sides of the proposed Bundelkhand Expressway. He said that nearly 10,000 hectares of land would be required and the process for its acquisition would begin soon. Bundelkhand is in an economic crisis as the people are starving because of non-availability of food. Further, water scarcity has made the condition worse and discouraged industrialists from setting up units.

Yogi Adityanath said that Uttar Pradesh is an ideal place and offers potential in the field of defence and aerospace. "We invite defence, automobile manufacturing, defence components, testing facility and test ranges, drone manufacturing and testing, aerospace parks fighter jets and helicopter manufacturing and asssembly."[57] He further said that Uttar Pradesh had an advantage as it was located on the Golden Quadrilateral road network, had access to the national capital region, strategic access to the market and resource depth of the eastern region, a large railway network and a dry port coming that was coming up in Jewar. The land bank in Bundelkhand, especially along the proposed Bundelkhand Expressway, would see defence units coming up. It is expected that the Uttar Pradesh corridor would generate production worth Rs. 50,000 crore in the next 10 years.

Thus, one can say that Yogi Adityanath's efforts are laudable. If everything goes well in and in the proper direction, the state will progress and will be soon equated with other states of India in terms of growth and prosperity. It will fulfil the aspirations of the people who want major changes in the structural development of Uttar Pradesh.

NOTES

1. Census, 2011, Government of India.
2. Ibid.
3. *The Times of India*, 5 October 2013.
4. Ibid.
5. http://www.indiatimes.com/news/india/up_cm_yogi_adityanath says all.
6. Ibid
7. *The Times of India*, 30 March 2018.
8. Liberation, April 1969, p. 53.
9. P.Singh, The Naxalite Movement in India, Rupa & Company, 1996, p. 59.
10. P.K.Agarwal, Land Reforms in India, M.D.Publication Limited, New Delhi, 1993, p. 115.
11. Ibid, p.116.
12. *The Times of India*, 3 February 2012.
13. Ibid
14. *Statesman*, 11 March 2001.
15. *Indian Express*, 29 March 2001.
16. *The Times of India*, 30 March 2018.
17. Ibid, 13 March 2018.
18. *Hindustan Times*, 28 July 2017.
19. www.outlookindia.com.
20. Ibid
21. *Hindustan Times*, 29 March 2018.
22. Ibid
23. Ibid
24. Census, 2011, Government of India.
25. S. Verma, S. Upadhyaya, D. Chadha, 'Demographic Challenges and

Opportunities in the Economically Marginalised Economic', *IOSR Journal of Business and Management*, vol. 6, issue 6, Jan-Feb 2013, p.18.
26. *Hindustan Times*, 12 July 2017.
27. http://pmjandhanyojana.co.in/yogi-rs-1000-reward-10th class-passed-girl-up.
28. Ibid.
29. http://pmjandhanyojana.co.in/list-yogi-adityanath-schemes-yojana-up.
30. Ibid.
31. Ibid.
32. Twelfth Plan, Government of India, vol. 130.
33. See note 27.
34. *Business Standard*, 25 March 2018.
35. *India Today*, 9 April 2018.
36. See note 25
37. Ibid.
38. Ibid.
39. *Hindustan Times*, 25 March 2018.
40. Ibid.
41. *Hindustan Times*, 9 July 2017.
42. Ibid, 31 March 2018.
43. Time of India, 22 February 2018.
44. 'Economic Survey', Government of India OI 2012-13, 278.
45. *Hindustan Times*, 12 July 2017.
46. Ibid, 24 December 2017.
47. Ibid, 30 March 2018.
48. Ibid, 12 July 2017.
49. *The Times of India*, 5 January 2018.
50. *Hindustan Times*, 5 July 2017.
51. Ibid.
52. Ibid, 22 February 2018.
53. Ibid.
54. *The Times of India*, 22 February 2018.
55. *Hindustan Times*, 22 February 2018.
56. *Times of India*, 23 February 2018.
57. *Hindustan Times*, 23 February 2018.

8

HINDU YUVA VAHINI: BRINGING PEOPLE CLOSER

In recent years, the formation of the Hindu Yuva Vahini by priest-turned-political leader, Yogi Adityanath has often been debated. It is said that the idea behind the formation was the promotion of Hindutva so that people from various streams could be united into a single national unit. But the task was not an easy one. One cannot forget 2002. On the one hand, the year witnessed a spate of barbaric communal riots that left Gujarat burning. On the other hand, the nation saw the rise of Yogi Adityanath who formed his own organisation, the Hindu Yuva Vahini.

It is believed that the Nath tradition has been carefully carried forward by Yogi Adityanath. When he conceived the Hindu Yuva Vahini, he followed the pattern set by the RSS. The organisation was more a socio-cultural rather than a political one because of the various problems that people had to face. His organisation was meant for Hindutva and to evoke the spirit of nationalism. The Vahini works within the socio-cultural and economic perimeters in order to realise its objective.

Before discussing the positive and negative features of the Hindu Yuva Vahini, it is essential to dwell on the term 'organisation'. Barnard has defined "organisation" as an identifiable group of people contributing efforts towards the attainment of goal."[1] Like any other organisation, the Hindu Yuva Vahini should be treated as a dynamic process which works for the fulfilment of its goal. The organisational goal must be given much importance within the larger framework of society. Generally, critics tend to equate the Vahini as a political organisation but in actual practice its purpose is to take up socio-cultural and economic causes. To understand the nature and functioning of the Hindu Yuva Vahini, it is desirable to discuss in general the social and cultural aspects of the organisation.

'Social organisation' refers to the system of obligation-relation which exists among and between groups constituting a given society. Within the given social organisation there is a social structure. It refers to the placement and positions of individuals and groups within that system of obligation-relation.[2] The system of obligation-relation must be keenly influenced by commonly-held sets of behaviour anticipation. The actual operation of a social system indicates that certain sets of obligation-relation are important for the proper maintenance of that system. On the other hand, a social structure is basically the social reality that influences our daily life. It is the way a society is organised into expected relationships. In other words, social structure refers to the way the units of a group or society relate to one another. It can be said that social structure refers to the overall composition of society. Social organisation and social structure give rise to a social system.

What is important in a social system? It is the functional relationship among the parts of a system and each part creates a new entity when they are functionally related. The social system of a country is also related with its cultural system. Culture determines the nature of inter-relations and inter-actions. Thus, social and cultural systems depend on the following factors:

- Belief and knowledge are the basis for social action.
- Sentiments are closely related to belief. A sentiment denotes feeling. It is the product of experience and cultural environment. It could be of various types like intellectual, ethical, religious, etc. Sentiments also have a background of historical and cultural legacy. In India, one is aware of the British policy of divide-and-rule that created strong

sentiments among Hindus and Muslims during the colonial era. These sentiments worked as a strong factor in the promotion of nationalism.

- Objectives or goals create a social and cultural system. Human needs and means and ends determine the nature of a social system.
- Facility is a means to justify an objective or end within the system. This is necessary because only then an individual can perform his or her role effectively.

Thus, social and cultural systems are closely interlinked. National culture influences people in good or bad ways. It creates an identity for the organisation. The characteristic of cultural organisation are individual initiative, risk tolerance, direction, integration, management support, control, identity, conflict, tolerance and communication patterns. Cultural organisation can be viewed as a descriptive feature of an independently defined stable social unit. Seen in this perspective, the Hindu Yuva Vahini is a social and cultural organisation based on these factors. These factors are important when one examines India as a nation and then figures out the necessity that motivated Yogi Adityanath to form such an organisation.

It is true that India is a nation with diverse features. It means the settlement of various kinds of people with their diverse customs, norms, beliefs, sentiments, traditions, etc. India is also a nation where people tend to acquire multiple identities based on region, language, religion, caste, etc. It represents a distinct social structure. However, there are threads which bind different regions into one single unit. Therefore, understanding the Hindu Yuva Vahini becomes important because it explains the bond that has developed between different communities in our country over a period of time.

Generally, critics tend to equate the Vahini with communal politics. This will be dealt with in detail later. But what is important in the Indian context is that every political party including the Congress, Samajwadi Party, Bahujan Samaj Party and other regional political parties have indulged in communal politics from time to time. The important question is why critics and political parties associate the Hindu Mahasabha, RSS and the BJP with communalism. These Hindu outfits have tried to bring diverse people into the mainstream of the national system. Communalism, based on hatred and separatist tendencies, is often understood in terms of Hindu and Muslim communities where the people of the Muslim community find themselves in isolation. Hence, the Muslim community is always antagonistic towards the Hindu who finds them to be aggressive and intolerant. The word 'communalism' in Indian politics is a misnomer and instead of communal parties one can speak of Hindu and Muslim groups as two distinct community organisations. Murray G. Ross defines community organisation as "a process by which community identifies its needs or objectives, gives priority to them, develops confidence and will to work, resources (internal and external) to deal with issues and in doing so extends and develops cooperative and collaborative attitude and practice in the community."[3]

Seen in this context, Indian communities refer to two or more major groupings of people. First, it may be all the people involved in a specific geographic area, i.e., village, town, city, neighbourhood or district. In a broader perspective, it may also include all people that constitute a nation. These people share some common interests and functions such as welfare, agriculture, education and religion. More or less, community organisation is involved in binding these people together so that awareness can be developed to work to solve common problems that do not harm the nation's identity. As such the Hindu Yuva Vahini is also a community organisation where its interest lies in promoting the identity of the nation through various ways.

Origin of Hindu Yuva Vahini

Before the Hindu Yuva Vahini, the Gau Raksha Manch was in existence. It influenced the followers of the Gau Raksha Peeth or the Gorakhpur temple. The organisation had a narrow vision to develop a wider people's base among Hindus. Hence, there was a need for a broader organisation and the Hindu Yuva Vahini replaced the Gau Raksha Manch. In order to fulfil Yogi Adityanath's aspirations, greater efforts were made to appeal to the masses by spreading its objectives beyond Gorakhpur. The organisation was created by him not as a political organisation but as a social and cultural one with emphasis on the idea of Hindutva and nationalism. The Mukhya Samraksha or chief guardian was Yogi Adityanath, the chief priest of Gorakhnath.

Objectives

The Hindu Yuva Vahini was created with the following objectives:

- In accordance with time and necessity, the purpose was to carry forward, establish and secure Hindu dharma, society and the cultural heritage of Hindustan.
- There was a need for social cohesiveness by integration and working for mutual harmony so that important issues like untouchability and caste differences may be curbed.
- To open avenues in an honourable and legal manner to bring back, under one single banner, all those brothers, if they so desired, who had either left the organisation because of misbehaviour or compelled to leave society.
- To create awareness among people for any age or gender to develop cow rearing and work against cow slaughter.
- Rising above politics, the need was to imbue the sentiment of nationalism among the people and thus promote the idea of Hinduism.
- There was also a need for the promotion, cooperation and fraternity among religious communities of Hindu society.
- There was also a greater need to provide assistance and services to those mothers, sisters and the aged who have been exploited and tortured.
- To eliminate nationwide corruption, there was urgency for more careful planning.
- Realisation to develop Hindustan into a prosperous nation as soon as possible.
- It was laid down that educated and unemployed youth may be made self-reliant by providing necessary opportunities

and assistance at governmental and non-governmental levels.

- The objective was also to work for the cooperation and coordination of the organisation by its members having the same ideology and then co-relate the national international organisations with similar ideologies to attain the above-mentioned goals. There is a need for Anushangik society.
- The organisation would have its own publications to promote Hindu Kosh.

Constitution

The Hindu Yuva Vahini's constitution offers a glimpse of Hindutva and Hinduism which it endorses. It also provides an insight into the meticulously organised internal structure. The constitution lays down the meaning of a Hindu. It means Vedic, Buddhist, Sikh, Jat, Jain, Naga and others who adhere to Indian culture. Several Hindu nationalists have earlier shown their faith and affinity with Buddhism, Sikhism and Jainism. It is based on what they perceive as ideational overlap. However, the appropriation of all these faiths as an element of Hindu culture is a much greater and untenable assertion.[4]

The constitution goes on to evince both the horizontal axis and the vertical axis of Hindu nationalism. It means that it appropriates not only Hindus but also the oppressed castes. The constitution speaks of the integration and imbuing of mutual good faith within the massive Hindu society through complete abolishment of the differentiation between the touchable and untouchable and high and low. It promotes the harmonious development of society.[5] Few would dispute the virtue of nurturing a harmonious society and in this process there are many who supported the abolishment of the caste system. The Hindu Yuva Vahini offers means and methods for the desired abolishment. The constitution reads that the caste system must end. This means that no subject should be dehumanised and degraded. In an interview before the Assembly Election of March 2017, Yogi Adityanath said, "castes play the same role in the Hindu society that furrows play in the farm and help in keeping it organised and orderly. Caste can be fine but casteism is not," he said.

Thus, the constitution of the Hindu Yuva Vahini is a startling document about Hindutva and the internal structure of the organisation. Not many political leaders in the country have based his organisation on the concept of Hindu Rashtra. It appears that it is structured like a mini corporation. This makes Yogi Adityanath different from other political leaders and he is even regarded as one of the most empowered individuals in the nation.

Internal Structure of Hindu Yuva Vahini

The Hindu Yuva Vahini consists of four categories of members. Its chief patron is Yogi Adityanath and Raghvendra Singh, a close aide of Yogi Adityanath, is the state coordinator. Both of them have held these positions since its inception. The organisation consists of life members, active members and those who are special invitees. Women are conspicuous by their absence in the organisation. It has been like this from the beginning including the gender disparity, in the Hindu Yuva Vahini. To Yogi Adityanath, what is important is the consolidation of the strength they already have. A member may be removed under certain circumstances if "an allegation of working against the objectives and interests of the organisation is proved."

The Hindu Yuva Vahini comprises an executive committee of 25 members. They hold positions that range from the chairmanship to media chief. The constitution delineates at length the rights and duties of the different office bearers. Ten of the 13 points of the chairman's rights and duties make it clear that the chairman shall have the right to acquire and maintain the movable and immovable property for the organisation. The General Secretary sends information gathered from the executive meetings and then prepares the minute book.

There is a time work schedule for Hindu Yuva Vahini leaders. They have to follow the rules strictly throughout the year. From mid-January to mid-February, these workers are supposed to mix with members of the scheduled castes and scheduled tribes by organising common feast (sambhoj) in their respective areas. From mid-February to mid–March, they conduct a membership drive. From mid-March to the end of May they are active in organising public meetings and rallies. In the remaining months of the year, the state office bearers have to visit different districts and do organisational work. Initially the work was limited as it was confined to Gorakhpur. After this, seven more districts are covered. These are Gorakhpur, Deoria, Kushinagar, Maharajganj, Basti, Sant Kabir Nagar and Siddharthnagar. In recent times, its organisational works could be seen in other parts of eastern UP. It includes Faizabad, Gonda, Mau and Azamgarh.

Gradually, the organisation expanded and the credit goes only to Yogi Adityanath whose efforts, after careful organisational planning, have placed the organisation in the forefront of the national mainstream. Further, the organisation consists of committees at several levels—state, district, block and panchayats. At the first three levels, the work has almost been completed to reach the strength of 101. At the panchayat level, the full strength of a committee has been achieved at 250. It includes vast numbers of young men in villages. Once the target is achieved, the committee members put up a hoarding in the panchayat. The members are given the task to put up triangular saffron flags of the Hindu Yuva Vahini on their houses. The organisational work of the district is assumed to be completed when all the panchayats have formed their committees. Till then the members of the Hindu Yuva Vahini tour specific villages every week to motivate the youth to join the organisation. According to Sunil Singh, the organisational work in Gorakhpur, Kushinagar, Maharajganj and Deoria was completed within time. For further motivation of the people, these members have now moved to other districts of eastern Uttar Pradesh.

One witnesses a major change in the membership drive of the organisation. Before the Assembly election in March 2017, membership was limited to eastern Uttar Pradesh. One of the reasons for this limitation was a political one as the state government had put a curb on its activities. As soon as Yogi Adityanath was made the supreme head of the state, the organisation received a fresh lease of life. Since March 2017, it has been stated that the organisational growth has been remarkable. The Hindu Yuva Vahini has now decided to move beyond Uttar Pradesh and make its presence felt in Bihar. The task was begun by enrolling thousands of youths. The Hindu Yuva Vahini state president said that youths in Bihar are now active in setting up various units in all the 38 districts. They will also select and appoint office bearers of the Vahini at district levels. The most important agenda is to promote Hindu interest.[6]

Caste-Based System

India is a country based on a caste system. Caste does effect and reflect Indian culture. But extreme politics of caste has a detrimental impact on Indian national culture. Though caste system cannot be abolished, its adverse role can be minimised. Even the constitution of the Hindu Yuva Vahini states that the caste system must end. It means that individuals should not be dehumanised and degraded. Yogi Adityanath believes that caste can be fine but casteism is not.

The image created by the media is that the Hindu Yuva Vahini indulges in caste politics. The high posts are dominated by Thakur Sunil Singh who was earlier elevated to the position of Uttar Pradesh president while Raghvendra Singh was made the state coordinator. Critics have often misled the people by equating caste politics with communal hatred. These critics often quote the Muslim community. Almost all the Vahini members opine that Yogi Adityanath is not against any community. A section of the Muslim community is radical. It has no respect for other religions. It protects anti-nationals and justifies criminal activities by citing religious scriptures. Today, as we see it, not only India but the entire world is under the shadow of Islamic (Muslim) terrorism. In India, to neutralise those Muslims promoting such violent ideology, the Hindu Yuva Vahini is the solution. The philosophy of the organisation is to have cordial relations with good people and destroy the evil ones.

Like other political parties, Yogi Adityanath's Hindu Yuva Vahini has supported the BJP's attempt to influence the Rajbhar OBCs through the legacy of King Suheldev. On 1th February, 2017, the Vahini celebrated "Suheldev Maharaj Jayanti." It was a determined effort to align the legacy of Suheldev with Hindu nationalism. A year earlier (24 February 2016), Amit Shah, the president of the BJP, unveiled a statue of the 11th century King Suheldev in Bahraich. The king had at one time ruled Shrasvati in Bahraich district of Uttar Pradesh. He lauded Suheldev as a figure whose name is revered not just in Uttar Pradesh but in the entire nation. It is said that Suheldev defeated the Muslim king Ghazi Saiyyad Salar Masud. Furthermore, it is noted that when Masud encountered Suheldev, he placed a herd of cows in front of his army to protect himself from attack. Suheldev and his army freed the cows at night and went to kill Masud.

The credibility of the narration shows that the BJP was keen in its pursuit to cement ties with the Rajbhar OBC. This has been the strategy that the BJP has deployed to please non-Jatav Dalit votes in Uttar Pradesh. In his book, "Fascinating Hindustan: Saffron Politics and Dalit Mobilisation" (2008), Badri Narayan noted that Hindutva entities have often used the "myth of Suheldev" to attract dalits. Both the Rajbhar and Pasi communities were cleared for inclusion in the Scheduled Caste list in December 2016. In an another article titled "The BJP Fascination with Dalit Icon" (2016), Omar Rashid wrote, "many non-BJP parties, especially the Samajwadi Party (SP) and the Bahujan Samaj Party (BSP) have over the years tried to influence the community for electoral benefits."

Later, in February 2017, when the Hindu Yuva Vahini observed Suheldev Maharaj Jayanti in Sarnath, the members chanted "Jai Shree Ram" and "Bharat Mata Ki Jai". Manish Pande, the vice-president of the Vahini in Uttar Pradesh invoked the history of Mughal rule and the British Raj by stating that "Hum ne ghulamon ki dasta ek hazar saal se dekhi hai." (We have witnessed the tale of slavery for a thousand years.) He continued that secular political parties like the Samajwadi Party (SP) and Congress are dividing society. He further said that if anybody sliced the circumcised Muslims like carrots and radishes, it was king Rajbhar.

On 19 February 2017, in Fatehpur, the Indian Prime Minister, Narendra Modi, said, "if there is a graveyard in a village then there must be a cremation ground as well." He continued, "if there is electricity "during Ramzan then there must be electricity during Diwali too; if there is electricity during Holi, then it must also be made available on Eid." Similarly, on 22 February 2017, Yogi Adityanath claimed during a television interview that development under the Samajwadi government had been "limited to the Kabristan." He then suggested that during Hindu festivals, households should receive four times the electricity supply that they receive during Muslim festivals. Soon after, on 2 March, 2017, Amit Shah, accompanied by Yogi Adityanath, held a road show in Gorakhpur. According to a report in the *Asian Age*, slogan such as "Ek hi naara, Jai Sri Ram, Jai Sri Ram" and "Gorakhpur mein rehna hai, Yogi-Yogi Kehna hai" was heard. Though critics and the media commented on the speakers of the Hindu Yuva Vahini by laying emphasis on communal divisive rhetoric, they have forgotten that these statements were made to broaden the Hindutva base by co-opting dalits. The members felt that Suheldev should not be seen as a Rajbhar or Pasi leader alone but as a leader of the entire Hindu community. Research and books written by historians have been biased and history has been mainly Mughal-centric.

Social Work 2009-2013

As mentioned earlier, critics and the media often equate Yogi Adityanath's meticulous work with communalism. But this is not true. He was fighting to improve the political and social system within the country by adopting the Hindutva philosophy so that the people of different communities can live peacefully. In doing so, during 2009-2013, his organisation undertook various works that could benefit the common man. Most of these works have been completed. They include:

- demand for Rs. 124 crore for Ramgarh Lal project.
- announcement of national medical care programme for such diseases like encephalitis.
- development of B.R.D. Medical College on the basis of All India Ayur Vigyan organisation.
- Rs. 624 crore for opening the Gorakhpur bypass.
- Rs. 9.25 crore for developing Mahsera bridge.
- Rs. 10.68 crore for developing Sasaighat.
- to start the project of Rampur Setu.
- to open avenues in Gorakhpur for a fertilizer factory.

- construction of a studio in Doordarshan Centre.
- agreement for opening of 10 kilowatt FM Channel in Akashwani.
- Rs. 915.74 lakh was given for the construction of Domingarh bridge.
- double line for Gorakhpur-Lucknow route.
- electricity work on Gorakhpur-Lucknow route.
- construction of overbridge in Sahjanwa.
- acceptance of funds from the Central Government to improve conditions in drought-stricken areas by strengthening ghats in Madhopur, Mahewa, Maniram and Bahuya.
- Consideration of Gorakhpur food park.
- construction of four-lane overbridge.
- initiative for Bhojpuri as a language in the Eighth Schedule of the Indian Constitution.
- effort to develop a Central University in Gorakhpur.
- plan to start a new train service from Gorakhpur to Durg and Gorakhpur to Mumbai.
- construction of Manchchariya and Kharkhariya ghats.
- construction of new overbridge in Tarang and Suryakund crossings.
- opening of trauma centre in B.R.D. Medical College.
- widening of Gorakhpur-Varanasi and Gorakhpur-Sonali routes.
- opening of Chandralok leprosy ashram for educating children.
- construction of 2,000 houses under Indira Housing Scheme.
- electrification of 225 villages in Gorakhpur parliamentary area.
- development of dharamsalas and libraries in 100 villages in Gorakhpur parliamentary area.
- development of 10 new community primary health centres in Gorakhpur.

Major Incidents

In the initial years of the Hindu Yuva Vahini, there were six major clashes in Eastern Uttar Pradesh. They occurred at Mohan Mundera village (Kushinagar district), Nathua village (Gorakhpur district), Turkamanpur locality (Gorakhpur city) in June 2002, Narkatahi village (Maharajganj district) in August 2002, Bhedahi village (Maharajganj district) and Dhanghata locality (Sant Kabirnagar district) in the first week of September 2002. Manoj Kumar, a local journalist has listed some 22 major riots in Gorakhpur and the neighbouring districts till Yogi Adityanath's arrest in 2007.

The cause of these incidents was political as the then Chief Minister, Mulayam Singh Yadav of the Samajwadi Party, decided to take stringent measures against Yogi Adityanath. This has been widely debated. It was said that Mulayam Singh had to take a hard decision because of the state assembly election that was due in April-May 2007. If he had not taken this decision, then the Muslims could have voted Mayavati to power. For these acts, Yogi Adityanath was not only arrested but his security guards were also withdrawn. This act was seen by him as a political conspiracy. He even alleged that it was done to malign and torment him.

This political vengeance had affected Yogi Adityanath and his organisation badly. For some time, the Hindu Yuva Vahini was on the back foot and Yogi Adityanath refrained from leading armed mobs against the Muslim community. But soon, he reactivated Hindu Yuva Vahini activities by participating in its demonstrations. In his speeches nothing changed but he became more sober and cautious. This could be seen from his involvement when a Hindu trader was murdered in December 2013 at Tanda in Ambedkar Nagar district though Yogi Adityanath intervened but from a distance. He even threatened to lead a march to Tanda if the culprit was not arrested within 15 days.

With the passage of time, Yogi Adityanath voiced his concern through various speeches but avoided direct confrontation with any community or political party. On 29 December 2016, Yogi Adityanath declared at Balrampur that "Muslims considered terrorists their protectors. Hindus must unite and remain alert wherever Muslims live and confront them if the situation so demands." This issue has been taken up separately in one of the chapters of this book.

The rise of the Hindu Yuva Vahini has many critics. One of them is Dhirendra K. Jha who wrote "Yogi Adityanath and the Hindu Yuva Vahini." A stern critic of Yogi Adityanath, Dhirendra Jha stressed that since its inception, the Hindu Yuva Vahini was involved in communal violence and projected minorities as the enemies of Hindus. The followers had only one leader and referred to Yogi Adityanath as "Gau Raksha Peethadishwar Parampujya Yogi Adityanath Ji Maharaj" and wore saffron stoles around their weeks. It was also reported in 2017 in the *Indian Express*[7] that communal riots had become a regular feature in Gorakhpur and adjoining areas since the Hindu Yuva Vahini came into existence. What was remarkable was that no hue and cry was made by the local administration on the activities of the organisation. One can say that this kind of reporting is a biased one as the numbers of incidents of communal violence have fallen sharply in Gorakhpur and the eastern part of Uttar Pradesh. The Hindu Yuva Vahini has also been criticised by the Left liberals. Christophe Jaffrelot[8] commented that the Hindu Yuva Vahini belongs to a militant Hinduism school of thought and in that sense is different from the BJP's political agenda.

These criticisms are baseless as the Hindu Yuva Vahini was constituted as a social and cultural organisation to strengthen Hindutva and Indian nationalism. The organisation combines the philosophy of Deen Dayal Upadhyaya's ideas of Antodaya and Narendra Modi's idea of new age reform. Thus, it can be said that the organisation was set up to eradicate corruption, generate employment and funds and improve the working conditions by not restricting the membership to local areas but to have a more wide-based area.

NOTES

1. http://www.pubslih your articles.net/knowledge-hub/business studies/organisation1978.
2. G. Gordon Brown and James H. Barnett, 'Social Organisation and Social Structure,' *American Anthropologists*, NS. 44, 1942, p. 31.

3. See Murray G. Ross, *Community Organization*, Harper and Row, New York, 1967.
4. http://www.caravanmagzin.in/vantage/hindu-yuva-vahini-constitution-tells-us-yogi-adityanath-regime-uttarpradesh.
5. Ibid.
6. *Economic Times*, 12 April 2017.
7. http://indianexpress.com/profile/columinist/christophe-jaffrelot.
8. http://indianexpress.com/article/what-is-yogi-adityanaths-hindu-yuva-vahini.

9

CONCLUSION

Kalhan once said that "there is a natural distinction of grade between man born to command and man born to serve." This statement is true in case of Yogi Adityanath. He is a man who has come to the world to command with his spiritualistic and political ideas. The world is well aware about his work in drawing a parallel between the conditions of India in general and Uttar Pradesh in particular where people could find a proper place in a divisive society. His early life illustrates the fact that a humble and ordinary man can rise to extraordinary heights. On account of his skilled intellect and diligent application, he became an illustrious and leading spiritual and political leader. His early life shows that whatever task was given to him, he immersed himself in it with dedication and sincerity. Such was the headiness of his influence that the people of the 21st century became intoxicated with Yogi Adityanath's growth of spiritual and political power. Thus, it was his inborn quality to perform his work with great perfection.

There was something in his mind that made Yogi Adityanath different from others. Being a science graduate, he was equally engrossed in the study of Indian history. Right from childhood, the independence of India and well-being of society became his only ambition. In search of these issues he turned to spiritualism and then the problems of India and Uttar Pradesh drew him into the political arena where he could play a more decisive role in

transforming society to his best ability. He felt that greater responsibilities had been thrust upon him to steer his state into a comfortable zone as compared to the well-established states of India. Therefore, there is a need to make greater sacrifices in restructuring the political and social systems than what the political leaders did for the country since independence. The time has come to mobilise the entire energy of frustrated youth into constructive and creative channels. Then, the country can be rid of its problems and we will be proud to call it Bharat.

Yogi Adityanath was gifted with a many-faceted personality. He was an extraordinary successful organiser and had the knack of keeping people together. His organisation, the Hindu Yuva Vahini, is a glaring example. Inspired by his guru, Avaidyanath, he is both a spiritual and a political leader.

Yogi Adityanath inherits the legacy of fiery politics of his guru, Mahant Avaidyanath. He represented politics that combined aggressive majoritarianism, vilification of the minority and use of muscle power to sustain activity. Under Mahant Avaidyanath, Yogi Adityanath also moved closer to the Sangh Parivar. The Vishwa Hindu Parishad gave him a larger social and political platform where he could perform a spiritual role as well as shape political opinion into the mould of Hindutva. This gave him ample opportunity to study the Hindu perspective on social and political matters. The Sangh Parivar brought this ascetic force to a decisive political level from which Yogi Adityanath gained immensely. To begin with, he served the nation by wining parliamentary elections five times but the poor conditions of Uttar Pradesh became the centre of his activity. Within a short span of time, he rose to become a spiritual and political leader of all-India stature. His ample work on Hindutva and the politics of the country in general and Uttar Pradesh in particular made him one of the leading national leaders of recent times. It shows his grooming as a spiritual and political leader that enabled Yogi Adityanath to serve the nation with great zeal.

One cannot deny the fact that he has good relations with the Bharatiya Janata Party because of its strong emotional and ethical values. He has developed good debating skill which has enabled him to correlate the past and present events to predict a future course of action. In other words, one can say that he is not just a believer of

Hinduism but in fact has immense knowledge of humanity. His fiery Hindutva approach on various occasions has turned the tables in favour of his party. This could be seen in the recent elections of Gujarat and Tripura.

Looking back into the pages of Indian history, our ancient period was a culmination of an age in which Yogi Adityanath saw the rise of great empires. It is also true that our ancient culture played an important role in binding the people into one single unit from time to time under great empires. From our history, we get ample opportunity to prove India's antiquity, priority and integrity. The great contribution of Kautilya and Samundragupta in making India a great power could not be digested by the European powers. That is why, in the colonial era, both their achievements were viewed from the Western perspective and history was re-written to suit the colonial powers.

Hindu Philosophy of Life

Yogi Adityanath says that India as a country that has to move away from the selfish interests of people or political parties that are dividing society. If this is not checked, India's unity and integrity will be in danger. He believes in the diction by stating **"सर्वम खल्विदं ब्रह्मम"**! It means that the visible world is only an expression of Brahma. This concept is the foundation of Hindu dharma, philosophy, life and culture. It is not confined to one particular sect but is extended beyond this realm where great spiritual leaders propagated religious ideas and tried to serve the national interests of the country.

Not only this, our holy men have also said "**आत्मवत् सर्वभूतेषु यः पष्यति स पश्यति**". It means that those who see all people as equala are those who are real and perfect. The message of our great gurus is reflected in the form of:

"सर्वे भवन्तु सुखिनः सर्वे सन्तु निरामयाः
सर्वे भद्राणि पष्यन्तु मा कष्चिद् दुःख भाग्भवेत् ।"

"Sarve Bhavantu Sukhinah
Sarve Santu Nir-Aamayaah
Sarve Bhadraanni Pashyantu
Maa Kashcid-Duhkha-Bhag-Bhavet."

It means that all should be happy, free from disease, lead a prosperous life and as such no one can be a party of sorrow. These moral ideas had a great influence on Yogi Adityanath's life. This has not occurred suddenly but was reflected in Indian culture and legacy. According to Hindu philosophy, the end of worldly existence is dharma, artha, kama and moksha. Dharma is an obligation to be discharged for the good of mankind. Artha is the material aspect of life, object, purpose and wealth. Kama is desire, greed and lust. Without kama there can neither be motivation nor creation. Wisdom and good conduct lead to moksha and ultimately liberation from the cycle of births and deaths.

But, in case of contradiction and conflict among them, the choice is left to the individual. In ancient India, there prevailed different schools of thought to solve these difficult problems. The Dharmasastra and the Smritis have given importance to dharma. Vyas in the Mahabharata has also attached importance to dharma because it is the source of both artha and kama. In the Santipurana, dharma is regarded as the best, arth is in the middle and Kama is the lowest goal of life and a man should follow dharma as the principal aim of life.[1] To Kalidas, dharma is more important than artha and kama. It seems he was greatly influenced by the Ramayana. Hence, representing the ideals of the Dharmashastra, he characterized King Dilipa as a king who gained wealth and gratified his desires thinking them as part of dharma. Like in our Vedas and Upanishads, Mahavir and Gautam Buddha spread the universal message of non-violence, friendship and fraternity and expressed the greatness of Indian culture. The universal message has been reflected in the culture of many countries. Hindu culture has always regarded the whole world as kutumbvat. The same feeling of our culture in reflected in the modern world as globalization.

It has been rightly said that Yogi Adityanath is a Hindu cleric, a monk, a sadhu with a private vigilante group. Many Indian politicians, including Mahatma Gandhi, have been religious, but no Indian state in modern times has ever been ruled by the leader of a religious order or institution.[2] Rajesh Pradhan has raised the question of the role of sadhus in politics. Pradhan followed the role of 30 sadhus from 1993 to 1996, probing why they got involved in the Ayodhya movement. He, then, returned to 10 in 2008. His interviewees included Mahant Avaidyanath. He met Yogi Adityanath but he says that he was not a major figure at that time. Two of Pradhan's conclusions are noteworthy. First, sadhus believe in spiritualism and not political discipline. They do get involved in politics to serve a larger religious perspective. Second, they are followers and do not follow political leaders. Sticking to political parties goes against their spiritual mission.[3]

In the case of Yogi Adityanath, the story is different. In him, one finds a rare blend of spiritualism and political realism. One could, then, argue which school of thought Yogi belongs to—idealism or realism. Noting his complete understanding of national and international politics as well as internal problems of India in general and Uttar Pradesh in particular, one can categorically state that he is a modern realist thinker. Though his study of ancient Indian history has helped him in producing rational and logical reasoning about the present Indian politico-socio-economic scenarios. He was quite perturbed about the developments of his time and readily concluded that these problems were not his own creation but the legacy he inherited from previous governments.

Development vs Hindutva

This leads to another important issue—development vs Hindutva. Yogi Adityanath's decided to solve the political and economic problems of Uttar Pradesh, which was once a debt-ridden state, in his own style. From the very beginning, he began to monitor all the weak sectors of the state. He wanted to improve its image by taking drastic steps in all directions so that Uttar Pradesh can be called Uttam State.

Viewed in this sense, I don't find any contradiction in Yogi's model of development and Hindutva. Perhaps, he was more influenced by Indian Prime Minister Narendra Modi's vision of India. He felt that modern Indian vision could be possible only when the state of Uttar Pradesh progressed. If we go by the BJP ideology, then it cannot be ruled out that India was subjugated for the last

1200 years and Modi's rise has put an end to that dark period. Modi often referred to the "1200 years of slavery" and to our "slave mentality." One of his goals is to end the slave mentality and revive the long-lost glory of Hindu civilization. At the core of Indian culture, is religious and cultural nationalism. But for survival it should be backed by a strong economy. Hence, economic development becomes important as it is a necessary pre-requisite for the political, social, military and cultural revival of Hindu civilization.

Though Yogi Adityanath has been criticised for being a radical Hindu leader, it would be wrong to assume that he neglected the growth of other communities, particularly Muslims. In Gorakhpur Math, there are plenty of Muslims earning their livelihood. As a Chief Minister of Uttar Pradesh, he endorses Narendra Modi's idea of Sabka Saath, Sabka Vikas. He says, "My government will be for everyone, not directed against any caste or community. We will work for the development of all sections and castes and create a new structure of progress." Yogi Adityanath insisted that everyone will be taken along on the path of development. "A body cannot be fully fit unless all its parts are fit. If one of my arms stop functioning, how can I work to my full potential? I will be called divyang. We will take every caste and community together on the road to progress. We will work for development of all. But, there will be no appeasement."[4]

Today, development has become his mantra because of the mistake committed by previous governments by not taking progressive steps in making UP a grand state. Hence, a state can be secured only when the people are protected and there is proper development. To overcome those obstacles that hamper development, recently in 2018, a conference was called by Yogi Adityanath inviting investors from all over the world and India. These investors participated and promised to invest in Uttar Pradesh as they thought the state had a vast potential market for investment.

It is in contrast to V. D. Savarkar's preaching that "it has been well said by Christ that man does not live by bread alone. As it is spiritually true, it is also true in the racial, cultural, national and several other aspects that go to constitute human nature. Therefore, the attempt to interpret all human history and human activities in economic terms alone is altogether one-sided. "Today, without a strong economy a nation cannot survive. The disintegration of the Soviet Union is a point to prove this. After 1991, the world saw the rise of globalization, liberalization and privatization. The impact of this was also seen in India. India saw market reform as essential to equate with other developed nations."

The impact of Kautilya's political philosophy was clearly visible in Yogi Adityanath's writings. Laying emphasis on artha, Kautilya had said that it should be the main goal of human life. Without artha, a man cannot sustain life. Similarly, the state of Uttar Pradesh is passing through a bad phase because of its non-economic performance. I have already discussed in detail the economic conditions and methods to solve the problem in Uttar Pradesh as it is passing through a bad phase because of its non-economic performance. Unless the state progresses in the economic sphere, it is doomed to be a failed state. Right now, the able leadership of Yogi Adityanath has done commendable work to improve its GDP and GNP growth and by doing so it will definitely emerge as a frontline state of India.

Similarly, on women empowerment and equal participation, Yogi Adityanath's views have changed. Once, in 2010, he opposed the Women's Reservation Bill. In an essay entitled "Matrishakti—Bharatiya Sanskriti Ke Sandarbh Mein," he wrote on the importance of women's participation in the development of society but limited the role of women to mother, sister, daughter and wife.[5] Women do not need freedom but they need protection and channelization. He gives examples by saying that a father offers protection to a girl; in her adulthood the role is taken up by her husband and in her old age it is the son who looks after her. But at some point, he acknowledges women's contribution to the independence movement and in the progress of the nation and lauds their success in various sectors. He saw women have progressed more in urban areas as compared to rural sectors. The recent budget of the Uttar Pradesh government has many packages for the upliftment of girls and women so that they can contribute more to the development of the state's society.

In India, we have a completely different situation. India has a well-developed parliamentary system network down to the village level. The ballot box and the people have been instrumental in bringing about major changes in the functioning of the government, both at the Centre and at the state level. We have seen active Left and democratic movements which have a deep impact on Indian politics. In fact, we have our Constitution which endorses various rights to solve the people's problems. But, in reality this is not the picture today where ultra radicals have used this in order to promote the party's selfish interests.

Soon after independence, the Congress party began focussing on its secular as well as socio-economic policies based on the concepts of development and non-alignment. Yogi Adityanath calls secularism a great lie and in the name of secularism it has not delivered the desired result at the appropriate time. Sixty years of Congress rule failed to promote and safeguard the rights of the minorities and backward classes. On the other hand, casteism, poverty, illiteracy and communalism were on the rise. That is why Yogi Adityanath has commented that casteism and dynasty rule can never bring social justice. He said the war of social justice was carried out by B. R. Ambedkar. Today, our government has launched schemes like 'Jan Dhan Yojana' and 'Ujjwala' to open bank accounts for all, providing LPG connection to five crore poor families, free power connections to the poor and introduction of the Goods and Service Tax (GST) which are part of the battle as they are aimed to uplift the living standards of the weaker sections of society.[6]

Furthermore, when we analyse the entire situation of India in general and Uttar Pradesh in particular, we find certain negative trends that are disturbing elements in the growth of nation and state. These are the law and order situation, role of civil society, common man's perspective on being deprived of their rights, terrorism and naxalism and problems of backward classes. All these problems have given rise to structural violence. This kind of violence is inherent in the present Indian political system. In understanding such problems, the following issues become important; poverty, relative deprivation, corruption, lack of governance and repression.

Poverty: Generally speaking, it is accepted that poverty and inequality are contributory factors that lead to human conflict. The standard measurement of poverty and inequality in economics begins with a definition of individual well-being which is specified in terms of fiscal-based measures such as income or consumption. This problem has affected other aspects of human development such as education, health and empowerment. It has been discussed in detail in the chapter on Uttar Pradesh; A Problematic State. But what is important to note is the comment of Amartya Sen that "there are two India's, the one which looks like a lot like California, the second and more populous, a lot like Sub-Sahara Africa."

Just before Yogi Adityanath took charge as Chief Minister, he found that there were many cases of hunger deaths in the state. He asked the government officials why this happened and why poor people were deprived of food. He did not get an answer. Later on, he found that the faulty policy of previous governments was responsible for it. It was found that there were 30 lakh fake ration cards while 37 lakh people were deprived of it. The government gave them ration cards. Still, the problem was not solved as the PDS shop owners did not provided full rations. The government realised this work cannot be done in a day when the coffers were empty. It was then decided to prepare ration cards on simple paper, link them with Aaadhar and have POS machines at every ration shop. In this way, the message was clear that if one shop owner was cheating beneficiaries he could choose another. Till now, the government has set up 14,000 POS machines and have ordered another 66,000.

The country is looking to set up "Ram Rajya." This, for Yogi Adityanath, means that the poor should have shelter and have electricity in their households. It is our endeavour that the administration should be sensitive and make this possible, as all of us have come to Uttar Pradesh with this dream. From 2014 to 2017, the SP government did not allot any house to the poor under the Prime Minister Awas Yojana Scheme. Our government will provide 8.85 lakh houses to the poor. The SP and the Congress failed to do so. From 2003 to 2017, nearly 1.75 crore people had no electricity connection. The Congress, SP and BSP tried to divide the people on the basis of religion and caste. They were shouting pro-poor slogans but our government gave 32 lakh electricity connections to the poor.[7]

Relative Deprivation: Poverty, in turn, leads to general disaffection among the people as they are deprived of the basic necessities of life—food, clothes and shelter. Relative deprivation points out the contradiction between expectations and reality as a breeding ground for internal disturbances.

Corruption: Corruption is another problem that the state of Uttar Pradesh has been facing for many years. Laying the foundation for various development projects at Sathiyaon in Azamgarh, Yogi Adityanath said, "those indulging in corruption will be treated as goondas and criminals. " He said that the properties of officers and mafias, who were taking away the rights of the poor, would be confiscated and distributed amongst the needy people."

Yogi Adityanath drew a parallel with Lord Hanuman while declaring a crackdown on corruption. He would burn down the Lanka of corruption in the state. He said, "kuch logon ko bandaron se bahut dar lagta hai...mai batana chahta hoon ki, yahan bhi ek bandar hai jo bhrasht tantra ko jala kar nasht kar dega" (some people are scared of monkeys. I want to tell them that there is a monkey here who will burn down the entire corruption system). He said that his government had identified over 400 corrupt officials and many of them were given compulsory retirement in the past year. This drive will continue." Moreover, he maintained that one year was not sufficient to assess his government's performance. The previous SP and BSP governments were responsible for devising policies which promoted corruption and nepotism and were largely driven by caste and communal politics. He even launched an anti-corruption web portal where people can post pictures and videos as proof of corruption so that the government can take harsh measures against the corrupt.

Governance: Uneasiness amongst the masses results from poor governance, corruption and non-implementation of government policies. Today, there is a need for reforms in the government setup. It is rightly said that "one cannot run a 21st century economy with a 19th century bureaucracy administering 18th century laws often with a 14th century mindset." This problem could be well addressed by political parties. Today, in Uttar Pradesh, we have the BJP as the ruling party. Even Yogi Adityanath had to face serious problems of governance, i.e., how to have a complete grip on the state administration. His hard decisions had enabled him to take a personal interest in the nitty-gritty of administration in order to make it more efficient, bring about a perceptible improvement in the law and order situation and mobilise additional resources to fund commitments and development.

Though Yogi Adityanath had made more than 200 promises, he still needs to do much more to satisfy the high aspirations of the common masses. The reason is that he was considered an outsider for not having sufficient administrative experience. The monk-turned-politician soon learnt the art of governance. His message to the bureaucrats is strong and said that red tapism needs to end to have investors coming in. Technology intervention will help in countering the menace of bureaucratic wrangles. The government has digitalized the system of single window clearance for industry and officers will monitor every step. Officials will be held responsible for the delay of files. Hence, they have to be accountable to keep one's job safe. His government has moved ahead at a faster pace fulfilling the party promise of crop loan waiver so that people in villages could benefit from such a scheme. But the challenges before him are daunting. He has accepted them and took major steps by cancelling 15 state holidays declared by previous governments in the name of caste icons and asked government officials to follow sanitation drive and punctuality. It is necessary for Yogi Adityanath to make the government machinery more efficient because people have high expectations from him.

Law and Order: Uttar Pradesh is generally considered as a Bimaru state. The reasons are poverty, corruption, bad governance, casteism, criminalisation of politics and threats posed by terrorists and naxalites that have become a stumbling block for the state's growth and prosperity. When Yogi Adityanath became the Chief Minister, the first step was to remove the tag of a Bimaru state. In the past one year, his government took a keen interest to improve the poor image of Uttar Pradesh. Most of the problems have been discussed above. But the problem of the earlier governments was that they could not fulfil the aspirations of the people. The entire state then was moving in another direction. People had no other way to achieve the desired result and had to resort to arms and not follow rules and laws. The situation become deplorable and the present government was much concerned of the state of affairs where anarchy, misrule and chaos became the order of the day. It became such a state as visualised by Hobbes and Rousseau. In other words, organised crime has emerged as a widespread and serious threat to society as a crime with no national boundaries. Furthermore, we have seen kidnapping, illegal mining , manufacturing and sale of illicit liquor, acquiring contracts on the basis of muscle power, organised exploitation of forest produce, trade in wild life and fake medicines and currencies, grabbing of government and private properties and extortion. These problems were not created in a single day. The state of Uttar Pradesh is burdened with the legacy left by the previous governments.

When Yogi Adityanath became Chief Minister, he was burdened with the task to improve the law-and-order situation. He claims that in one year, his government did not allow any riots. The government cracked down on criminals without any bias. Pick and choose was the first priority but the officials warned them and acted. The government said, if you fire, you will have to face the consequences. If you kill, the result would not be good for you. "Police pe goli chalaoge toh thik nahi hoga." (If you fire on the police you will have to pay for it). We can see the result today.[8] He further said that "this is a sanyasi's government and considers everyone without discrimination. The SP, BSP and Congress allowed the mafia to grow. Today, criminals prefer to stay in jail and more are surrendering. They do not wish to move out of jail due to fear of the police"[9]

In one of his interviews, Yogi Adityanath was reminded of the violence in Saharanpur and Kasganj which the state witnessed in the last 10 months since the BJP came to power. He said that these were incidents and not riots. "Yeh samanya ghatnayen hain. Isse aap danga nahi kah sakte" (These are routine incidents of crime. You cannot call them riots). Both the incidents were brought under control by the Uttar Pradesh police. There was no need to impose curfew. No military or paramilitary forces had to be called in. Action was taken without any bias.

Yogi Adityanath says that these incidents have not changed his image. He is still what he was earlier. But the people's perception has changed. The development of the state's 22-crore population is his responsibility. For this, he has taken stringent measures. Recently, the State Legislative Assembly passed the Uttar Pradesh Control of Organised Crime Bill (UPCOCB). The purpose is to check organised crime and terror activities in the state and deal strictly with those trying to foment terror or dislodge the government forcibly or through violent means. The proposed legislation is on the lines of the Maharashtra Control of Organized Crime Act (MCOCA). Yogi Adityanath said that there was a need for a stringent law to break the nexus of politicians, corrupt officers and the mafia. The law will not be misused. The bill proposes that properties amassed through organised crime will be taken over by the government with the permission of the court during the course of investigation. The property will be confiscated by the state government after conviction.[10] In 1986, the government had passed the Gangster Act. But, today, there is a need to implement UPCOCA. The penal and procedural laws of the Gangster Act were found to be rather inadequate to control organised crime. Hence, if the implementation of UPCOCA finds no obstacle in both the Houses of the State Assembly, then one can say that where there are good laws there are good arms and where there are good arms there are good laws. Good laws and arms are the only solution to take Uttar Pradesh out of this critical stage.

Terrorism and Naxalism: Today, the nation is passing through a critical stage in the form of terrorism and naxalism. Both are diseases and hence there is a need to curb separatist tendencies. Both of them have led to structural violence where they are trying to spread their wings through nefarious designs. These have to be checked immediately otherwise the state and the nation will suffer immensely. The government will have to take such harsh measures so that there could be no more fragmentation of the state. Kashmir is a hot-bed of terrorist activities. It is not only the local people who are involved but it has been sponsored by external powers. If not checked, its repercussions could be seen in other states. In the case of Uttar Pradesh, there are many incidents of terrorist activities. How to check it is the biggest challenge the state is facing today.

The late K. Subrahmanyan, noted defence analyst, noted that the Central government cannot abdicate its responsibility and seek refuge behind the plea that law and order is the responsibility of the states. Ultimately, all people of India would have to look to the Central government for exercising the fundamental right of peaceful living. Even Article 355 of Indian Constitution states that "it shall be the duty of the Union government to protect every state and to ensure that the governance of every state is carried out in accordance with the provisions of the Constitution. The Union government will have to work out a coordinated plan of operations by all states and carried in an integrated manner." The Union government is in constant touch with the state of Uttar Pradesh as the state is reeling under numerous internal security problems. In curbing the threats of separatist tendencies, Yogi Adityanath has highlighted the significance of the National Investigative Agency (NIA) towards national security. The NIA was constituted in 2009 to combat incremental terror attacks. He has even proposed the idea of holding high-level meetings between the agency and state agencies once in every six months to overcome terrorism. He also informed that four northern states, namely, Uttar Pradesh, Uttarakhand, Madhya Pradesh and Bihar will be affiliated to the Lucknow office.

Hinting on problematic neighbouring countries that have adopted terrorism as a tool of foreign policy, Yogi Adityanath said that India would be successful in breaking the backbone of terrorists with an institution like the NIA. He even communicated to Home Minister Rajnath Singh about better coordination between the NIA and state agencies and work has already been done without any delay. Rajnath Singh said that the central government had directed the NIA to probe the smuggling of fake Indian currency. "During investigation, it was found that fake currency was smuggled into the country for funding terror. The NIA took measures to check both smuggling of fake currency as well terror funding. We will secure victory on terrorism soon."[11]

Further elaborating, Yogi Adityanath says, "the terror activities can be effectively countered with latest technology, coordination and exchange of information." Even the porous India-Nepal border has posed a threat to national security. The state government is equipping the Anti Terrorist Squad (ATS) with technology and human resources. There is a need for more cooperation between the NIA and the ATS.

How can one judge Yogi Adityanath's contribution in the spiritual and political world? It is not easy to answer. But his performance will enlighten us about the greatness of such a man. Can we analyse his perception at the moment by his Hindutva utterances of the past or the promises of the present. As Uttar Pradesh Chief Minister, he has promised to free the state of corruption and communal violence. He has viewed a development model based on Modi's slogan Sabka Saath, Sabka Vikas. In the initial few months as Chief Minister he has come up with so much schemes and programmes that might fulfil Narendra Modi's dream to turn Uttar Pradesh into a Sarvottam Pradesh. Mukesh Ambani sees in Yogi Adityanath all those qualities that may fulfil the aspiration of the masses. The state is fortunate to have him as Chief Minister and "we will all join together to make it a grand state." Yogi Adityanath himself admitted that this is only the beginning and the second year will be more shaandar for the State as the agenda for development is right on track.

Yogi Adityanath is up against his cultivated image of a Hindu nationalist firebrand Hindutva. The people are still seeing him through his prism and choosing to ignore the fact that he is much more than that.[11] With his Hindutva philosophy, he remains a nationalist to the core of his heart. All the great leaders have made valuable contributions towards the development of their countries by following extreme ideologies. The basic difference between Hindutva and Western philosophy is that Hinduism had accommodated everyone from time to time. But this has never been in the case of the Western world. Manu, the ancient thinker, believed that the king was formed out of the eternal particles drawn from eight guardian deities, Indra, Vayu, Yama, Surya, Agni, Varuna, Chandra and Kubera. Similarly, one can say that Yogi Adityanath's works are like the sun. His thought is his dew and sunshine. His thought is the beacon that lightens Indian culture. Without the sun, the moon would give no light and without the study of Yogi Adityanath's spiritual and political thoughts we are like blind men upon the road.

NOTES

1. *Mahabharata Udyoga*, 124, 37-38.
2. *The Indian Express*, 18 April 2017.
3. Ibid.
4. *The Times of India*, 19 February 2018.
5. www.yogiadityanath.in.
6. *Hindustan Times*, 31 March 2018.
7. *Hindustan Times*, 3 July 2017.
8. *Hindustan Times*, 19 February 2018.
9. Ibid, 31 March 2018.
10. Ibid, 28 March 2018.
11. *The Hitavada*, Nagpur, 26 March 2017.

INDEX